# REWRITING RIGHTS IN EUROPE

# Rewriting Rights in Europe

*Edited by*
LINDA HANCOCK
*School of Australian and International Studies,*
*Deakin University, Melbourne, Australia*

CAROLYN O'BRIEN
*Department of Political Science,*
*University of Melbourne, Australia*

## Ashgate

Aldershot • Burlington USA • Singapore • Sydney

Published by
Ashgate Publishing Ltd
Gower House
Croft Road
Aldershot
Hants GU11 3HR
England

Ashgate Publishing Company
131 Main Street
Burlington, VT 05401-5600
USA

Ashgate website: http://www.ashgate.com

**British Library Cataloguing in Publication Data**
Rewriting rights in Europe
    1.Human rights - European Union countries  2. Citizenship - European Union countries  3.Sovereignty  4.Minorities - Legal status, laws, etc. - European Union countries
    I.Hancock, Linda  II.O'Brien, Carolyn

**Library of Congress Control Number:** 00-134485


ISBN 0 7546 2002 6



Printed in Great Britain by
Antony Rowe Ltd, Chippenham, Wiltshire

# Table of Contents

*Acknowledgments*                                    vii

*About the Contributors*                              ix

*Acronyms and Abbreviations*                         xiii


**Foreword**                                          xv
Elizabeth Meehan

1.  **Introduction: Rewriting Rights in Europe**       1
    Linda Hancock and Carolyn O'Brien

2.  **Rights and the Dignity of Humanity**             9
    Attracta Ingram

3.  **Women and Human Rights in Europe:**
    **Views from France**                             25
    Bronwyn Winter

4.  **From Joan of Arc to Bardot: Immigration, Nationalism,**
    **Rights and the *Front National***               53
    Paul Hainsworth

5.  **Reflections on Minority Rights and the Liberal State**
    **in Central Europe**                             69
    Stefan Auer

6.  **Rights, Institutions and Culture after Communism**   91
    Martin Krygier

v

7.  **Economic Rights in Contemporary Europe**                     109
    Donald MacLaren

8.  **Towards a Wider Europe: Eastern Europe's
    Rocky Road into the European Union**                          121
    Harald Sander

9.  **Legal Rights and State Responsibilities under
    the ECHR**                                                    151
    David Kinley

10. **The International Criminal Court and State Sovereignty**    169
    Helen Durham

11. **Fundamental Rights, National Sovereignty
    and Europe's New Citizens**                                   191
    Stephen Hall

*Index*                                                          217

# Acknowledgments

The editors are grateful to the contributors for their scholarship and commitment to completing this volume. We also thank the reviewers: Alistair Davidson, Bernadette Dejean de la Bâtie, John Dryzek, Heather Field, James Goodman, Leslie Holmes, Peter McPhee, Elim Papadekis and David Tucker, who assisted in refereeing the chapters and Elizabeth Meehan for her apposite comments in the Foreword. We are grateful to those who supported the initial Contemporary European Studies Association of Australia (CESAA) symposium, from which the idea for the book arose and in particular, to the Delegation of the European Commission to Australia and New Zealand and to the Ambassador, Aneurin Hughes. We thank our publisher, John Irwin from Ashgate, for his encouragement and patience, our colleagues for their conviviality and intellectual support and the Politics Department and Centre for Public Policy, University of Melbourne for supporting our work on this project.

# About the Contributors

**Stefan Auer** has studied political philosophy and German literature at the University of Cologne and worked for the Czech and Slovak department of the Radio *Deutsche Welle*. He is currently completing a PhD in Political Science at the University of Melbourne, writing on Liberal Nationalism and the Postcommunist Transition of Central Europe. His most recent published work is 'Nationalism in Central Europe—A Chance or a Threat for the Emerging Liberal Democratic Order?', in *East European Politics and Societies*, Vol. 14, No. 2, 2000.

**Helen Durham** is the National Manager of International Humanitarian Law (aka the Law of War) for Australian Red Cross. She graduated from The University of Melbourne with a Bachelor of Laws with Honours and a Bachelor of Arts and has recently completed a Doctorate of Juridical Science, reviewing the role of non-governmental organisations in the development of the Statute for an International Criminal Court. In 1995 Helen was chosen by the Academic Council of the United Nations to attend a two week seminar in The Hague. A year later she was awarded a Queens Trust Grant and spent six months in New York working on her Doctorate at the United Nations and New York University. In 1997 Helen was awarded a Gareth Evans Grawemeyer Award to enable her to complete her research at the United Nations. In 1998 Helen was a member of the International Committee of the Red Cross (ICRC) delegation to the Rome Diplomatic Conference on the Establishment of an International Criminal Court. She has lectured academics and members of the military in Jakarta and Aceh, Indonesia. Helen has published numerous articles in the area of international law and edited a book soon to be released on the effectiveness of International Humanitarian Law.

**Paul Hainsworth** is Senior Lecturer in Politics/Humanities at the University of Ulster. His research interests include contemporary French politics, Northern Ireland and the European Community, Communist-Catholic relations and regional politics and policy. He has published a number of books on the above issues, including *Border Crossing: Film in Ireland, Britain and Europe* (Institute of Irish Studies, 1994), co-edited with J.Hill and M.McLoone, and *Divided society: ethnic minorities and racism in Northern Ireland*, (Pluto Press, 1998). He has also published a great deal of articles and contributed chapters to journals and books, including *Parliamentary Affairs, Studies in French Language, Literature and Society, Regional Politics and Policy, Electoral Studies* and *Irish Political Studies*.

**Stephen Hall** is Director of the European Law Centre and Senior Lecturer in law at the University of New South Wales and formerly Counsel in the Australian Federal Attorney-General's Department. Dr Hall teaches a range of European Union law subjects and has taught European Union law in the postgraduate law programme at Monash University. He practiced law for nine years and retains a consultancy role at the Attorney-General's Department. Among his publications on the subject of European Union citizenship is his book *Nationality, Migration Rights and Citizenship of the Union* (Martinus Nijhoff, 1995). His most recent publication is *The Rule of Law after Communism: Problems and Prospects in East-Central Europe* (Ashgate, 1999). His current field of research is Union citizenship, external relations law, federalism and human rights.

**Linda Hancock** is Associate Professor in public policy at Deakin University, Victoria and President of CESAA (the Contemporary European Studies Association of Australia). She teaches a range of social and public policy subjects with a particular interest in comparative welfare states, social policy and social protection. Recent edited monographs include: *Women, Public Policy and the State* (Macmillan Australia, 1999) and *Health Policy in the Market State* (Allen and Unwin, 1999). She has been Visiting Professor at the University of California at Berkeley, Duke University and the European University Institute, Florence, and has written chapters and articles for journals and books; the most recent for the Canadian Social Union Project and *Citizenship and National Identity in Europe* (eds. L. Holmes and P. Murray). Recent research includes The Women's Audit Project and she is currently working on a two year project: From Welfare State to New Social Settlement.

**Attracta Ingram** teaches philosophy and women's studies at University College, Dublin. She is the author of *A Political Theory of Rights* (Oxford, 1994). Recent work includes publications on normative issues of European integration, justice and pluralism, and changing conceptions of the nation-state. She is currently working on a book on political membership.

**David Kinley** is Director of the Castan Centre for Human Rights and Professor in law at Monash University, and is a legal specialist in human rights and constitutional law. He holds a Doctorate in Constitutional Law from Cambridge University, as well as an MA in Socio-Legal Studies from Sheffield University. Dr Kinley has lectured in and written on a range of subjects in public law, human rights and EU law. His publications include *The European Convention on Human Rights: Compliance Without Incorporation* (Dartmouth,

1993) and *Principles of European Community Law* (Law Book Co., 1995). He also has written chapters and articles for a number of books, his most recent in the forthcoming publication entitled *Protecting Human Rights Through Bills of Rights*.

**Martin Krygier** is a Professor of Law at the University of New South Wales. In 1995-96, he was Visiting Fellow at Collegium Budapest, and part of a focus group on the political psychology of post-communism. He has studied politics, philosophy and law, and his doctorate is in the history of ideas. Prof Krygier has been Visiting Professor at the University of California, Berkeley and Nicolaus Copernicus University, Torun. He has published in a number of areas, including politics, law and society after communism, political and legal philosophy, sociology of law, and the history of political and social thought. His work has been translated into French, Hungarian, Italian, Polish and Spanish. His present work involves civil society and the rule of law, before and after communism. His most recent publication is *The Rule of Law after Communism: Problems and Prospects in East-Central Europe* (Ashgate, 1999).

**Donald MacLaren** is Associate Professor in the Department of Economics, University of Melbourne, and the Associate Dean of Undergraduate Studies in the Faculty of Economics and Commerce. His main research interests currently involve agricultural trade policy, with particular reference to the World Trade Organisation, the Asia Pacific Economic Cooperation forum (APEC) and the European Union. He has also been a consultant with the Regional Directorate of the European Commission, and with the Socialist group of the European Parliament while working at the University of Aberdeen.

**Carolyn O'Brien** teaches European Studies in the Department of Political Science at the University of Melbourne. She graduated from Bath University with a Bachelor of Arts and has completed an MA at Monash University, Melbourne, both in European Studies. She has been an member of the executive committee of the Contemporary European Studies Association of Australia since 1994, was co-editor of the *CESAA Review* from 1994 to 1999, and co-edited *Teaching European Studies in Australia: Problems and Prospects* (CESAA, 1999) with A.Pavkovic and C.Welch. She researches in the area of European nationalism and the politics of the European Union, and is currently completing a PhD at Monash University.

**Harald Sander** is Associate Professor at the Maastricht School of Management in Maastricht, The Netherlands. He has studies economics, business administration, and development theory and policy at the Universities of Bochum, Essen and Duisburg in Germany. Dr Sander specialises in international trade and its macroeconomic consequences on developing countries and countries in transition. He has published widely, his most recent work including an edited volume entitled *World Trade after the Uruguay Round* (Routledge, 1996).

**Bronwyn Winter** teaches in the Department of French Studies at the University of Sydney. Her doctoral thesis (1995) centred on women of Maghrebian background and discourses of national and cultural identity in France. She is committed to contributing to critical thinking on women and the gendered nature of racism, class and cultural/national identity, and to maintaining connection between (radical) feminism and women's studies. Her recent research interests include the concept of 'human rights' as it relates to women and the possibilities and limitation so supranational and international organisations in ensuring that women's human rights are respected. Recent publications include 'Identity, Choice and Power: Politics of Difference in Context', *Journal of Australian Lesbian Feminist Studies* (1995). She also has a number of forthcoming publications in *Women's Studies International Forum* and *Proceedings of the 5th Women and Labour Conference* (Macquarie University).

# Acronyms and Abbreviations

| | |
|---|---|
| AA | Association Agreement |
| ASEAN | Association of South East Asian Nations |
| CAP | Common Agricultural Policy |
| CEECs | Central and Eastern European Countries |
| CESAA | Contemporary European Studies Association of Australia |
| CGE | Computable General Equilibrium Model |
| CU | Customs Union |
| EC | European Community |
| ECHR | European Convention on Human Rights |
| ECJ | European Court of Justice |
| EFTA | European Free Trade Association |
| EMU | Economic and Monetary Union |
| EU | European Union |
| FDI | Foreign Direct Investment |
| FN | *Front national* (French National Front) |
| FTA | Free Trade Agreement |
| GA | General Assembly (UN) |
| GATT | General Agreement on Tariffs and Trade |
| GDP | Gross Domestic Product |
| GNP | Gross National Product |
| ICC | International Criminal Court |
| ICRC | International Committee of the Red Cross |
| ICTR | International Criminal Tribunal for Rwanda |
| ICTY | International Criminal Tribunal for the Former Yugoslavia |
| ILA | International Law Association |
| ILC | International Law Commission |
| IMF | International Monetary Fund |
| NAFTA | North American Free Trade Organisation |
| NGO | Non-Government Organisation |
| SC | Security Council |

| | |
|---|---|
| SEA | Single European Act |
| TEU | Treaty on European Union (Maastricht Treaty) |
| UDHR | Universal Declaration of Human Rights |
| UN | United Nations |
| UNCTAD | United Nations Conference on Trade and Development |
| UNHCR | United Nations High Commissioner for Refugees |
| UNTS | United Nations Treaty Series |
| WTO | World Trade Organisation |

# Foreword

**ELIZABETH MEEHAN**
The Queen's University of Belfast

Through the prism of the European Union (EU), but also by way of the European Convention on Human Rights and the International Criminal Court, this book tackles a wide range of issues relating to rights, citizenship and sovereignty in the European context. For example, it deals with philosophical and economic ways of thinking about rights; the legal formulation and protection of rights; women's rights and human rights; immigrants who may have formal rights but are dispossessed or 'scape-goated'; and conditions in states which may become members of the EU.

Such issues are also of concern in debates elsewhere about shifting conceptions and practices in international human rights law. This raises the question of how much European rights and human rights interact and how much they must do so if Europe as a whole is to be an arena of 'belonging' and effective participation for all its residents.

Hall's chapter in this book suggests that the jurisprudence of the European Court of Justice and the Maastricht Treaty's introduction of 'Citizenship of the Union' represent a legal diminution of national sovereignty. If this is so, then his case may lend comfort to Carlos Closa (1998) who argues that, in principle, there is more potential in supranational than national arenas for the realisation of democratic citizenship.

His argument is not a legal one but rests on a critique of the case that a shared national identity is a pre-condition for citizenship. For, by insisting that citizenship can be built only on such bonds, such theories propose that a democratic practice be based on a commonality that was formed under pre-democratic conditions. In contrast, a site of democratic citizenship is one in which people live together under a set of principled bonds, such as those identified by Robert Dahl: voting equality, effective participation, enlightened understanding, control of agendas and inclusiveness. In drawing this contrast, Closa suggests that supranational citizenship is less vulnerable than national citizenship to exclusion and discrimination because, being unable to draw on comparable non-principled bonds, its success must depend on democratic and human rights norms.

Hainsworth's chapter in this book about the French right and immigrants demonstrates the validity of Closa's concerns about national citizenship.

In practice, Closa suggests however, west European civil society may be too fragile to transform EU citizenship into an arena for democratic self-determination from what he calls an enhanced set of private rights to make the most of new market opportunities (or be sheltered a little from its threats)—as discussed in MacLaren's chapter in this book, it is unclear whether economic rights can be re-established to the standards of their 'golden age'.

If Closa is right about the weakness of civil society in the west in combatting a privatised, liberal or libertarian conception of citizenship, then enlargement of the EU may reinforce the challenge—as shown in several of the chapters in this book. The prospective member states, while having to subscribe to principles of liberty, democracy and human rights as a condition of entry, are not well placed to do so in practice—emerging as they are from totalitarianism which suppressed civil society or bent it to the will of the state. At a conference during the 1998 UK presidency, harrowing tales were told of the vulnerability of emergent civil society associations in the Balkans and of discrimination against minorities in east and east-central Europe.

With or without minority problems, the concept of liberty—perhaps necessitated by dire economic conditions—is even more libertarian than that which Closa sees in the EU. It is the negative one of 'freedom from' restraint—not the 'freedom to' which is implicit in Christian- and social-democracy and still has some place in the link in the EU model between social inclusion and economic progress.

The point that can be drawn about enlargement from Closa is not about the addition of more nationalities, either *per se* or in their further reduction of an overlap between nationality and citizenship. It is that growing mismatches amongst sets of principled bonds, not a more complex collection of pre-democratic identifications, may inhibit the transformation of EU citizenship along the lines aspired to by democrats.

However, the potential members do introduce more dramatically than before the possibility of ethnic conflict within the borders of the EU. There is, of course, inter-ethnic discrimination in a number of Member States, including France, as discussed in this volume; for decades, there was open violence between two nationalisms in Northern Ireland. But, by and large, the EU has not had to consider, for internal purposes, how the international human rights community has been rethinking self-determination and the relationship between individual and group rights—as the basis of new forms of peace-brokering between majorities and minorities occupying the same territory (Bell, 1999).

As Bell aptly notes, another factor, yet to be resolved, is how to make such agreements stick—a matter which has, of course, been on the EU's external agenda.

The internalisation of group conflict, as a result of enlargement, would place an even heavier burden on the European political realm, which, even in its present form, needs to democratise the public space so that the various associations of people can come face to face with their different interests and agendas (Tassin, 1992). If enlargement entails not merely a more diverse set of principled norms, but also deeply entrenched non- or pre-democratic forms of identification, the process of dialogue will have to be robust indeed for the achievements of outcomes that are, if not satisfactory to all, at least reasonable. There may be lessons in Winter's chapter in this book on women's rights, since the 'transversal politics' of postmodern feminism has been shown in Northern Ireland, and elsewhere, to be one method of moving forward.[1]

Thus it can be seen that this book provides much food for thought in respect of the issues facing citizens in the EU as currently constituted and it lays important groundwork for thinking about the new challenges of the future.

## Note

[1]   The work of other thinkers about this is summarised in Lister (1997).

## References

Bell, C. (1999), 'Minority Rights', in P. Emerson (ed.), *Majoritarianism or Democracy?*, The de Borda Institute and The Society for Social Choice and Welfare, Belfast.

Closa, C. (1998), 'Supranational Citizenship and Democracy: Normative and Empirical Dimensions', in M. Torre (ed.), *European Citizenship. An International Challenge*, Kluwer Law International, The Hague.

Lister, R. (1997), *Citizenship: Feminist Perspectives*, Macmillan, Basingstoke.

Tassin, E. (1992), 'Europe: A Political Community?', in C. Mouffe (ed.), *Dimensions of Radical Democracy*, Verso, London.

# 1 Introduction: Rewriting Rights in Europe

LINDA HANCOCK and CAROLYN O'BRIEN

With wide ranging debates about the effects of the sweeping forces of globalisation the European Union (EU) stands as a relatively newly consolidated supranational regional entity; surrounded by potential new members to the east, north and south. Forged first in economic terms, albeit with political aims, and post Maastricht and Treaty of Amsterdam, with enhanced political, economic, civil and social commitments, the EU has consolidated its commitment to rights. On the one hand this has been accomplished through individual Member States' ratification of United Nations International Covenants on Civil and Political Rights and on Economic, Social and Cultural Rights and through the European Convention on Human Rights (ECHR). On the other, the EU itself has taken the leadership, for example via the European Social Charter. As Stephen Hall points out in this volume, cases decided in the European Court of Justice since 1969 have also consolidated community law's protection of interests interpreted as falling within the scope of fundamental rights.

Rights are central to the understanding of a 'new' Europe and central to rights are the two recurring concepts of citizenship and sovereignty. Tackling economic and political security, social protection and social exclusion remain unmet challenges. Sorting out the layers of sovereignty and of citizenship rights, duties and obligations is the project of the early new century.

This book responds to and reflects the increasing focus on rights in Europe. Ongoing debates concerning immigration and minority rights, rising concerns about social exclusion, social protection, war crimes, the role of supranational institutions in relation to nation-state sovereignty, and the expansion of the European Union to incorporate the countries of Eastern and Central Europe, place rights firmly on the political, social and legal European agenda.

At an international level, this volume follows the 50th anniversary of the UN Universal Declaration on Human Rights in 1999. As has been widely commented, this anniversary coincided with shocking human rights abuses which were seen as belonging in the past and playing no further part in contemporary Europe—even if elsewhere such abuses remained widespread. Notwithstanding

1

European guilt over the atrocities on its doorstep, or within its own boundaries, Europe however, was seen as a 'privileged' bastion of fundamental rights and indeed, as incarnated in the EU, has sought to entrench a conception of rights in its expansion plans and in its legal relations with so-called 'third countries'.

Moreover, this UN anniversary also coincided with an increasing emphasis on human rights in the international political arena. The creation of the International Criminal Court highlights the increasing significance of rights: Helen Durham taps into the area of international rights and duties in her analysis of the role of an international court to try war criminals. She argues that the International Criminal Court is important in highlighting the onus on sovereign states to enforce international law. International duties transcend national obligations of obedience. A right of international citizenship is to have contravention of internationally agreed standards tried in a forum that rises above national level partiality, conceptual differences and cultural or historical relativity.

Such developments as the NATO-led forces in Kosovo and the establishment of the International Criminal Court, may, arguably, foreshadow the emergence of human rights as a new organising principle in international relations, taking precedence over traditional rationales of national sovereignty. The basis of such thinking is that individual, universal human rights may form the basis for action which contravenes the 'rules' of national sovereignty, thus 'weakening the presumption in favor of state sovereignty' (Ignatieff, 1999). Similarly, it has been suggested that the extension and codification of human rights norms at an international level may also form a basis for the protection of (non-citizen) immigrant rights within the nation-states of western Europe—rights that traditionally inhered within national citizenship (Soysal, 1994). Such actions and developments in favour of 'human rights' thus raise many complex issues particularly in the area of citizenship and national sovereignty.

**Rights and Rights**

The book explores various dimensions or layers of civil, political, social, legal and economic rights in contemporary Europe, east and west. Contributors address the nature of human rights, women's rights and equality debates, human rights as embodied in national and international covenants; minority and immigrant rights and citizenship; economic and social rights in an integrating Europe, and national sovereignty and the development of an EU supranational form of citizenship.

There remains much debate over what constitutes inalienable and universal rights: for example, the idea of liberty as 'freedom from'—a negative conception of liberty as opposed to the 'freedom to'. The Australian High Court Judge, Michael Kirby observes the finding that some countries such as the US have been more successful in their protection of fundamental civil and political rights than their protection of fundamental social and economic rights essential for equitable development. This can be related to the 'particular liberal conception that the best government is one that leaves its citizens alone. For government to provide positive freedoms to the disempowered would be to limit the content of the individual freedoms of others' (Kirby, 1997, p.5). Having rights is one thing, structurally positioning individuals to exercise them is another.[1]

Attracta Ingram's chapter explores the conceptualisation of rights: 'that distinctive strand of rights thinking which takes rights as basic building blocks of political morality'. Democracy is underlaid by the right to equal respect and the concept of a right, Ingram argues, includes both the presupposition of freedom as absence of constraint and, the idea that coercion can be used to protect freedom. Conceptualising rights as giving liberties as well as powers and bearers of rights as having their own moral sovereignty, enables a critique of regimes or structures which do not respect individual freedoms. Rights are 'the shields that protect our vulnerable normative status as free and equal human beings'. As Ingram argues, human rights norms have been central to the development of modern political organisation. However, uneven enjoyment of the development of rights and entitlements characterises divisions within and outside the EU—for instance regarding refugee policy, citizenship for resident aliens within the EU and global human rights and democracy projects.

Rights talk encourages the analysis of different classes of rights: Women's rights as human rights (Winter); Human rights as legal rights (Kinley and Hall) and Economic rights in the context of globalisation and free market economics (MacLaren). Winter identifies the problems of defining and defending European women's rights in human rights terms and the hollow rhetoric of EU women's rights promotion. Drawing on the French context, she highlights the problematic for women, of masculinist conceptions of human rights—ironic given French pride in claims to key rights concepts like equality and freedom. Winter highlights the ineffectiveness of the equality reform agenda with inadequate enactment of EU Directives and resolutions at Member State level and the problem of dismissing minority women's rights as an 'immigrant problem'. Nonetheless, the EU as a supranational entity is an important focus for women's rights claims that might recognise class and race/ethnic inequalities. As Winter and others[2] observe, there is potential to extend beyond the important but limited EU equal opportunity reform focus on employment and work place issues.

Kinley and Hall both examine the relevance of legal rights in relation to those (40) States which are signatories to the European Convention on Human Rights. Kinley focuses on aspects of ECHR implementation and the qualifications that may allow states to limit the right at issue. New questions of accountability and responsibility are raised by shifts in the boundaries between public and private with privatisation, corporatisation and the contracting out to private entities of previously state owned, managed or delivered services. This is particularly problematic in the new democracies in Eastern Europe. Since obligations under the Convention are owed by the state to individuals, there is therefore an onus on states (via legislatures, executives and bureaucracies) to protect human rights between private legal persons or entities. Courts, Kinley argues, are less effective than elected legislators and state officials for enforcing Human Rights principles. Hall reminds us though, since it is Member States and not the Community that are signatories to the ECHR, in the absence of the Community becoming a legal party to the Convention, the EU's Court of Justice has played an important role in reinforcing fundamental rights protections in Community law.

MacLaren examines the economic rights expected by citizens in the European Union. Since the 'golden age' of economic growth of the post war years, the goals of macro-economic policy have undergone a considerable shift, with the drive towards increasing integration, the introduction of a single European currency and the subsequent loss of national control over monetary policy. One example is the changing relationship between unemployment and social welfare in Member States. EU economic policy and the European Central Bank constrain and limit government control and government capacity to reduce unemployment. Balancing market and social agendas is one of the key challenges for both the EU and its Member States in the future.

According to Harald Sander, a further impediment to a wider Europe might be the reticence of current Member States to shoulder the economic burden of Eastern European states' demand for structural funds. Aside from these costs, with integration of some Eastern European states, secondary impacts could include the economic adjustment costs of industrial relocations. In any event, accession will be uneven, with an assessment of risks and costs made on a country-by-country basis.

## Making Rights Work

It would seem that it is in Europe where the concept of rights 'counts' the most, as the NATO-led intervention in Kosovo in 1999 suggests. More specifically, the 370 million people living within the EU, Stephen Hall suggests in this volume, are 'probably the most human rights-protected people in world history'! Certainly, the European Union is increasingly concerned with rights at a number of levels, both within and outside the Union. As Meehan alludes to in her preface, the EU is explicitly tying in adherence to human rights principles to its political and economic agreements with third countries—an initiative emanating from the European Parliament.[3] The 1997 European Year against Racism concluded with the setting up of a European Monitoring Centre on Racism in Vienna. Likewise, the inclusion of a commitment to ensuring human rights as a criterion for admission into the European Union, highlights the increased political importance of human rights in the EU context. The countries of Eastern and Central Europe, it would seem, may only be classed as 'European' and admitted to the European club, when they explicitly defend minority rights. The Copenhagen criteria—decided at the 1993 EU Summit in that city—set out the political criteria to be met by applicant countries (see Sander in this volume), and stated that 'membership requires that the candidate country has achieved stability of institutions guaranteeing democracy, the rule of law, human rights and respect for and protection of minorities'. Underlining the increased focus on rights, the Maastricht Treaty set out that all Member States should have regard for and promote the ECHR (as noted by Kinley in this volume). Respect for human rights has also been explicitly spelt out as a founding principle of the EU in its most recent Treaty: the Amsterdam Treaty (entered into force 1.5.99). This states that the Union 'is founded on the principles of liberty, democracy, respect for human rights and fundamental freedoms, and the rule of law, principles which are common to the Member States'.

The stipulation of rights-based entrance criteria for the EU, as Martin Krygier discusses, raises the issue of how the post-Communist states of Central and Eastern Europe, with vastly differing socio-cultural milieux, traditions and histories, will cope with major institutional innovations. After all, institutions are culturally embedded and may or may not graft successfully onto recipient cultures. The attempt to do so, may in itself be flawed. Krygier's analysis tempers what he calls 'institutional optimism'. As he observes, we need to question assumptions that rights, developed and institutionalised in the West will thrive in post-Communist Central and Eastern Europe. In any event, it is not the 'technical equipment' of change but cultures and societies that ultimately mediate change. The future of human rights and the rule of law in individual Eastern European states will vary, depending on both tradition and agency. Krygier is probably realistic when he says it is impossible to predict the future, because we do not know in advance the intermixture of surviving traditions and the role of various agents.

## Rights, Citizenship and National Sovereignty

The ongoing process of European integration focuses attention on the nexus between rights and citizenship both within the EU and in relation to expansion. As Hall notes, post Maastricht, 'the new rights of Union citizenship relieve Member States of their previously sovereign power to restrict a range of important political and civil rights to their own nationals'. Rights that are conferred universally and which are effectively bound to the nation-state raise issues about what role transnational entities such as the EU might play in more effectively monitoring and enforcing rights beyond national borders.[4]

Nonetheless, as chapters in this book remind us, the up-grading of rights is not a one-way street. Despite the institutionalisation of human rights in the political workings of the European Union, there remain many fields where rights are the subject of dispute, or abuse, within Europe. Paul Hainsworth's chapter suggests that despite the formal inclusion of minority rights as a criterion for joining the EU, the status and rights of minorities within contemporary France is undermined at a number of levels. The discourse and proposals of the French National Front (FN) are targeted particularly at immigrants and this has involved considerable scape-goating and stereotyping.

Stefan Auer tries to reconcile the needs and aspirations of minority cultures in Eastern and Central Europe in the context of their developing liberal democratic order. It becomes clear that respect for and acknowledgment of minority rights is not a simple transaction. More visceral forms of nationalism which aim to wipe out different nationalities within the nation-state may be easy to identify and denounce, but the questions raised by demands for minority recognition and in some cases, self-determination, remain complex. They not only challenge the development of the new democracies in this part of Europe but also pose questions for the West in its treatment of both settled ethnic minorities and of more recently arrived immigrants.

The rights debate, then, is closely bound up with notions of democracy and national sovereignty. National sovereignty is undoubtedly being eroded at a number of levels, and nowhere is this more apparent than in Western Europe. While forces of 'globalisation' may be the order of the day at the international level, at the European (EU) level, the economic and political integration into a new type of polity has cut yet further into the traditional thinking on national sovereignty and the more traditional forms of economic and political cooperation. The introduction of the Single European currency in January 1999—a political as much as an economic decision—is one example of this far-reaching change.

The meaning of citizenship, the rights and obligations that come with it, access to citizenship and the notion of multiple, overlapping and potentially conflicting citizenship rights and obligations are contested terrain. In the context of the European Union, questions arise as to where and at what level rights are best protected. There is a fuzzy relationship between the 'pooling of national sovereignty' on the one hand, and democratic rights of citizens on the other. Where rights of citizens were once seen as fundamentally tied to national belonging and the civil, social and political rights which (however imperfectly) inhered in national citizenship, the introduction of a new level of citizenship and the erosion of the sovereignty of the nation-state raises new questions. As Hall argues, there has been a one-way, irreversible 'invisible seepage of power', resulting in a legal diminution of national sovereignty in favor of the Union, and not merely a pooling or sharing of sovereignties. The establishment of a citizenship of the Union, in particular, represents a further erosion of national sovereignty and an enhancement of Union sovereignty. Such trends, he observes, are inescapably tied to the 'gradual emergence of the individual as the beneficiary of the Community's unwritten and steadily unwinding code of fundamental rights'. Community law goes further than classical international law, entitling individuals to both a confirmation of Community law rights at the national court level as well as providing aggrieved citizens with a supranational remedy for national failure to recognise a right. Of course this begs the question of exclusion from some nationally bestowed rights and thus a more complete claim on Community citizenship.

Certainly, the nation-state has been, and remains, a major point of reference, in both the protection of rights—via citizenship and constitutional provisions—and the elaboration of future national and international treaties and charters concerning rights. However as this volume demonstrates, human rights cannot be understood in isolation, or in relation solely to the national. The increasing salience both of international norms as well as the increased spread of supranational and international covenants and treaties need to be taken into account; as does the driving force of international markets in setting national and regional agendas. The increasing scope of the EU, economically, politically and territorially, and the possibility of a European (EU) Bill of Rights in the future, suggests a radical rewriting of the relationship between rights and the nation states of Europe.

## Notes

[1]    Women are a case in point. Historically and in the present, women's citizenship has been derivative and relational and the vast majority of women have not been positioned structurally to exercise rights. See Hancock (1999).

[2]    See Blossfield and Hakim (1997); Hoskyns (1996); Lister (1997); Mazey (1998) and Meehan (1993).

[3]    One example is the Australian government's reluctance to include a human rights clause in a Framework Agreement with the EU which led to the ditching of the Agreement in 1997 and the signing of a weakened 'Political Declaration', 26.6.97.

[4]    The European Court of Human Rights has of course contributed to this development within the 41-member Council of Europe; however the creation of a European (EU) citizenship raises possibilities of specific citizenship rights being directly conferred—and defended—at this level.

## References

Blossfield, H. and Hakim, C. (eds) (1997), *Between Equalization and Marginalization: Women Working Part-Time in Europe and the United States of America*, Oxford University Press, Oxford.

Falk, R. (1998), 'A Half Century of Human Rights', *Australian Journal of International Affairs*, Vol. 52, No. 3, pp.255-272.

Hancock, L. (1999), 'Citizenship on the Margins', in P. Murray and L. Holmes (eds), *Citizenship and National Identity in Europe*, Ashgate, Aldershot.

Hoskyns, C. (1996), *Integrating Gender: Women, Law and Politics in the EU*, Verso, London.

Ignatieff, M. (1999), 'Human rights: The Midlife Crisis', *New York Review of Books*, May 20.

Kirby, M. (1997), 'Human Rights: an Agenda for the Future', in B. Galligan and C. Sampford (eds), *Rethinking Human Rights*, Federation Press, Leichardt, NSW.

Lister, R. (1997), *Citizenship: Feminist Perspectives*, Macmillan, Basingstoke.

Mazey, S. (1998), 'The European Union and Women's Rights', in E. Hine, and H. Kassim (eds), *Beyond the Market: The EU and National Social Policy*, Routledge, London.

Meehan, E. (1993), *Citizenship and the European Community*, Sage, London.

Soysal, Y. (1994), *Limits of Citizenship: migrants and postnational membership in Europe*, University of Chicago, Chicago.

# 2 Rights and the Dignity of Humanity

ATTRACTA INGRAM

The United Nations organisation committed itself from the start to human rights, taking one of its fundamental aims 'to reaffirm faith in fundamental human rights, in the dignity and worth of the human person, in the equal rights of men and women and of nations large and small' (Wild, 1968, p. 5). In 1948 all the member states of the UN adopted its Universal Declaration of Human Rights. Subsequent documents such as the European Convention on Human Rights, the African Charter, and many more, reinforced the growing consensus on the political importance of human rights. Now, 50 years after the UN declaration, human rights have become a core policy instrument of ethical international relations, and a standard aspect of domestic relations between state and citizen. Each of the main international human rights covenants has been ratified by 140 or so out of some 185 states. The post-1945 emergence of an international human rights regime has featured the development of a framework of global norms, a body of international law, and the growth of institutions for implementation and monitoring. These institutional developments take for granted, to some extent, the capital of Enlightenment universalism. This bank of moral ideas has been maintained in value by conceptual innovation and theoretical development in moral and political philosophy, especially on the normative foundations for human rights. This is the less visible work of the 'underlabourer'. We need a picture of the kind of work going on there, if we are to understand something of the deeper ideas that inspire and justify the vast resources that are going into the international human rights agenda. The focus of this chapter is one view of the normative foundations for human rights, a view of the kind of considerations that should direct the detailed work of specifying human rights. This view has deep roots in European thought. It is not the only view, but it has been of seminal importance in setting the legitimation standards for modern political organisation in Europe and in countries that have drawn on the European heritage of moral and political ideas.

I am going to identify one powerful strand of human rights doctrine. I want to argue that it rests on a view about the importance of respect for the fundamental moral capacity of individual human beings to think for themselves, and that this view helps us to understand what is distinctive about rights-based moral and political ideologies.[1] I do not want to deny that different moral and religious views can generate different understandings of rights from the one advanced here. But I do want to say that insofar as a doctrine of rights is based on individual liberty as pre-eminent among values, we have a distinctive rights position, one in which rights are a core element of a theory of justice rather than a useful, but theoretically redundant, way of talking about duties; or a contingent, but violable, means for pursuing a fundamental social ideal. My focus, then, is on that distinctive strand of rights thinking which takes rights as basic building blocks of political morality. I shall draw out the characteristic features of this conception of rights and argue that what links these into the distinctive doctrine that gives rights pride of place in political morality is a commitment to individual moral independence, and that this commitment in turn requires social arrangements that are hospitable to free moral thinking.

As I understand this doctrine of rights, it is a fighting doctrine. It gives people not just liberties but *powers*. It therefore involves the recognition of an original coercive power of people to institute a framework of government in which their collective power can be regulated for the pursuit of their vital interests, and thus redeemed from arbitrary use. The interpretation I shall give is not uncontroversial, but I believe it underpins the characteristic claims that make for a right-based theory of political morality.

So what follows is a view that takes the connection between rights and coercion seriously, that is mindful of John Locke's view that outside properly constituted government, individuals enjoy the executive power of 'the law of nature' to defend their own rights, and that shares his insistence that the best fence against tyranny, indeed the best guarantee of peace, is a form of political authority invented in the knowledge that the people have a right of resistance to arbitrary power (Locke, 1960, pp. 128–131).

Locke was not alone in connecting rights with coercion. Immanuel Kant did likewise. ' ... justice [a right] is united with the authorisation to use coercion against anyone who violates justice [or a right] (Kant, 1965, p. 36).[2] These theorists are members of a long family of contract theorists, currently represented by John Rawls, which connects the special status of rights with the claim that political authority is not self-justifying. The family line is dominated by concern for a moral principle of equal respect for persons conceived as capable of rational agency. This principle prohibits coercing people to do things that cannot win their rational assent. Since political principles are precisely those that we believe can be enforced, the idea that such principles must be rationally acceptable translates into the requirement that they be defensible to all who are coercively subject to them. The final guarantee of the principle of equal respect is not democratic self-rule, as civic republicans claim, but the right to equal respect that underlies democracy. This right is given concrete expression in constitutional recognition of certain fundamental rights—the rights of man, as they were called in the eighteenth century—additional to the political rights of the citizen.

The difficulty for political authority is seen, therefore, as arising from the fact that it curtails our liberty to exercise our own capacity for rational agency. Granted an original moral right to liberty on the ground of equal respect, authority is legitimate only if it secures that liberty and curtails it only to the extent demanded by important aims to which we freely assent. A bill of rights gives institutional expression to this understanding. It marks the distinctive importance of liberty and reflects our intuition that we have a right to act freely except when there is very good reason for restriction.

## Rights and Self-Command

The numerous declarations of human rights all give long lists of rights. But it is clear enough that what lies at the heart of these declarations is a conviction about a single right—the equal right of every human being to be free. Thus Kant writes: 'Freedom (independence from the constraint of another's will), insofar as it is compatible with the freedom of everyone else … is the one sole and original right that belongs to every human being by virtue of his humanity (Kant, 1965, p. 44). Kant had his own way of arguing for freedom as implied in his famous categorical imperative which enjoins people to act only on those maxims that they can will as universal rules. Here is a more accessible argument, due to H.L.A. Hart.

The concept of a right, Hart writes, is the concept of a legitimate exercise of force by one person over another. To assert a moral right to be just, is to assert that there is a moral justification for determining how another person should act. The idea that coercion of another requires justification entails the equal right of all persons to be free. Hence, each person is viewed as having a 'master right' to be free, that is, a natural right to liberty (Hart, 1984, pp. 87–8). This natural right to be free may be differentiated into a list of basic liberties, powers and opportunities, which under equal distribution form spheres of personal sovereignty.

So the concept of a right carries two components—the presupposition of freedom as absence of constraint, and the idea that coercion may be used to protect freedom. The concept of a just right is the concept of a power by which one person blocks another's encroachment on his/her liberty. The argument for coercion in defence of freedom draws on Kant. He says that interference with the freedom of another is wrong as contrary to a universal moral law. So, if we value freedom, we must be able to place obstacles in the way of obstacles to freedom, and this entitlement derives from the very law of freedom itself. For, Kant holds, law, of its nature, contains the authority to compel (Kant, 1965, pp. 35–6). Our moral title to use force in defence of freedom ultimately rests on these facts about what it is to value freedom and about the nature of law.

So far we have concentrated on the concept of a right. We need to re-introduce the bearers or subjects of rights. Again Hart is useful.

> Rights are typically conceived of as *possessed* or *owned by* or *belonging to* individuals and these expressions reflect the conception of moral rules as not only prescribing conduct but as forming a kind of moral property of individuals to which they are as individuals entitled; only when rules are conceived in this way can we conceive of *rights* and *wrongs* as well as right and wrong actions (Hart, 1984, p. 83).

We may be uneasy about Hart's description of rights as properties of individuals on the ground that it commodifies objects of rights such as our bodies and bodily powers, though it is worth noting that this kind of description has been prevalent in the tradition of rights theory I am describing.[3] Leaving this aside, the point I want to focus on is the idea of a rule at the disposal of individuals in Hart's account, because this seems to me to be of central importance. It captures the idea that a right is always somebody's right as a matter of the logical form of rights. Now the significance of this is that individuals are thus recognised as the basic units of moral and political power. For if each person has an equal right to be free and that entails a right to resist the intrusions of others, then no person or group of persons can claim an original right to the moral or political governance of others.

This image of individuals as self-masters is a legacy of Reformation thought that cannot be stressed too much. The Reformation was characterised by a burgeoning confidence in individual human ability to make sense of God and his commands. As Ryle (1949, p. 159) has summed up the Protestant view, it is the belief that the individual can know 'the moral state of his soul and the wishes of God without the aid of confessors and scholars'. The crucial point here is the belief that the individual is equipped with sufficient resources of reason and understanding to be treated as her own moral authority. Belief in the priesthood of all believers replaces belief in a hierarchical religious caste system in which the ignorant masses submit to the moral governance of the Holy and the Wise. The democratisation of moral authority underpins the demand for recognition of a right of private conscience and the case for religious toleration. And it is also why the right to conscience, or right to religious liberty, becomes the paradigm for rights generally. Under this paradigm, all rights are seen as protected freedoms from interference vested in individuals by virtue of their moral sovereignty.

The Reformation optimism about individual moral power to determine the content of a Christian life is matched by an optimism about the possibility of a *political* order designed around the idea of individual moral sovereignty. If the authority of the Holy and the Wise is rejected in matters of moral governance then it cannot continue to function in matters of political governance. If no one has superior moral authority then there is no basis for the idea that some people are naturally fitted to rule over others. Thus Locke observes that rulers are not evidently superior in wisdom or goodness to those they rule, and there is no evidence that God intended some to rule over others. On the contrary, he claims:

> all the Power and Jurisdiction is reciprocal, no one having more than another: there being nothing more evident, than the Creatures of the same species and rank promiscuously born to the same advantages of Nature, and the use of the same faculties, should also be equal one amongst another without Subordination or Subjection, unless the Lord and master of them all, should by any manifest declaration of his Will set one above another, and confer on him by an evident and clear appointment an undoubted right to Dominion and Sovereignty (Locke, 1960, p. 309).

Being governed, on this view, is not natural to human persons. It should be viewed as something invented, as something people bring on themselves in an exercise of free choice. This suggests that the constitution of political society is best thought of as a contractual arrangement, something which people agree to put themselves under for certain purposes. So Locke again:

> Men being ... by Nature, all free, equal, and independent, no one can be put out of his Estate, and subjected to the Political Power of another, without his own *Consent.* The only way whereby anyone divests himself of his natural liberty and puts on the bonds of civil Society is by agreeing with other Men to joyn and unite into a community, for their comfortable, safe and peaceable living one amongst another, in a secure Enjoyment of their Properties, and a greater Security against any that are not of it (Locke, 1960, p. 374).

Of course, this view cannot ignore the fact that people, for the most part, do not find themselves in a *chosen* community. Instead, they find themselves in social and political communities governed by hereditary rulers or political aristocracies, communities that have evolved complex traditions, customs, and systems of ascribed statuses and social roles. These generate obligations which people simply find themselves with as members of this or that community. But, the Lockean insists, it is nevertheless possible and desirable to stand back from all such arrangements and put them to the test of individual critical evaluation.

Individuals are thus credited with the native ability to assess their social and political arrangements not only against the standards set by those arrangements but also against the standard of the individual mind or reason itself. They are enabled to ask of any existing moral practice or social arrangement not merely: 'how does it stand in relation to its own goals?' but also: 'how does it stand with me and others like me?'.

So the view that I want to identify as a source of rights is based on this Reformation idea that individuals can legitimately demand that moral and political authority should answer to the tribunal of individual reason. This view describes individuals as their own masters, or as having dominion over themselves, or as being a kind of moral sovereign. What this means is that individuals are rightly in charge of their own lives. For Thomas Hobbes this is an inevitable feature of beings motivated by a strong desire to preserve their own lives. They *take* charge of their own lives. Thus he identifies right and liberty as a natural fact of the human condition. For Locke, self-sovereignty is a feature of beings created in the likeness of God with powers of intellect and agency or free will. Since Locke thinks of divine sovereignty as ownership, he is led to think of the dependent sovereignty of created beings as a kind of ownership too. Thus he famously describes individuals as having a property in their lives and liberties. What this means is that individuals are the morally rightful owners of their persons and personal powers. They may do with them as they please within the bounds, as Locke says, of the laws of reason, which basically means, within the limits set by the equal self-ownership of others, though suicide and voluntary slavery would also be condemned by Locke as contrary to God's law. But Locke, like Kant in the next century, does not think that he is proposing a doctrine for Christians only. Our right to be in charge of our own lives, derives from the natural freedom innate to our humanity and is therefore independent of any social order in which we find ourselves.

We have seen that one key Reformation bequest to modernity is the idea that all individuals have a kind of moral sovereignty that entitles them to be recognised as bearers of rights. The metaphor of moral sovereignty is meant to conjure up an image of individuals laden with the moral equivalents of sovereign political powers, something like full internal control over one's own affairs, and external independence of the powers of others. So the view I am moving towards is that a rights doctrine is basically a doctrine about working up this image of individual moral sovereignty into principles for the basic structure of society. The claim that I want to say is fundamentally deontological is this:

a social structure is unjust unless it is based on a set of common equal rights and liberties; the installation of rights in the social structure is a fundamental condition of its being right for the state to substitute its rule of law and coercion for the self-defence that is justified in a world without civil law.

Understood in this way, a rights doctrine provides a basis for arguing *against* some political regimes and criticising aspects of others, inasmuch as one can show that they are bastions of arbitrary power, or fail to fully respect aspects of individual freedom. And it provides a basis for arguing in *favour* of a regime if one can show that no coercive social order which lacked reverence for fundamental rights and freedoms, could possibly be just.

But we must remember that rights become important when coercion or the threat of coercion is in the air. Their function is to mark out the moral borders where political struggle is most likely, and most dangerous. Moreover, they perform this function by putting the state on notice that the people have a moral right to resist its coercive rule if it fails *their* test of fundamental justice. Now the right to resist is not an all-or-nothing right. There are degrees and forms of resistance that fall short of the use of physical force. Nevertheless, what gives teeth to a doctrine of rights is that rights legitimate resistance to authority, and may in some cases legitimate political violence.

What then is the test of fundamental justice that a government must observe if it is not to merit dissolution by the people? The canonical text is chapter XIX of Locke's *Second Treatise*. There, Locke makes it clear that there are two conditions: government should proceed through a representative legislative assembly and never on arbitrary will; and it should observe the people's trust by refraining from any arbitrary disposal of their lives, liberties, or fortunes. In modern terms, these tests require governments to meet the claims of democracy and human rights: democracy because that is our fence against invasion of our rights by what Locke called 'the boundless will of tyranny' (Locke, 1960, p. 466) and rights because these are the shields that protect our vulnerable normative status as free and equal human beings. Commenting on the charge that this doctrine is destructive of peace in the world, Locke says that it is those, especially governments, who invade the rights of others that destroy peace. What is so admirable about a peace that is maintained for the benefit of 'robbers and oppressors', that calls on 'the Lamb, without resistance' to yield 'his throat to be torn by the imperious wolf?' (Locke, 1960, p. 465).

At the deepest level, then, doctrines of individual rights have an insurrectionary potential that we overlook at our peril. One historical response has been to deny the validity and coherence of any doctrine of pre-political rights. This was the response of Burke, Bentham, and Marx, for their own very different reasons.[4] A more common response, nowadays, is to acknowledge a doctrine of rights while pre-empting its subversive force by installing and improving democratic structures and rights-regarding legislation. Thus Locke's defence of a right of resistance as the most probable means of hindering arbitrary government (Locke, 1960, p. 464) is vindicated by the historical efforts that have gone in to creating systems of limited and accountable government.

## Rights and Free Moral Thinking

The thesis I have outlined is a doctrine of moral individualism. It holds that the primary subjects of moral concern are individuals taken one by one. As a doctrine of rights it also holds that there are moral barriers that limit what may be done to individuals for the sake of society as a whole. The claim as Rawls puts it is: 'Each person has an inviolability founded on justice that even the welfare of society as a whole cannot override' (Rawls, 1981, p. 3). This states an understanding of 'rights as trumps' over some general principle for political decisions that asserts a view of the common good. One such principle is developed in utilitarianism which takes as the common good of politics the fulfillment of as many people's preferences for their own lives as possible. But there are other understandings of the common good. The point of saying that rights are trumps is that whichever view of the common good provides the normal justification for political decisions in a society, it cannot be an unrestricted doctrine.

Now there is more than one way of arguing for a right that restricts the operation of a background common good principle. Effective argument will often be in a mode that *draws* on the basic justification for the background common good doctrine. Thus, as Dworkin argues (1984, p. 154), utilitarianism may yield the case for its own restriction by certain rights. Similarly, for other doctrines. Catholic natural law theory may yield its own doctrine of rights, and even ways of accommodating particular rights that conflict with orthodoxy in particular areas, such as family morality. For example, the case made for the introduction of a right to divorce in Ireland in 1995 by politicians on the pro-divorce side, did not appeal to respect for individual liberty, but to compassion. This seemed an odd strategy of argument, especially to liberals, but it signalled appreciation that a major aspect of the common good culture being addressed holds that individual liberty is not the only thing of importance.

The possibility of finding arguments for rights that draw on the internal resources of different moral and political traditions is a major reason people are able to moderate their claims on the design of public institutions to ones that can accommodate citizens who do not share their substantive religious or moral views. But this is no guarantee that the adherents of different doctrines will always be able to agree on a common scheme of rights in practice. Their understanding of the force of rights as conveyed by the image of rights as trumps may be very different from one another, and so too may their views about which rights there are. For example, some may hold that rights are absolute and there are strict constraints on action that can never be overridden. Others view rights as principles to be balanced against other principles and values in practical deliberation. And some may give rights a certain lexical priority over considerations like general welfare, but countenance trade-offs when rights themselves conflict.

So we cannot suppose that different ethical views will simply converge on the thesis that rights are overriding. Yet this thesis seems central to the idea that certain vital interests of individuals may not be sacrificed for the sake of society as a whole. Is there a more promising approach to defending the thesis?

Suppose we start from the fact that among adherents of different views, there is widespread agreement on the introduction of rights into political morality and institutions. What does that tell us about the deeper idea people must share to make this agreement in difference possible? And does it give us a basis for insisting on the priority of rights over other considerations in political practice?

An account of the deeper idea can be drawn out of Kant. Kant's favorite moral injunction is: 'think for yourself'. The point of his famous distinction between autonomy and heteronomy is to decry the person who simply accepts unthinkingly the moral system handed down by parents and teachers and authority figures. According to Kant, the heteronomous person refuses to think for him/herself, and simply obeys rules laid down by others. This has no moral merit in his view. He views the medieval Church as trying to produce heteronomous people, something that all churches at times try to do. But his point is not that traditions of moral teaching should try to produce critical people who *reflectively* appropriate their doctrines. Thomas Aquinas and Alastair MacIntyre would both endorse that idea. What is really different about Kant's view is that he thinks that the moral world does not harbour a single truth about happiness or how best to live. The project of trying to discover such a truth about human nature, of finding for ourselves an independent standard, and then trying to live up to it, is, for Kant, a great delusion. There are many views of human flourishing and reason does not select one as true. Kant thinks that this is something to be welcomed. The picture of an independent moral world by which we have to discover and shape our conduct, is, for him, a picture that forces on us a certain form of heteronomy. And we should not want that.

Moving to the autonomy side of the distinction, Kant has two important things to tell us. One is that 'thinking for oneself' entails attaching particular value to an individual's organisation of her own life—to her own reflection on desires, plans, and projects, and to her own deliberative effort to shape her life into a meaningful whole. This does not mean that every view of a meaningful life is as good as any other. There are better and worse among forms of life. But life generally goes better for an individual if it is led from the *inside* according to her own beliefs about value.[5] On this account, we should be free to critically evaluate our moral inheritances, and to endorse or reject them. And this freedom cannot exist if legislation is used to install a conception of the good. This would mean that employment of legislation usurps and interferes with the effort to live life from the inside, leaving at best an individual life that has been shaped from the outside in accordance with someone else's conception of the good. Then it has none of the peculiar value attaching to an autonomously organised life. Here then is one kind of reason for accepting a restricted form of moral utilitarianism or other doctrine. The Kantian idea is that it is the *way* we hold our doctrines of happiness that really counts morally, and this we cannot legislate for. Instead we should have the protected liberties and resources that enable us to 'think for ourselves', even if these ultimately give people what, from within our own moral view, appears as a licence to do wrong.

The second thing we may learn from Kant is that the fact of reasonable disagreements about ethics and religion makes these views problematic in a way that is very helpful to us. Kant says that it would be a bad thing if the truths of religion could be deduced by reason because that would produce fanaticism. The fanatic is not one who is necessarily wrong in his beliefs or arguments. What makes the fanatic is his hostility to others thinking for themselves. And this comes from his certain grip on the truth and his conviction that contrary opinion has no merit, even as evidence of another's effort to work things out for him/herself. So the second reason that people may have for restricting their own doctrines in favor of a shared framework of rights is that they may think it necessary to douse the fundamentalist fervour and intolerance that can accompany people's most important convictions.

The injunction 'think for yourself' undercuts the notion of submission to a certain kind of moral teaching about the good and what is right. 'Think for yourself' gives a reading of what it means for all people to be equal in dignity, namely, they each have the capacity and need for free moral thinking. This is a notion of equality to which freedom of thought and the like are essential and so we find it associated with making civil and political rights of the first importance, and with rejection of totalitarianism even in the name of economic equality.

If 'think for yourself' is an element of most standard versions of the major moral and even religious doctrines, as it seems to be, we have a basis for respecting and protecting different conscientiously held views. We may explain the pluralism that results from freedom of thought under free institutions as due to what Rawls calls 'the burdens of judgment'—the fact that human reason is limited, and time short, that we bring different knowledge and experience to the solution of practical problems, that they are in any case difficult, that the balancing of different values may be done differently by different people, and so on (Rawls, 1993, pp. 56–7). This is the basis for an appeal for reasonableness as willingness to moderate our demands on the character of the basic social structure, provided others do so, for the sake of willing social cooperation between different groups.

How do these considerations help us with the thesis of rights as trumps? While it is true that many ethical positions reject the Kantian notion of autonomy as a criterion of morality, the Kantian insight seems to me illuminating on the priority of rights because that flows from a widely shared belief in the importance of thinking for oneself, that is, of reflection in ethics. Reflection is often seen as the route to self-discovery and appreciation of the attachments that constitute identity. The Kantian insight is that self-discovery is not all there is. Having found the aims and goods that constitute the identities we inherit, we can go on to ask whether these aims and their internal goods are indeed valuable. Reflection and questioning do not stop at means but address ends as well. We may endorse our inherited way of life and its internal goals, but we may also revise, and even reject it. So reflection opens the way to reconstitution of the self and redefinition of identity.

Once we admit that individuals are capable of questioning and rejecting the value of their community's way of life, then the attempt must be made to provide them with appropriate conditions for the re-examination that is indispensable to their being able to make judgments about final value. Among these conditions should be the guarantees of personal independence necessary to make these judgments freely. Here too should be guarantees of political and social participation without which people's self-determination is restricted. The defence of the priority of rights then is that they are the indispensable means of guaranteeing to every last individual what Kant called the dignity of humanity—the *freedom* to be a member of the realm of ends, a being who can regard him/herself as a person whose duties are self-imposed in accordance with his or her own reason (Kant, 1964, p. 97).

## Conclusions and Challenges

I have focused my discussion on the notion of free moral thinking because it expresses in a clear and insightful way the deep idea that links the various aspects of rights we have been considering. In sum, the thought that the respect in which we are all equally human is our capacity to think for ourselves, grounds the claim that individuals should be free to live their own lives in the light of their own reflectively held convictions. We have seen that the Reformation inspiration on which this is based is the belief that individuals can take care of their own souls and determine for themselves the content of a good life. Individuals should be treated as moral sovereigns, in the sense that their own reason should be the final arbiter in determining how to live. This image of a world of individual moral sovereigns, or of Lockean self-owners, to mention a still popular view,[6] functions as a picture of how moral lives can and should be organised both personally and socially. The image is not a declaration of an extra value or ideal in the world. It is rather a picture of the proper way of organising values and ideals in particular moral lives. It conveys a claim about what might be called the management structure of society, that the level at which values and ideals are to be fashioned into particular lives is the level of individuals themselves. The case for this allocation of power to individuals and its implications for social order comes together in a series of moves that give us the characteristics of a right-based theory of justice. The claim that the dignity of humanity lies in our capacity for free moral thinking, a capacity that all normally functioning men and women are thought to have to an adequate degree, stakes our very humanity on recognition of an original coercive power at the disposal of individuals to secure this vital interest—the generic claim of a right of all human beings to be free. The step from individual capacity for moral thought to its exercise as a matter of a right is mediated by the powerful association of humanity itself with moral independence. The pre-eminence of individual liberty among values is thus explained as the general condition under which people can realise their humanity. The claim that considerations of individual liberty, (properly specified in a scheme of liberties, of course), should trump other considerations in social decision, makes sense as observing the parameters set by the background ideal of a universal human community depicted as a world of moral sovereigns.

There are important differences between rights theorists operating within the broad outline of ideas I have been laying out. There are major disputes about which entitlements to specific rights—for example, to private property or equal resources[7]—fit the framework conviction that people should be in charge of their own lives. These are not my concern here; it is rather to offer an account that shows how the key elements in a right-based theory of political morality can be fitted together. This is not to suggest that the resulting picture is its own justification. It is to show what the distinctive approach on offer is, and what has to be defended or attacked when we come to the overall assessment of rival approaches to political morality.

I began by observing that human rights norms have been highly influential in setting the legitimation criteria for modern political organisation. I hope it is now clear how the idea that the state exists to provide security, freedom and other rights, fits into a pattern of argument that links human dignity and moral independence to government by consent. But the argument for state power does not justify the powers of states. Any argument from human rights opens further questions about the justice of a plurality of states. Given that states are thought to be entitled to perform their tasks within secure territorial boundaries, it is evident that the state system establishes distinctions between the rights and life chances of those whom they divide. This is a problem for a theory wedded to universal rights. The problem of uneven enjoyment of rights and entitlements is recognised in the transnational character of the developing institutions for human rights standard setting and monitoring. But there is a yawning gap between standard setting and monitoring functions and enforcement, because we lack wider agreements on the permeability of state boundaries and thus of state sovereignty with respect to rights enforcing institutions.

The European Union provides one model of a piecemeal approach that fills the gap in the context of a wider regional project of integration. The relevant factors are the willingness of Member States to adopt the common standard of the European convention and to recognise and implement the rulings of the European Court of Justice. These factors exist in the context of a larger set of agreements and common interests and (some) pooled sovereignty. The impermeability of the external boundaries of the EU as a region remains untouched by these internal developments. The porous internal boundaries leave external sovereignty intact. This has raised acute problems in relation to refugee policy and citizenship for resident aliens in the EU. It is also unclear how the Union can justify the distinctions between the rights and expectations of the human lives its boundaries segment from a standpoint that fosters commitment to common human rights among its citizens as a force for integration. The levels of human rights awareness being cultivated through the development of human rights law and educational programs in the EU may be expected to lead to strong internal demands for initiatives that address the conflict between universal principles of human rights and their egregious segmentation by territorial boundaries.

In principle, the EU model of piecemeal negotiation and subsidiarity can be extended to a project of global human rights, perhaps, in concert with what is now called the global democracy project.[8] There are now several proposals for the kinds of supranational institutions we could aim to build, and there are powerful interpretations of the EU model which show that such institutions need not be thought to involve frightening transfers of national sovereignty.[9] The general practical problem is that wider agreements on effective human rights institutions may be dependent on levels of economic development that cannot be achieved without the positive support of better-off countries and regions. The human rights agenda is not separable from engagement with development projects, humanitarian assistance, and some control of the international economic order. In the context of the EU, these considerations raise difficult questions about the balance between the energies and resources devoted to solving the problems of its own integration, and those needed for the moral responsibilities to the wider world inherent in its commitment to human rights principles.

## Notes

[1]    Dworkin (1977, pp. 171–2) distinguishes theories of political morality into right-based, duty-based, and goal-based.

[2]    Material in parenthesis supplied in Ladd's translation.

[3]    This view is criticised in Ingram (1994).

[4]    For texts and commentary, see Waldron (1987).

[5]    See Kymlicka (1991), pp. 62–3.

[6]    For a strong contemporary defence that combines libertarianism with egalitarianism, see Steiner (1994).

[7]    The most extensive defence of Lockean right to private property is Nozick (1974). Waldron (1988) gives a critical analysis of this and other views. A classic socialist response to Nozick is given by Cohen (1986a and 1986b).

[8]    For a useful collection of articles see Archibungi, Held, and Köhler (1998).

[9]    For general institutional proposals see the articles by Held and Rosenau; for an interpretation of subsidiarity in the EU, see the article by Bellamy and Castiglione, in Archibungi, Held and Köhler (1998).

# References

Archibungi, D., Held, D., and Köhler, M. (1998), *Re-imagining Political Community: Studies in Cosmopolitan Democracy*, Polity Press, Oxford.

Cohen, G.A. (1986a), 'Self-Ownership, World-Ownership, and Equality', in E. Lucash (ed.), *Justice and Equality Here and Now*, Cornell Press, Ithaca, New York, pp. 108–135.

Cohen, G.A. (1986b), 'Self-Ownership, World-Ownership, and Equality: Part 2', *Social Philosophy and Policy,* Vol. 3, No. 2, pp. 77–96.

Dworkin, R.M. (1977), *Taking Rights Seriously*, Duckworth, London.

Dworkin, R.M. (1984), 'Rights as Trumps', in J. Waldron (ed.), *Theories of Rights*, Oxford University Press, Oxford, pp. 153–167.

Hart, H.L.A. (1984), 'Are There Any Natural Rights?', in J. Waldron (ed.), *Theories of Rights*, Oxford University Press, Oxford, pp. 77–90.

Ingram, A. (1994), *A Political Theory of Rights*, Clarendon Press, Oxford.

Kant, I. (1964), 'The Metaphysical Principles of Virtue', in *The Metaphysics of Morals*, translated by J. Ellington, Bobbs-Merrill, Indianapolis.

Kant, I. (1965), *The Metaphysical Elements of Justice* (1797), translated by J. Ladd, Bobbs-Merrill, Indianapolis.

Kymlicka, W. (1991), *Liberalism, Community and Culture*, Clarendon Press, Oxford.

Locke, J. (1960), *Two Treatises of Government* (1689), in P. Laslett, (ed.), vol. 11, Cambridge University Press, Cambridge.

Nozick, R. (1974), *Anarchy, State, and Utopia*, Basic Books, New York.

Rawls, J. (1981), *A Theory of Justice*, Harvard University Press, Harvard, Massachusetts.

Rawls, J. (1993), *Political Liberalism*, Columbia University Press, New York.

Ryle, G. (1949), *The Concept of Mind*, Hutchinson, London.

Steiner, H. (1994), *An Essay on Rights*, Blackwell, Oxford.

Waldron, J. (ed.) (1987), *Nonsense Upon Stilts: Bentham, Burke and Marx on the Rights of Man*, Methuen, London and New York.

Waldron, J. (1988), *The Right to Private Property,* Clarendon Press, Oxford.

Wild, R. (1968), 'Human Rights in Retrospect', in K.J. Keith (ed.), *Essays on Human Rights,* Sweet and Maxwell, Wellington, pp. 1–13.

# 3 Women and Human Rights in Europe: Views from France

BRONWYN WINTER

The slogan 'women's rights are human rights' has gained considerable international currency in the 1990s. In 1998, the year of the 50th Anniversary of the Universal Declaration of Human Rights, the 53rd General Assembly of the UN incorporated a 'gender perspective on human rights' into its discussions on the elaboration of a new declaration for the 21st Century.[1] In Europe, the European Union has moved increasingly towards 'mainstreaming' of women's rights issues (ie. incorporation of a gender perspective into all EU policy). Both the UN and the EU have created or officially recognised a number of fora and committees (such as the UN Division for the Advancement of Women, the Women's Rights Committee of the European Parliament and the European Women's Union) devoted to the elaboration of various initiatives for the advancement of women's rights.

With all this apparent official recognition of women's human rights, few but the radical right would now question women's right to human dignity, to freedom of movement, to an education, to freedom from violence and so on. Or at least, they would not do so 'out loud'.[2] However, such superficial quasi-unanimity hides a number of problems that muddy western thinking about 'women's rights'. These problems can be grouped under six interconnected themes.

The first issue of 'women's rights' is generally limited in national and international political discourse to a question of 'equality', usually defined narrowly as 'some women being able to do what some men currently do in the public sphere'. Not only is this model based on the assumption that it is in women's interest to imitate 'male' roles in a male-dominated world, but most oppressions of women, and indeed most women, are excluded from the model in the first place. Even those cases of 'sex discrimination' or of 'sexual violence' specifically referred to in EU documents—usually within the context of the workplace or education—are not necessarily considered to be 'human rights' issues as such.[3]

Second, violations of 'human rights' is invariably deemed a 'Third World' problem, or else perceived to be restricted to the treatment of ethnic minorities

25

or, occasionally, the disabled, in western societies. Where sex-specific violations of 'minority' women *are* recognised as occurring, they are deemed a 'cultural' problem and the responsibility is thus attributed to minority men. The ideas that majority men can violate the sex-specific human rights of minority women and that the rights of white gentile women in Europe can be violated outside wartime, thus have little to no currency.

Third, in any case, the term 'human rights' continues to be understood as synonymous with 'men's rights'. Violations of 'women's rights' in whatever country are simply not taken as seriously as violations of 'men's rights', if they are perceived to exist at all (unless it can be argued that men are also affected). Even the narrow 'equality' model is not fully enforced in any country in the world.

Fourth, 'women's rights' can also be redefined to mean 'the "right" to do whatever men want women to do in order to maintain male privilege and domination of women'. This is rationalised through the western liberal interpretation of rights as 'self-ownership' and the ensuing libertarian-contractarian approach to 'market exchange' of oneself as of any other 'property'. The currently fashionable idea of western women's 'right' to prostitute themselves is an example of this sort of analysis.

Fifth, another fashionable conservative discourse that parades as 'oppositional', using the theoretical model of cultural relativism, is the questioning of the very notion of 'human rights', based on the reasoning that it is an ethnocentric, phallocentric and individualistic western concept. This leads, somewhat paradoxically, to a claiming of a kind of 'right' *not* to have 'rights', and may or may not be associated with the development of a notion of 'group rights', to which all individual rights are subordinated.

Sixth, a variant of the above problem is the rewriting of the concept of 'human rights' as one of 'national (or cultural) sovereignty'. In the Franco-European context, for example, campaigns for the protection of other social rights have typically been strongly tied to arguments for national autonomy. In the case of women, however, the exercise of such 'national sovereignty' has invariably depended on the *violation* of their human rights.

So, what at the outset could seem a fairly straightforward activity, that of defining and defending European 'women's rights' in human rights terms, starts to seem like a rather slippery endeavour once one attempts to move beyond the political platitudes.

To look at how these six sets of problems manifest themselves within Europe, I will draw on some examples from the French context. However, while each national context in Europe will present its own peculiarities, there is sufficient similarity between the various countries with regard to the issue of 'women's rights', for extrapolation from the French context to be meaningful. The French context is particularly illuminating in that while France prides itself on being the 'inventor' of human rights, it remains attached to a peculiarly masculinist definition of the concept.

## Equality with whom and for whom?

Problem number one is that 'women's rights' are seen as fitting into an 'equality' paradigm within the public sphere—that is, public education, the workplace and politics. Thus the conditions currently enjoyed by middle-class white heterosexual western men are taken not only as the norm but as the ideal. This is usually understood to mean that once a significant minority of women has succeeded in aligning itself to this norm in certain areas of public life, the problem of 'women's rights' is well on the way to being solved. This particular discourse has been quite prevalent in France, as it has in the EU, from its inception with the Treaty of Rome (1957) and throughout the following decades.[4] Jane Lewis goes as far as to say that 'gender equality was virtually the be-all and end-all of Community social policy' during the 50s, 60s and 70s (Lewis, 1993, p. 23). However, as both Lewis and Elizabeth Meehan point out, although the then EC's policies on women led to considerable gains, they have been characterised by three major problems: first, the failure of formal EU anti-discrimination legislation to address structural and indirect problems of discrimination within the workforce and welfare agencies; second, the plethora of litigation cases resulting in the acceptance of a number of instances of national exception to EU anti-discrimination policies; and third, the fact that 'equality' is in any case considered synonymous with 'sameness' with (some) men (Lewis, 1993; Meehan, 1993). Even attention to other issues of major concern to women, such as child-rearing and male violence, has tended to centre on the workplace, with recommendations concerning maternity leave and sexual harassment, for example, although this is not to deny that such measures nonetheless represent important advances for European women (Gregory, 1995; Collins, 1996). It is also noteworthy that much feminist research on women and the EU has similarly centred on what is broadly referred to as 'social policy', that is, policies on the workplace, education, welfare and family needs (eg. Lewis, 1993; Duncan, 1996; García-Ramon and Monk, 1996).

More recently, a major European focus has been on equal representation in politics and other spheres of decision-making. The first EU-sponsored Summit of Women in Power took place in Athens in November 1992, and the ensuing declaration (3 November) launched 'a campaign to reinforce European democracy' through the provision of 'equal access to instances of decision-making'. On 8 March, 1994, the European Parliament issued a resolution on the situation of women in the EU (Resolution B3-0225, 0258, 0264, 0265 and 0267/94). Of the 20 articles comprising this resolution, five directly concerned the participation of women in politics and decision-making and four directly concerned workplace, welfare and educational equality. Other articles were devoted to reaffirming the principle of equality. Two years later, another women's summit took place ('Women in Decision-making'), and its Charter of Rome (18 May 1996) focused on women's participation in parliamentary politics. The same year, the EU launched its Fourth Action Program for equal opportunity between the sexes. The major objectives of this program focused on the promotion of equal opportunity 'in a changing economy'; of policies that enable the combining of professional and family life for both sexes; and equal participation by women and men in decision-making, along with the reinforcement of protections for women's rights in these areas.

So the EU seems to have gone largely the way of the United Nations before it in limiting its major articulation of 'women's rights' to the 'equality model'. This is not to say there is no mention whatsoever of violence against women. In UN documents in particular, there are specific articles referring to the traffic in women, rape, domestic violence and other abuses of women. However, such violence is never put at the centre of the picture. It is included in a clause among many, or as an addendum to the 'main' document, which is based on the 'equality' model and remains the primary reference (Winter, 1996a). Now, few would deny that women in the workforce should be paid the same wages as men and have the same rights to job security, training, superannuation and so on, or that women should be able to participate effectively in instances of decision-making. Nor would any feminist deny that if the EU has taken such issues on board, it is only because it was forced to do so by women themselves through years of relentless campaigning. 'Equality', however limited, *is* an important issue, given that women who do not have the independent means to provide adequately for themselves and who are systematically excluded from national, supranational or international decision-making have immense difficulty in effecting any sort of major change in their own or other women's lives. However, such observations do not change the fact that the 'equality' model remains limited and defective, for it is based on three main errors in logic.

First, the fact that a minority of women manage to 'succeed'—that is, obtain (usually) some professional or post-secondary academic qualification along with salary equity—within a particular male-dominated socio-economic stratum hardly means that structural inequalities between women and men (or between different groups of women) have been removed (Hoskyns, 1996). As far as the area of work is concerned, even EU directives such as that of 1975 (75/117) on 'equal pay for work of equal value', and training and equal opportunity programs launched under the EU's Third Action Program in the first half of the 1990s, have done little either to counter the devaluing of 'feminised industries' (eg. clothing trade, nursing, primary school teaching) or to remove the barriers of entrenched class systems that reproduce unequal distributions of wealth. The majority of low-paid workers in precarious employment, even in an 'equal pay' situation, remain female. In 1991, the European Network of Women found that what lay at the basis of women's poverty in Europe was the sexual division of labour, with women doing unpaid domestic labour and dominating the lowest-paid sectors of the workforce (ENOW/CEF 1991). In France in 1990, 60 per cent of waged women worked in the six most feminised sectors of employment, and in 1993 14 per cent of women were unemployed as compared with 10 per cent of men (this figure reached 25.7 per cent and 19.3 per cent respectively for the under-25 age group). Of the French women who *do* have a job, over 25 per cent work part-time, as against 3 per cent of men (Maruani and Reynaud, 1993, cited by Delphy, 1995, p. 42, and CNIDFF/INSEE, 1995, p. 133). As concerns income, 1992 figures showed that the average base rate for men over all sectors was 22.7 per cent more than that for women; this figure rose to 26.7 per cent more for the average actual wage paid (CNIDFF/INSEE, 1995, p. 151).

Moreover, even feminist campaigns in the area of 'work' do not always challenge the assumptions on which 'work' is based, namely, the division of 'work' into labour and capital, into hierarchies of 'white' and 'blue' collar work (or, particularly for women, 'professional' and 'service' work), the former attracting significantly greater remuneration and better working conditions. Nor do they always challenge the explicit 'sex-objectification' of work in the advertising, fashion, 'beauty', 'sex' and service industries, although attention is frequently drawn to employers' and colleagues' sexist expectations of female workers in other sectors (eg. expectations of 'good grooming', sexual harassment, allocation of hackwork and 'servicing' work allocated to women who are ostensibly in 'equal' employment).

Second, the 'equality' model, by reinforcing the division between the 'public' and the 'private' (Hoskyns, 1996), provides no means of addressing the sex-specific oppressions that affect women, such as rape, incest, pornography, prostitution, wife-beating, woman-hating cultural imagery and male-dominated educational models, the infringement of reproductive rights, lack of collective social responsibility for child rearing, and disregard for women's specific health. EU treaties and policy documents may address some aspects of these issues:

article 7 of the Convention on Transfrontier Broadcasting states that transfrontier broadcasts must not contain pornography, and the 1986 Resolution on Violence Against Women was designed to combat trafficking in women. However, they are rarely either central to EU legislation or really enforceable. Often they are resolutions or policy documents rather than directives or treaties, and are thus easily sidelined, particularly given the absence of national legislation and strong lobbies such as the pornography industry and the pro-prostitution lobby (Itzin, 1996; Leidholdt, 1996).

This lack of central focus either on the capitalist rationale behind 'work', on work dependent to some degree on the sexual exploitation of women or on other sex-specific violations of women's rights not directly linked to 'employment', is in fact directly attributable to the third flaw in logic. Put simply, the insufficiencies of the 'equality' model reside in the presumption that the solution to women's oppression resides in slotting women more easily and visibly into a phallocratic social structure. This hardly corresponds to a feminist idea of equality.

## Equality and the French Context

Despite the pitfalls of the 'equality' model—of which many feminists are indeed aware—it remains a significant area of feminist political activity within the EU. One French campaign that has attracted considerable attention in the 1990s is that of equal political representation.

The tardiness with which French women were given the vote (1944) and their continuing under-representation in political institutions seems paradoxical in a country that was one of the first to embrace republican democracy. This paradox stems from the limited definition given at the time of the Revolution, and prevailing long thereafter, of both political rights and those qualified to exercise them, as well as from the strongly individualistic character of the French definition of rights which both excluded women who were not perceived as 'individuals', and operated against the idea of any representation of women's collective interests (Perrot, 1993).

So, the fact that French feminist campaigns for 'equal rights' have only recently started to focus on political participation, now known as 'parity' (*parité*), is hardly surprising. However, now that (some) French women *have* decided to focus on it, they have quickly moved to the forefront of the European campaign. The association *Parité* was created in mid-1992 by a number of women active both in politics and in the women's movement, with the specific objective of ensuring equal representation of women in all elected political bodies.

While feminist accountability is not an explicit objective of the parity move-ment, many of its followers believe it should be supported by and answerable to the feminist movement, so that elected women are not isolated and their voices not drowned out and so that elected women will not 'sell out' to the male-supremacist agenda (Dental, 1993). In this way, it is hoped by some in-volved in the campaign that the pitfalls of the 'equality' model can be avoided, because the women in power would work to bring about real advancement for *all* women. Further, it is argued, the specificity of women's oppression will not be overlooked, as the actions of the women in power would be informed by a feminist analysis; and the goal will no longer be 'sameness' with men on male-supremacist terms, but a transformation of the exercise of political voice and political power. How well this actually works in practice remains to be seen, although current evidence indicates that pro-feminist women in parliament have had limited opportunity to support feminist campaigns, either through personal adherence to party politics or through being marginalised by their own parties (Adler, 1993).

*Parité* has been extremely active since its inception, and its *Manifeste des 577 pour une démocratie paritaire*, signed by a number of well-known women, and published in the national daily *Le Monde* in November 1993, attracted considerable public attention and sympathy for their cause (Barzach *et al*, 1996; Sensier, 1996). In 1996, the association organised a European conference spon-sored by the European Commission and the French Women's Rights Bureau (Gaspard, 1997). Unfortunately, the growing popularity of the campaign has led to cooption and lip service of the parity issue by male politicians of both the right-wing coalition, in power between 1993 and 1997, and the current socialist-led coalition government.

In 1994, women represented 6 per cent of *députés* in the *Assemblée Nationale*, the lower house of the French parliament (with hardly any of these ministers), and roughly 4.5 per cent of senior civil servants. Compare this with French women in the European Parliament, where women represented almost 30 per cent of elected members in 1994. Following the 1995 election of the French Gaullist president, Jacques Chirac, and the appointment of his prime minister, Alain Juppé, (from the same party), the two made much of their ap-pointment of twelve women ministers—the greatest number ever. Most of the new female ministers' portfolios, however, remained the traditionally 'soft' ('social') ones of environment, the family, health and school education. The women were perceived as ineffectual figureheads, to the extent that they were dubbed the 'Juppettes' (miniskirts) by the media and only four of the twelve were fully-fledged ministers. The rest were Secretaries of State attached to a ministry held by someone else. Moreover, during a ministerial reshuffle less than a year later, eight of these women lost their portfolios to men, or the portfolios in question were abolished.

After the 1997 legislative elections, France moved up the scale of women's political representation in the EU Member States: from number fifteen to number thirteen. The proportion of women in the lower house moved from 35 out of 577 (6 per cent) to 63 out of 577 (11 per cent), and in December 1998, women made up 30 per cent of the ministers in Lionel Jospin's socialist government. Moreover, some of them have been given typically male-dominated ministries such as Employment (Martine Aubry), Justice (Elisabeth Guigou), and Culture (Catherine Trautmann), which seems to indicate a definite movement from tokenism to political representation with 'teeth'. Unfortunately, the flawed logic of the 'equality' model still remains: equal representation in parliament, even through the presence of women on the party-political left, does not guarantee a feminist agenda. Guigou and Aubry are not known for putting forward any overtly feminist agenda (although the Women's Rights Bureau is attached to Aubry's ministry), and Trautmann, although popular with women because of her outspokenness against the National Front in her capacity as Mayor of Strasbourg, is still far from being a radical by any feminist criterion.

In fact, the *Parité* campaign throws into very clear focus the problems with the 'equality' model: without a clear feminist agenda, the mere presence of numbers (even equal numbers) of women in instances of decision-making, whether in politics or on the company board, will not guarantee any sort of transformation of either the polity or the workplace in ways that ensure respect of all women's rights (Le Dœuff, 1995).

Certainly, many feminists are aware of the limitations of such 'equality campaigns', seeing them only as the bare minimum necessary for women to both survive materially and participate (at least to some extent) as social actors. Notably, such battles for (limited) equality are also the most easily winnable within the EU context. The institutions of a liberal male-supremacist society can afford to take on 'equal rights' issues as they do not, for the time being, threaten current structures of social organisation. It is this reason, I would argue, these issues are pushed so strongly by institutions such as the EU, to the detriment of others which could be seen as infinitely more urgent and which would require social, political and cultural change that would reach far beyond the incorporation of a handful of women into the current status quo. Women campaigning against various forms of male violence and intimidation of women that occur outside the office or factory have a significantly harder time. Interestingly, we also hear significantly less about such campaigns, including within feminist political and academic circles. Unfortunately, a number of women's rights campaigners appear to see the 'bare minimum' of the 'equality model', not as a stepping stone towards a more far reaching goal, but *as the goal in itself.*

## 'Human Rights': A Non-Issue?

This brings us to the second set of problems, namely, the association of the idea of violations of 'human rights' with images of dictatorships, child prostitution and labour, oppression of ethnic minorities and exploitation of workers in general and women in particular in the so-called 'Third World'. In Europe, this means the oppression either of European ethnic minorities or of non-European immigrants, or particular forms of violence in situations of civil war; or wars between neighbouring countries in non-EU regions or countries such as Chechnya, Bosnia or Kosovo. In other words, 'human rights' is rarely understood to refer to *western women in peacetime*, nor is it usually understood to refer to ways in which the situation of ethnic minority women (immigrant or not) may *differ* from that of minority men. Even in such cases, it is usually perceived as being 'an ethnic minority issue only'. This may well be so, as in cases of culturally specific practices such as the imposition of Islamic personal law or female genital mutilation (FGM) among North African or sub-Saharan minorities in France, but it is often not, as in cases of trafficking in non-western women, or rape of non-western women in domestic service (more on this presently). Even where such problems are acknowledged to exist, they tend to be considered as marginal cases, and have certainly not been taken up in any concerted way within the European Union.

The French are as proficient as any at this form of denial of women's rights abuses in the west. Observe, for example, this remark from well-known historian François Furet, identified with the intellectual centre-left: 'In Islamic countries, the situation of women is frightening ... We cannot tolerate this sort of thing here' (Furet, 1989). This dismissal of minority women's rights as an 'immigrant problem' and the concurrent denial that white French women's rights are being violated, is common-place in France. The dominant myth is that the 'woman question' has been solved or is well on the way to being solved, the few 'discriminations' that remain being the last vestiges of the *ancien régime.* Officially media-accredited voices of 'feminism' lend weight to such fantasies. One of the most strident is that of Elisabeth Badinter, whose 1986 book, *L'Un est l'Autre*, affirms that the French revolution struck the first major blows against patriarchy and that the years since the start of the 'second wave' of feminism have 'sounded its death knell' (Badinter, 1986, p. 215). Using Simone de Beauvoir's concept of women as the 'Other' (both object and peripheral) while men are the subject, the 'One' at the centre (de Beauvoir, 1949), Badinter argued in this book that women had become 'one' with men as it were, in terms of rights.

In the wider European context, 'human rights' have generally been associated with notions of citizenship and the attendant exercise of political rights, focused on central and eastern Europe and on regional minorities in EU countries. This focus, along with the context of war, is perhaps why the mass rape of Bosnian women by the Serbian military was taken seriously as a crime against women. This was, however, only after massive feminist mobilisation throughout Europe, including France, over several years. Although not attracting a large turnout at regular twilight vigils held in Paris from autumn 1992 onwards, the association *Solidarité avec les femmes de l'ex-Yougoslavie* nonetheless succeeded in heightening public awareness and in raising money to send various items to Bosnian women. The campaign was joined in January 1993 by women politicians of the EU, who, under the aegis of *Femmes d'Europe—femmes de cœur et d'action*, launched a national fundraising appeal and participated in a much-publicised EU delegation to Bosnia later that year. This combined grassroots and party-political feminist campaign succeeded, for the first time in European history, in obtaining official acknowledgment of rape as both a war crime and a crime against humanity.

One wonders, however, how successful the feminist campaign would have been if the mass rape of Bosnian women had not *also*—and even, in many cases, *primarily*—been represented as a form of 'ethnic cleansing' through Serbian impregnation of Bosnian women (even though pre-pubescent girls and post-menopausal women were raped in similarly great numbers). While the real violence suffered by Bosnian women was perceived as horrible indeed, the *symbolic* violence perpetrated against the *men* through the bodies of the women, I would argue, was ultimately what counted the most in international opinion, with comparisons with Hitler's 'final solution' abounding.[5] Had the crimes against Bosnian women not been represented as part of an assault on a people (and thus on men), would the feminist campaign have obtained as much sympathy? Would it have obtained as much sympathy without the demonisation of the Serbs, without the distancing superiority that French men were able to feel in deploring the 'balkanisation' of central Europe? Would it have obtained as much sympathy if it had concerned the rape of French women in a country not at war?

The answer, I would argue, is probably no in the first case, and definitely no in the second and third. The sad truth is that apart from extreme exceptions such as Bosnia, women in Europe, particularly of western European descent, are not generally perceived as suffering from any major violation of their human rights that *is specific to them as women*. Even those cases of 'sex discrimination' or of 'sexual violence' specifically referred to in EU documents—usually within the context of the workplace or education—are not considered to be 'human rights' issues as such. Women suffering these 'discriminations' or acts of 'physical abuse' are not seen as being denied freedom of movement or expression, as suffering repression or imprisonment or slavery. Within such a discursive context, the assertion that women in countries such as France are suffering in great numbers from human rights abuses is made to appear rather odd.

Yet this is precisely what is happening, not only through the denial of political voice or through the maintenance of women in situations of poverty, but through the daily perpetration of acts of physical and/or psychological violence against women and female children. Such acts of violence are rarely denounced as human rights abuses or even made public. When they are, they are usually sensationalised as the isolated act of a madman, as was evidenced through reporting of the Montreal massacre of 1989, when a male student gunned down fourteen female engineering students in their classroom[6]. A European example is the reporting of Marc Dutroux's serial rapes and murders of pre-pubescent girls in Belgium in 1996, an affair in which Belgian police were said to be implicated. It is significant that the media reporting of the latter case focused, not on the issue of male violence against girls, but on the issue of 'pædophilia', seen as sex-neutral, when in fact the majority (90-95 per cent) of paedophilia victims are female (Clarac and Bonnin, 1985, p. 141).[7] In other words, not only are widespread crimes against women sensationalised as isolated incidents, but even in these rare cases, they are not always clearly spelt out as crimes *against women*. Nor are they described as 'human rights' abuses, for they are seen as neither political (read 'part of the public sphere') nor perpetrated with state collusion, an assumption contested by feminists such as Charlotte Bunch:

> The assumption that states are not responsible for violations of women's rights in the private or cultural sphere ignores the fact that such abuses are often condoned or even sanctioned by states even when the immediate perpetrator is a private citizen. The distinction between private and public is a dichotomy largely used to justify female subordination and to exclude human rights abuses in the home from public scrutiny. Yet human rights activists readily pressure states to prevent other forms of abuse, such as slavery and racial discrimination, that also occur in the private sphere (Bunch, 1995, p. 14).

## Human Rights, Men's Rights, Women's Rights

This leads to the third and related problem area: the fact that violence and discrimination against women are not taken as seriously as other human rights violations. A change in terminology from 'the rights of man' to 'human rights' has not necessarily been accompanied by a change in thinking concerning *women's* rights as a central, rather than secondary, human rights issue. Rather, the term 'human' has, in fact, taken on some of the connotations of the term 'man' that it superseded. (Guillaumin (1992b) has made a similar point in relation to the replacement of the term 'race' by terms such as 'ethnicity' or 'culture'). Of course, the majority of the French have not embraced a change of terminology, justifying the continued use of the expression *les droits de l'homme* by France's specific historical connection and enduring political attachment to the *Déclaration des droits de l'homme et du citoyen* of 1789. Even UNESCO's bilingual guide to non-sexist language allows this 'historically significant' exception. Such a justification is, however, spurious in the light of the facts that masculine nouns also tend to dominate in other areas where maleness is perceived as the norm, and in any case, in 1789 the expression really did only refer to (some) men! Despite the sidelining, however, there *has* been considerable feminist debate in France, in political, academic and activist circles, concerning sexism in language, with a particular focus on the pros and cons of feminising names of professions (Michard and Viollet, 1989; Michard, 1991; Groult, 1997).

Men's experience is still taken as the general, while that of women is the particular, often being subsumed under some 'human' oppression that is perceived as much nastier. Some European women's lobby groups, such as the NGO European Union of Women (*Union Européenne de Femmes*) have been attempting to change this mind set. On 28 January 1993, the French section of this NGO published a motion condemning the 'torture and degrading treatment' of women and girls. While a number of paragraphs in the motion referred specifically to Bosnia, a number of other observations and demands were made, including the following:

The French Section of the European Union of Women [...]

Observes that the [European] Charter of Human Rights is interpreted as rights belonging to men. Observes that half of the human race, those belonging to the female sex, are mostly excluded from rights in the name of customs, religions and of the State (UEF, 1993).

This text clearly challenges the assumption that the violation of women's rights is an isolated, private act committed by deviant individuals.

The assertion that rape is a violation of human rights has been accompanied by campaigns for women's acts of self-defence against their rapists to be considered acts in defence of their human rights, and as such, treated with leniency by institutions of justice. In 1996 the French case of Véronique Akobé received much media attention. In 1990, Akobé, a clandestine domestic worker from the Ivory Coast, had been tried in Nice and sentenced to twenty years' prison for having killed her employer's son and seriously injured her employer, both of whom had repeatedly raped her. During the trial, Akobé, who had already spent two years in prison prior to the trial, testified that the two men would come into her room and one would hold her down while the other raped her. The rapes were not recognised by the court and the jury actually pronounced a *heavier* sentence than the 15 years recommended by the prosecuting attorney. A feminist campaign was launched immediately and spread throughout Europe and beyond; over nine months during 1995–1996, the *Association Européenne contre les Violences faites aux Femmes au Travail* collected 44,000 signatures on a petition demanding Akobé's release. At the beginning of July 1996, Akobé was granted a pardon by the French president, on the basis that there were 'extenuating circumstances', but the rapes were still not officially acknowledged to have happened.

There was general public recognition that if Akobé had been pardoned, it was because she had been unjustly imprisoned in the first place. Her case also focused attention both on the abusive treatment of domestic workers (who are mainly female) in western Europe, and on the specific violence and discrimination suffered *in Europe* by women of non-European background. As such, the case represents a landmark, and a significant feminist victory in putting violence against women *as a violation of their human rights* on the French, and by extension, European, agenda.

Unfortunately, in spite of such tenuous indications that acts of violence against women are starting to be recognised as violations of women's *human* rights, much work remains to be done. As sketched out in the introduction, the crux of the problem here concerns the double-thinking of female submission to male domination into a 'right' for women. This is made possible by the dominant definition of 'rights' in terms of self-ownership and of human interaction in terms of contractual relationships. One of the implications of this is that if an individual has a 'right' to contract to sell her property, then, given that she is, in fact, her own 'property', nothing prevents her from selling herself into various forms of slavery. Conversely, any given individual has the right to 'buy' and amass property, which frequently includes other individuals or the products of those individuals' labour. Such a libertarian-contractarian model does not allow clear identification and challenging of relationships of domination (Pateman, 1988; Ingram, 1994).

A classic example of such double-think is the argument for the legalisation of prostitution, on the basis that not to do so would constitute a denial of a woman's 'right' to exercise her profession publicly and 'safely'. This presentation of prostitution as an 'emancipation' issue seems reminiscent of the 'equality' model, in that it takes currently prevailing male desires and methods of social organisation as the ideal, but it is in fact quite different. At issue here is not the 'emancipation' of (some) women so they can do the same things men do in the public sphere, but the removal of legal and moral restrictions on the exercise of woman-specific activities in the service of the male-dominant social order (Pateman, 1988; Jeffreys, 1997).

A further problem with the presentation of prostitution as a 'right' is a perceived difference between the prostitution of western women in western countries and that of non-western women in both western and non-western countries. A greater element of 'choice' is assumed to exist among 'emancipated' western women, whereas non-western women are seen as passive victims by definition (Leidholdt, 1996). Racist-sexist stereotyping of the 'downtrodden Third World woman' thus manages both to refuse agency to these women while appearing to be sympathetic to their cause, as well as to reinforce the myth of the 'emancipated' western woman. At the same time, however, it contributes to the perpetuation of her oppression, because it is simply not perceived as such. Unfortunately, many self-identified feminists have espoused this line of thinking and have become champions of prostitution, pornography, sado-masochism, pædophilia, and so on, although this tendency is considerably less marked in France than elsewhere, and there is some evidence that the French media are less sympathetic to prostitution than their counterparts in English-speaking countries.

What is more immediately obvious in France is the defence of 'femininity' as expressed through the work of women identified with so-called 'difference feminism' or *féminitude*, such as Julia Kristeva, Luce Irigaray and Hélène Cixous. It should be noted, however, that the school of so-called 'difference feminism' is not particularly concerned with the issue of 'rights' as such, but rather with setting up a theory of 'difference' in opposition to phallocentric 'equality' (Brodribb, 1992; Guillaumin, 1992a, pp. 83–106). More 'mainstream' pseudo-feminist defences of 'femininity' pursue another variation: the 'different-but-equal' line. Elisabeth Badinter, for example, has argued in favour of 'sexual difference' within a context of 'equality' and extolled the joys of flirting as 'a sweetness of life', criticising those prudish American feminists for complaining about sexual harassment (Badinter, 1994, p. 43).[8]

The championing of 'femininity' as a matter of 'choice' is particularly evident, moreover, in the imagery of 'fashion' and in advertising. Of course, such imagery exists elsewhere, and would appear to be on the increase, but it is arguable that it is attributed particular cultural significance in France. For example, considerable exposure is given to the fashion industry on national television news programs: daily reports on the new collections of French and foreign couturiers are featured at the start of each season, as an important item on the cultural agenda. The effect of such exposure is reinforcement of the anorexic fashion model wearing constraining clothes as a role model for women. One could indeed be forgiven for assuming that the encouragement of anorexic behaviour is part of French cultural policy, given the relative lack of either medical or public attention given to female eating disorders, and the alarmingly high number of advertisements for slimming creams, pills and so on, that appear in even the most 'pro-feminist' of mainstream women's magazines.

## 'Women's Rights' vs. 'Cultural/National' Interests

The fifth area of muddy thinking around the issue of 'women's rights' is the somewhat fashionable questioning of the notion of individual rights altogether, on the grounds that it is a product of western and phallocentric ideology. According to this line of reasoning, we must therefore throw individual rights out along with anything else that might resemble 'ideology', and replace it with an 'anything goes' potpourri based on individual or 'cultural' self-definition. Such thinking shows limited imagination and great intellectual sloth, not to mention a singular lack of common sense. In such action the male-supremacist or white-supremacist definition of 'rights' is assumed to be the only one around; there is no attempt to find any practical alternative to this 'rights' model that may allow for some coherent social interaction based on respect for human dignity; and, it seems to be a case of the disposal of babies with their bathwater. Western men invented this, so we had better 'get rid of it quickly' and do it all over again. Or not do it at all.[9]

It is difficult to see how this wholesale ditching of the notion of 'rights' can help any oppressed group fight its oppression, as there is no acknowledgment of the material existence of a social order, with its hierarchies and subgroups, which means there is no suggestion as to what might be done to *change* this social order. One cannot change what one refuses to identify. In fact, the relativisation of rights based on 'self-definition' can only advantage those individuals or groups that are *already* privileged, powerful and articulate, that is, those that are in a material position to impose their own self-definitions, as well as their interpretations of the self-definitions of others.

This is not in any way reconcilable with a feminist project for social change that is inclusive of *all* women. Quite the contrary: far from doing women greater service than the 'equality' model, the 'difference' model takes us back into socio-biologising and essentialising notions of 'women's specificity' of the type defended by the 'difference' feminists referred to above or by socio-biologists, notions that many of us had hoped to have left behind in some dark pre-feminist age (Hubbard, 1990; Kay, 1990; Guillaumin, 1992a, pp. 153–170).

Other schools of thought have not entirely ditched the notion of rights, but subordinate individual rights to those of the group or culture. The cause of group or cultural rights has been defended in intellectual circles by cultural relativists such as Will Kymlicka (1989, 1990, 1995), Michel Erlich (1986) and Raymond Verdier (1990), and in international circles by transnational governmental or non-governmental cultural and/or religious groups. These groups have produced 'culturally specific' human rights declarations such as the *Cairo Declaration of Human Rights in Islam* (Organisation of Islamic States, 1990, see also Mayer, 1995); a similar document has been produced within the Asian context (Bangkok Declaration).

The relativisation of 'rights' is further enabled by ambiguities and contradictions contained in UN and European human rights documents. For example, the Universal Declaration of Human Rights contains tensions between the exercise of public and private rights, and between women's rights and religious rights (UN Division for the Advancement of Women, in Moghadam, 1994, chapter 21; Sullivan, 1995; Mayer, 1995). There exist fairly obvious contradictions between the Convention of the Elimination of All Forms of Discrimination Against Women (CEDAW), 1979,[10] and documents such as the Declaration on the Elimination of All Forms of Intolerance and Discrimination Based on Religion or Belief, 1981, in particular Article 5 on parental religious rights. In the European context, Articles 8, 9, 10 and 12 of the European Convention for Protection of Human Rights and Fundamental Freedoms (1950)—on private and family life, freedom of religion, freedom of expression and the 'right to marry' respectively—sit uneasily beside Article 14 (prohibition of discrimination on the grounds of sex, among other things) and the various agreements and action programs on the elimination of discrimination against women. Such contradictions are rarely exploited in favour of women, and it is arguable that this is particularly the case at this point in time, as Europe finds itself in an increasingly 'multicultural' context, both materially and discursively.

In France as elsewhere, the cultural relativist lobby has been particularly vocal in its defence of 'group rights' to exercise 'cultural practices' that are clearly directed specifically at the control of women within the private (and to a certain extent, public) sphere, such as polygamy, Islamic female dress and FGM (Moghadam, 1994; Winter, 1994; Okin, 1998). The culture-specific and sex-specific interpretation of the concept of 'persecution', for example, has been spectacularly demonstrated during French trials for FGM. Both 'custom' and the supposed relativity of the 'notions' of pain and mutilation have been invoked by 'expert' witnesses for the defence (Winter, 1994).

Allowance for 'cultural specificity' within both the European and wider international contexts is also made by provisions for 'a margin of appreciation' of local conditions when applying international directives (van Dijk and van Hoof, 1990; van der Vyver, 1996). This has led to a number of cases of 'national exception' being established concerning the application of international conventions and laws on women's rights (Lewis, 1993; Meehan, 1993). Moreover, as I have noted elsewhere in relation to the UN, such international treaties often do not carry the force of law and even where they are assumed to, enforcement is difficult (Winter, 1996b). France is particularly good at playing the 'national exception' card and at taking advantage of the weaknesses in EU provisions on women's rights, even where such provisions have been applauded by women as a breakthrough. EU policy on sexual harassment, for example, has had little influence on French legislation, which compares unfavourably with that of a number of other EU countries (Mazur, 1996).

Such weaknesses and contradictions in EU legislation and policy, along with the influence of cultural relativist lobbies, have provided the perfect ideological justification for governments and legal institutions to continue to disregard violations of women's and also of (female) children's rights. This intertwining of 'group rights' relativism and national strategies of avoidance has fed into the final area of problem thinking about 'women's rights', namely, the incompatibility of women's rights with 'national sovereignty'.

When one looks outside the area of 'women's rights', it becomes evident that most if not all 'rights' campaigns led by groups of French nationals within the EU context have been strongly linked to some form of national self-interest. For example, concerned by the possible dismantling of a national system of social and worker protection that is perceived, with reason, to be one of the best in Europe, the French Communist Party voted, in a referendum held in France in September 1992, against ratification of the Maastricht Treaty. The fear was that the policies underpinning the formation of the European Union would lead to an erosion of French workers' rights through a realignment of social provisions to the 'lowest common denominator'. It was thus perceived as being in French workers' self-interest to support French autonomy within the EU, at least as far as economic and social policy were concerned.

French women's rights, on the contrary, are not even remotely tied to national self-interest. In fact, it has often been argued that women can only continue to prop up national identity and serve national sovereignty if their own well-being is consistently ignored and even overtly denied (eg. Enloe, 1990; Hélie-Lucas, 1990; Kandiyoti, 1991; Yuval-Davis, 1992, 1997; Pettman, 1996). I would add that an idea of 'national sovereignty' that did *not* involve the subordination of women's interests to those of 'the group' is a conceptual impossibility, unless one were to radically redefine what a nation—or nation-state—is. At the same time, women are allocated a central role in safeguarding both national and cultural identity and in propping up the economic structures of the nation state—even if the importance of these roles is rarely acknowledged (Enloe, 1990). The most obvious example of national and supranational structures' simultaneous dependence on women's self-sacrifice and disregard for women's rights—even where women's participation in the national project is actively encouraged—is that of women's role in child bearing and raising, including the 'passing on' of cultural norms to ensuing generations through the domestic and institutional education of children.

Many feminists, both within and outside Europe, have thus long been aware that for women to get anywhere at all in defining and exercising their rights, it is imperative to reach beyond the confines of nation-states and their particular interests. In short, it is imperative to think and act internationally. So, while many French feminists cherish no illusions about the possibilities offered by the EU, they have realised its usefulness as a bridge across and beyond national boundaries. In much the same way as feminist NGOs worldwide have been able to use the United Nations as a public forum and as a source of political and financial support (however imperfect the forum and limited the support), French feminists have used the EU to seek funding for international feminist solidarity initiatives and to bring pressure to bear on the French government and on other European governments concerning women's rights.

Unfortunately, women lobbying European institutions come up against the same difficulties and contradictions as women lobbying the UN, namely, the fact that the EU remains a sum of its parts, ie. the individual Member States. Its policies and agenda are largely driven by Member States. In spite of the fact that the EU possesses a forum that the UN does not, namely, a parliament with members directly elected through universal suffrage, feminist attempts to influence political and social policy at the European level are often stymied at

both European and national levels, as women's needs are frequently antagonistic to those of the EU Member States.[11]

The issue of political asylum for victims of sexism is a case in point here.
This issue has been pushed particularly hard by a number of French feminist
groups, as France has (at least until recent years) prided itself on being a *terre
d'asile* (land of asylum). Of course, there has always been a huge discrepancy
between the rhetoric and the reality. It has, however, informed a number of
feminist campaigns, within European countries, for the rights of non-European minority women. Some of these campaigns have had limited success,
notably in the case of Iranian women fleeing the Khomeiny regime, and more
recently, in the highly-publicised case of Taslima Nasreen, but all have been
seriously hampered by the combined negative effects of cultural relativism,
national self-interest and the automatic precedence of 'men's rights' over wom-
en's rights.

A case in point is that of Aminata Diop, a Malian women who had sought
political asylum in France on the grounds that, had she stayed in Mali, she
would have risked genital mutilation. In 1991, the French OFPRA (*Office
français de protection des réfugiés et apatrides*) refused political asylum on
the grounds that FGM did not constitute a persecution in the sense of the 1951
Geneva Convention Relating to the Status of Refugees, ie. fear of FGM did not
constitute a 'well-founded fear of being persecuted for reasons of race, religion, nationality, membership of a particular social group or political opinion'.
It was subsequently ruled that FGM *did* constitute such a persecution, but Diop
was refused refugee status on the grounds that her dossier presented insufficiencies and contradictions. In the end, she was granted residency in France,
*but not refugee status*. In other words, the violation of her human rights was
not officially recognised as a reason for granting residency.

According to Linda Weil-Curiel, the lawyer who handled Diop's case, it
was clear to all that if refugee status had been granted, this would have created
a precedent that would have made it significantly more difficult for French
authorities to control African immigration (Weil-Curiel interview, 1992).[12] In
other words, even where violation of women's human rights is acknowledged,
France's perceived national self-interest in keeping its borders as impermeable
as possible to non-European immigrants is of far greater importance. This is
also more generally the case in Europe, as the 1995 Schengen accord has clearly
shown.[13]

The closer the EU countries move together, the stronger the exclusion of
people of non-European background, even those born in Europe. In 1993, the
so-called 'Pasqua laws' (named after the then immigration minister who drafted

them) severely restricted the application of the hitherto sacrosanct principle of *jus soli* (the granting of automatic citizenship to those born on French soil, whatever the nationality of their parents) in French immigration citizenship law.[14]

Within such a context, the human rights of *women* of non-European background have a low priority indeed. Certainly, lobby groups exist, some of which are directly attached to the EU, such as the Women's Conference of the Migrants Forum of the European Communities,[15] but such groups are generally restricted to defending the rights of legal immigrants. This continues to exclude women seeking asylum, as they have invariably arrived clandestinely in France, fleeing threats to their health, personal freedom of movement or even their lives. This is not to say that men seeking asylum do not face such threats, simply that threats to women are taken less seriously, as both the OFPRA decision in Diop's case and the influence of cultural relativist arguments in FGM trials clearly demonstrate. However, both the issue of the inadequacy of the Geneva Convention and of European law to deal with human rights abuses not related to the actions of states and that of right of asylum for women fleeing sex-specific oppression, have come under some recent public scrutiny in relation to Algerian women fleeing the Islamic Salvation Front (also known by its French acronym as *FIS*) (eg. *Le Monde*, 1 August 1997). The French government, in agreement with the Algerian government, is not currently granting refugee status to those fleeing the FIS (although some have been able to obtain limited residency through other means). There has been considerable feminist and human rights mobilisation around the issue and the public debate continues.

It would be wrong to assume, however, that cultural relativism combined with French affirmation of national self-interest only works against non-western women. European women also suffer, both in the name of nationalism and in the name of 'diplomacy' (which basically amounts to national respect for the nationalisms of other nations), as was demonstrated through the case of a group of women who became known as *les Mères d'Alger*. These women, most of whom were French, launched a campaign following the kidnapping of their children by their Algerian ex-husbands. The children had been taken to Algeria and in most cases hidden at undisclosed addresses. Following a feminist campaign that lasted many years, a Franco-Algerian Convention on the children of mixed marriages (covering custody, visiting rights and so on), was finally signed in 1988, but a series of annual reports by the *Collectif de Solidarité aux Mères des Enfants Enlevés* show that its most positive effect has been dissuasive, as litigation over kidnappings dragged on for years in most cases, not all of which have been satisfactorily resolved.

It is significant that the French government, unwilling to offend or put pressure on its Algerian counterpart (which did not recognise the French women's legally granted custody of the children), had been not only reluctant to move towards signing a Convention or obtaining the return of the children (even after the Convention had been signed), but was positively obstructive of the mothers' attempts to see their children. It was only after the women started lobbying the UN and the European Parliament, with the support of women EU politicians such as the Belgian Anne-Marie Lizin, that the French government started to sit up and take notice. And even then, it took a 600 kilometre walk through freezing temperatures (to the UN in Geneva via the European Parliament in Strasbourg, in February 1987) plus a hunger strike (at Orly airport in 1989) to make this happen.

As in so many other cases involving the rights of women—and here, those of children, particularly female children, for whom the risks to their personal freedom associated with kidnapping and removal to Algeria were considerably greater than for their brothers—the French women's voices were only heard *once they stepped outside national boundaries*. In this case in particular, the rights of French women and children were subordinated not only to perceived *French* national self-interest, but to the national self-interest of an *allied* country and its *male* citizens. (Had the interests at stake been those of French men and Algerian women, one wonders if France would have been equally reluctant to intervene on its citizens' behalf.) The women also met with misogynist and cultural-relativist opposition to their cause in some of the French media, notably the post-'68 left-leaning national daily *Libération*, which, in a July 1984 article, presented the fathers as poor, misunderstood beings who were genuinely fond of their children, and who only kidnapped them to protect them from their mothers' loose morals (one father used this argument to justify having beaten his wife and children). The French women ended up coming across as bad mothers at best and racist sluts at worst (Duroy, 1984). Like the French government, the immediate solidarity of the 'progressive' French media lay not with French women (or any women, for that matter), but with men, whatever their national background.

## Conclusion: 'Women's Human Rights'—A European Priority?

Despite all the rhetoric, it remains that international organisations, like the nation states that comprise them, are dominated by men and subscribe, by and large, to male-supremacist value-systems (including male-supremacist definitions of 'human rights'). These value-systems are articulated through the defence of 'free specch', of formal 'equality' narrowly defined, in the public sphere, of the private sphere as escaping public scrutiny and of national and/or cultural sovereignty. The notions of 'nation' and 'culture', like the notions of 'equality' and 'freedom', are defined in masculinist terms. The most spectacular 'human rights' successes for women are thus in those areas that are least likely to threaten those value-systems and the social order that they inform. Hence, women have made significantly more progress in achieving token 'equality' on middle-class male terms within the public sphere, than in combating male violence against women (with the possible exception of sexual harassment)—particularly in a cross-cultural context. As we have seen in the case of France, however, even in those public-sphere areas that have been a strong focus of EU policy on women, such as employment and salary equity, and anti-discrimination and anti-harassment measures in the workplace, EU directives and resolutions are far from being fully enacted. At the same time, it would seem that, whatever the failings of European policy on women's rights, many women are increasingly looking to the EU both to provide infrastructure for international networking and to bring pressure to bear on Member States. For, even if feminist voices have only half a chance of being heard on the international stage, this is arguably better than no chance at all.

Unfortunately, however, while women's human rights continue to be double-thought into something less than, or qualitatively different from, those of men, and as in any case applicable only to those European women whose class and ethnic backgrounds, sexuality and professional status put them in a position of privilege in relation to most female residents of Europe, the EU will continue to go largely the way of the UN in its promotion of women's rights. That is, the package will look very pretty, and will no doubt contain enough to satisfy some customers, but the reality will continue to fall far short of the rhetoric.

## Notes

[1]   On 10 December 1998, CLADEM (Carribean and Latin American Committee for the Defence of Women's Rights) presented its 'Human Rights Declaration from a Gender Perspective' to the 53rd UN General Assembly (UN Document No. E/CN.4/1998/NGO/3). The articles of CLADEM's document are grouped into the five subject areas of identity and citizenship, the right to peace and a life free from violence in both the public and the private sphere, sexual and reproductive rights, the right to development and human fulfilment and the right to a sustainable environment.

2  In the early 1980s, French National Front leader Jean-Marie Le Pen insisted that he 'said out loud what others thought to themselves' (*je dis tout haut ce que les autres pensent tout bas*), and to a great extent he was probably right, as subsequent increases in the right in France seemed to indicate.

3  At their meeting of 29 May 1990, for example, EC employment ministers condemned sexual harassment as 'contrary to the principle of equality' and 'a violation of women workers' dignity', but not as a violation of 'human rights'.

4  See for example Article 119 of the Rome Treaty on equal remuneration between men and women, and the Equal Treatment directive of February 1976 which stipulated that women and men be allowed equal access to training and employment. Mariagrazia Rossilli points out, however, that 'Article 119 remained a dead letter for 20 years' until the European Court of Justice ruled in 1976 that it must have direct effect in member countries even where those countries do not have equal pay legislation in place (Rossilli, 1997, pp. 64 and 66).

5  This comparison was quite openly made in a poster campaign by the French medical volunteer organisation *Médecins sans frontières*. This campaign was criticised, not because women's suffering was subsumed under Holocaust imagery, but because it was considered inappropriate and disrespectful of Jewish 'people' to compare Serbian military behaviour with that of Hitler's executioners.

6  Colette Guillaumin (1992a, pp. 143–149) has written an excellent critique of the creation of the idea of male violence as 'deviance', using the Montreal massacre as a case study.

7  According to UN statistics, from 12 per cent to 34 per cent of all girls, depending on the reporting country, suffer sexual abuse. (The UN, 1995, p. 160, and footnote 23, pp. 166–67). According to Clarac and Bonnin, 72 per cent of all child sexual abuse is committed by the child's father (p. 142). In France, the CNIDFF/INSEE (1995) reports that sentences for sexual abuse of girls under 15 went up by 700 per cent between 1984 and 1991, but provides little other information on pædophilia and incest (pp. 208–209).

8  Elisabeth Badinter, 'Ici, en droit, nous avons tout obtenu' (interview with Elisabeth Schemla), *Le Nouvel Observateur*, N° 1541, 19 May 1994, pp. 40–43, esp. 43. The original reads: 'La coquetterie féminine est vécue par les femmes [américaines] comme un aveu déjà de soumission; la séduction masculine est vécue par les hommes comme l'espression déjà d'un désir de domination. C'est stupéfiant: ce qui nous paraît à nous un jeu, une douceur de la vie, l'expression de la nature même leur apparaît comme une menace pour l'égalité! Nous, nous ne voulons pas de la séparation des sexes, ce n'est pas notre plaisir ni notre bonheur'.

9  In that case, let us immediately dispense with those many aspects of modern technology, culture and social organisation that have made our lives easier, safer and more pleasant than they otherwise might have been, that happen to have been developed by western men (a number of whom may well have pinched women's ideas in the first place. See, for example, Spender, 1982).

10 In any case, CEDAW has not been signed by a number of Muslim, Asian and Pacific Countries, nor has it been ratified by some western countries such as the United States.

[11]　The Parliament also does not possess the right to initiate legislation: this is held by the European Commission.

[12]　'On sait que ce qui a déterminé la Commission à refuser à Aminata le bénéfice du statut, c'est qu'en créant un tel précédent, c'était une voie, je dirais, facile pour les femmes africaines de demander le statut de réfugiée et court-circuiter, naturellement, toutes les limitations de l'immigration'.

[13]　This accord has, among other things, led to a significant increase in the policing of movements by non-Europeans across the external borders of participating countries, and to restrictions on the rights of potential refugees to apply for asylum in participating countries (the granting or refusal of refugee status by one of the signatories is now valid for all participating countries).

[14]　These have now largely been repealed by the socialist-led government.

[15]　The Migrants Forum (head office in Brussels) was founded by the European Parliament in 1991 and is financed by the European Commission. It is ostensibly politically independent of both. Its stated double obejctive is '(a) to advise EC institutions in all areas connected to immigration, ethnic minorities and race relations in Europe, and (b) circulate EC information among migrant and ethnic minority associations throughout Europe'. My translation from the preamble to the French-language version of recommendations to the Maastricht conference of December 1991: *Racisme et discriminations en Europe à l'heure du marché intégré.*

# References

Adler, L. (1993), *Les Femmes politiques,* Seuil, Paris.

Badinter, E. (1986), *L'Un est l'Autre: des relations entre hommes et femmes,* Odile Jacob, Paris.

Badinter, E. (1994), 'Ici, en droit, nous avons tout obtenu' (interview with Elisabeth Schemla), *Le Nouvel Observateur,* No. 1541, 19 May, pp. 40–43.

Barzach, M. *et al.* (1996), 'Manifeste des dix pour la parité', *L'Express,* 6 June.

de Beauvoir, S. (1949), *Le Deuxième sexe,* Gallimard, Paris.

Brodribb, S. (1992), *Nothing Mat(t)ers. A Feminist Critique of Postmodernism,* Spinifex, Melbourne.

Bunch, C. (1995), 'Transforming Human Rights from a Feminist Perspective', in J. Peter and A. Wolper (eds), *Women's Rights, Human Rights,* Routledge, New York/London, pp. 11–17.

Centre National d'Information et de Documentation sur les Femmes Françaises/Institut National de la Statistique et des Etudes Economiques (CNIDFF/INSEE) (1995), *Les Femmes,* INSEE, Paris.

Clarac, V. and Bonnin, N. (1985), *De la honte à la colère. Viols par inceste,* Les Publications Anonymes, Paris.

Collins, E. (1996), 'European Union Sexual Harassment Policy', in R.A. Elman (ed.), *Sexual Politics and the European Union: The New Feminist Challenge,* Berghahn Books, Providence/Oxford, pp. 23–33.

Delphy, C. (1995), 'Egalité, équivalence et équité: la position de l'Etat français au regard du droit international', *Nouvelles Questions Féministes*, Vol. 16, No. 1, pp. 5–58.

Dental, M. (1993), Interview with B. Winter, Paris, 11 January.

Duncan, S. (1996), 'Obstacles to a Successful Equal Opportunities Policy in the European Union', *European Journal of Women's Studies*, Vol. 3, No. 4, pp. 399–422.

Duroy, L. (1984), 'Algérie, des enfants à qui père gagne', *Libération*, 6th July.

van Dijk, P. and van Hoof, G. (1990), *Theory and Practice of the European Convention of Human Rights*, Kluwer, Denver.

Enloe, C. (1990), *Bananas, Beaches and Bases: Making Feminist Sense of International Politics*, UC Press, Berkeley.

Erlich, M. (1986), *La femme blessée. Essai sur les mutilations sexuelles féminines*, L'Harmattan, Paris.

European Migrants' Forum (1991), *Racisme et discriminations en Europe à l'heure du marché intégré,* Recommendations to the Maastricht conference, December, 1991. Self-published.

European Network of Women/Coordination Européenne des Femmes (1991), *Rapport final des séminaires sur la féminisation de la pauvreté en Europe*, ENOW/CEF, Brussels.

Furet, F. (1989), 'Pour un nouveau concordat', *Le Nouvel Observateur,* No. 1300, p. 17.

García-Ramon, M. and Monk, J. (1996), *Women of the European Union: The Politics of Work and Daily Life*, Routledge, London.

Gaspard, F. (1997), *Les femmes dans la prise de décision en France et en Europe*, L'Harmattan, Paris.

Gregory, J. (1995), 'Sexual Harassment: Making the Best Use of European Law', *The European Journal of Women's Studies*, Vol. 2, No. 4, pp. 421–440.

Groult, B. (1997), *Histoire d'une Evasion,* Bernard Grasset, Paris.

Guillaumin, C. (1992a), *Sexe, Race et Pratique du Pouvoir. L'idée de Nature*, côté-femmes, Paris.

Guillaumin, C. (1992b), 'Usages théoriques et usages banals du terme *race*', *Mots: les langages du politique*, No. 33 (special issue entitled *Sans Distinction de...race*), pp. 59–66.

Hélie-Lucas, M. (1990), 'Women, Nationalism and Religion in the Algerian Liberation Struggle', in M. Badran and M. Cooke (eds), *Opening the Gates: A Century of Arab Feminist Writing*, Virago, London, pp. 105–114.

Hoskyns, C. (1996), 'The European Union and the Women Within: An Overview of Women's Rights Policy', in R.A. Elman (ed.), *Sexual Politics and the European Union: The New Feminist Challenge*, Berghahn Books, Providence/Oxford, pp. 13–22.

Hubbard, R. (1990), 'The Political Nature of "Human Nature"', in L.R. Deborah (ed.), *Theoretical Perspectives on Sexual Difference*, Yale University Press, New Haven, pp. 63–73.

Ingram, A. (1994), *A Political Theory of Rights,* Clarendon Press, Oxford.

Itzin, C. (1996), 'Pornography, Harm and Human Rights: The UK in European Context', in R.A. Elman (ed.), *Sexual Politics and the European Union: The New Feminist Challenge*, Berghahn Books, Providence/Oxford, pp. 67–81.

Jeffreys, S. (1997), *The Idea of Prostitution*, Spinifex, Melbourne.

Kandiyoti, D. (1991), 'Bargaining with Patriarchy', in J. Lorber and S. Farrell (eds), *The Social Construction of Gender*, Sage, Newbury Park, Ca, pp. 104–118.

Kay, H. (1990), 'Perspectives on Socio-biology, Feminism, and the Law', in D. Rhode (ed.), *Theoretical Perspectives on Sexual Difference*, Yale University Press, New Haven, pp. 74–85.

Kymlicka, W. (1989), *Liberalism, Community and Culture,* Clarendon Press, Oxford.

Kymlicka, W. (1990), *Contemporary Political Philosophy: An Introduction,* Oxford University Press, Oxford.

Kymlicka, W. (1995), *Multicultural Citizenship: A Liberal Theory of Minority Rights*, Oxford University Press, Oxford.

Le Dœuff, M. (1995), 'Problèmes d'investiture (De la parité, etc.)', *Nouvelles Questions Féministes*, Vol. 16. No. 2, pp. 5–80.

Leidholdt, D. (1996) 'Sexual Trafficking of Women in Europe: A Human Rights Crisis for the European Union', in R.A. Elman (ed.), *Sexual Politics and the European Union: The New Feminist Challenge*. Berghahn Books, Providence/Oxford, pp. 83–95.

Lewis, J. (1993), 'Women, Work, Family and Social Policies in Europe', in J. Lewis (ed.), *Women and Social Policies in Europe: Work, Family and the State*, Edward Elgar, London, pp. 1–24.

Maruani, M. and Reynaud, E. (1993), *Sociologie de l'emploi,* La Découverte, Paris.

Mayer, A. (1995), 'Cultural Particularism as a Bar to Women's Rights: Reflections on the Middle Eastern Experience', in J. Peters and A. Wolper (eds), *Womens Rights, Human Rights: International Feminist Perspectives*, Routledge, New York/London, pp. 176–188.

Mazur, A. (1996), 'Interplay: The Formation of Sexual Harassment Legislation in France and EU Policy Initiatives', in R.A. Elman (ed.), *Sexual Politics and the European Union: The New Feminist Challenge*, Berghahn Books, Providence/Oxford, pp. 35–49.

Meehan, E. (1993), 'Women's Rights in the European Community', in J. Lewis (ed.), *Women and Social Policies in Europe: Work, Family and the State*, Edward Elgar, London, pp. 194–205.

Michard, C. and Viollet, C. (1989), 'Le genre en français contemporain: matérialisations linguistiques de la catégorie socio-conceptuelle de sexe', in *Recherches sur les femmes et recherches féministes: présentation des travaux 1984-1987*, Editions du Centre National de la Recherche Scientifique, Paris, pp. 41–46.

Michard, C. (1991), 'Approche matérialiste de la sémantique du genre en français contemporain', in M-C. Hurtig, M. Kail et H. Rouch (eds), *Sexe et genre: de la hiérarchie entre les sexes*, Editions du Centre National de la Recherche Scientifique, Paris, pp. 147–157.

Moghadam, V. (ed.) (1994), *Identity Politics and Women: Cultural Reassertions and Feminisms in International Perspective*, Westview Press, Boulder, Colorado.

Okin, S.M. (1998), 'Is Multiculturalism Bad for Women? When minority cultures win group rights, women lose out', article distributed on the Internet list of the Coalition Against Trafficking in Women.

Pateman, C. (1988), *The Sexual Contract*, Polity Press, Cambridge.

Perrot, M. (1993), 'Femmes et démocratie: l'exclusion française', speech delivered at a feminist conference held on International Women's Day 1993, and subsequently published in *Vendredi-Idées*, No. 3.

Pettman, J. (1996), *Worlding Women,* Allen and Unwin, Sydney.

Rossilli, M. (1997), 'The European Community's Policy on the Equality of Women: From the Treaty of Rome to the Present', *European Journal of Women's Studies,* Vol. 4, No. 1, pp. 63–82.

Sensier, S. (1996), 'La démocratie sans les femmes', *Le Monde diplomatique*, May.

Spender, D. (1982), *Women of Ideas—and What Men Have Done to Them*, Routledge, London.

Sullivan, D. (1995), 'The Public/Private Distinction in International Human Rights Law', in J. Peters and A. Wolper (eds), *Womens Rights, Human Rights: International Feminist Perspectives*, Routledge, New York/London, pp. 126–134.

UNESCO (undated, circa 1993), *Guidelines on Non-Sexist Language/Pour un langage non sexiste*, UNESCO, Paris.

Union Européenne des Femmes (1993), *Motion du 28/01/1993*, Maison de l'Europe (self-published document), Paris.

United Nations (1995), *The World's Women 1995: Trends and Statistics*, United Nations, New York.

Verdier, R. (1990), 'Chercher remède à l'excision: une nécessaire concertation', *Droit et Cultures: revue semestrielle d'anthropologie et d'histoire*, No. 20, pp. 147–150.

van der Vyver, J. (1996), 'Religious fundamentalism and human rights', *Journal of International Affairs*, Vol. 50, No. 1, pp. 21–40.

Weil-Curiel, L. (1992), Interview with B. Winter, Paris, 9 December.

Winter, B. (1994), 'Women, the Law and Cultural Relativism in France: the Case of Excision', *Signs: A Journal of Women in Culture and Society*, Vol. 19, No. 4, pp. 939–974.

Winter, B. (1996a), 'Learning the Hard Way: the debate on women, cultural difference and secular schooling in France', in *Europe: Retrospects and Prospects: Proceedings of the Australasian Association of European Historians Tenth Biennial Conference*, South End Press, Manly.

Winter, B. (1996b), 'Down the River: The Political Marketing of Women's Rights', paper presented at the Sixth International Interdisciplinary Conference on Women, Adelaide (unpublished),

Yuval-Davis, N. (1992), 'Racism, Nationalism and Gender Relations', *Working Paper Series No. 130*, Institute of Social Studies, The Hague.

Yuval-Davis, N. (1997), *Gender and Nation*, Sage, London.

# 4   From Joan of Arc to Bardot: Immigration, Nationalism, Rights and the *Front National*

PAUL HAINSWORTH

In the early 1980s, the prospect of the French extreme right resuscitating itself was questionable. However, a complex alchemy of factors combined in this period to provide a momentum for the then ailing National Front/*Front national* (FN). These factors included: popular disillusionment with mainstream political parties; the effects of political change in 1981, which brought the left to office after twenty-three years of right-wing rule; the official racialisation of immigration policy over the previous decade or so; the radicalisation of the right-wing opposition's discourse after 1981 (notably on the issue of immigration); the persistence of national economic problems; the willingness of right-wing politicians to strike a legitimating deal with the FN in local elections at Dreux in 1983; and the nature, circumstances and voting system (proportional representation) used in the 1984 European elections.

The National Front emerged as a significant force in French politics and society, then, in the local and European elections of 1983-84. Breakthrough in the European elections bought the party 11 per cent of the vote and 10 seats in the European Parliament. From thereafter, the movement proceeded to perform well in a succession of diverse electoral contests (local, regional, national and European), taking between 10 and 15 per cent of the poll and establishing itself as a durable enough political force. Undoubtedly, the electoral high spots have been the 1988 and 1995 French presidential elections, when party leader Jean-Marie Le Pen won 14.4 per cent and 15 per cent shares of the polls, respectively. In contrast, Le Pen had polled only 0.74 per cent in the 1974 presidential election while in 1981 he had failed to win sufficient initial backing (from 500 elected office-holders) to sponsor his candidacy.

After its birth in 1972, the FN experienced an initial decade marked by electoral failure, internal divisions, external rivalry on the extreme right, a low public profile and difficulties in lasting out as a viable organisation. The FN of the 1970s served as an umbrella movement for various extreme right-wing causes: notably French Algeria, Vichy, holocaust revisionism, neo-fascism,

Poujadism, anti-Semitism, Catholic fundamentalist reaction and so on. Party conferences and literature marked out the reference points and models for the party, including Pinochet's Chile, Salazar's Portugal, Videla's Argentina and the apartheid regime of South Africa. Party literature too eulogised collaborationist and anti-Semitic intellectuals while early campaigning focussed upon immigration control.

## Immigration

Immigration control was certainly an aspect of the early FN discourse but it was not the central theme. Anti-communism was more of a feature of the party's policy orientation. Indeed, the creation of the party was largely a reaction against the leftism of the May 1968 events, nascent Euro-communism and the growing left-wing party political unity which culminated in the 1972 Communist (PCF)-Socialist (PS) Common Program for Government.

Immigration emerged as a more pronounced policy theme for the FN in 1977, as the movement contested local elections in the capital city under the slogan 'Paris to the Parisians'. The local electoral campaign was organised by leading party activist and theoretician, François Duprat, who predicted that 'the struggle against immigration is going to become a more and more burning theme'. Duprat contended that immigration had not yet become a significant determinant of voting behaviour, but would do so with rising unemployment (Bresson and Lionet, 1995, pp. 381–2). Duprat did not live to witness FN popularisation and success via immigration policy discourse: he was killed in 1977, somewhat mysteriously in a car 'accident'. However, Jean-Pierre Stirbois now joined the FN and the propagation of immigration control as the party's key electoral and campaigning issue paralleled his rapid ascent to second in command within the movement.

Stirbois, a longstanding activist on the French extreme right, began immediately, with his wife Marie-France, 'to work the ground' in Dreux. The terrain was ideal: a small boom and bust town just outside Paris, which experienced rapid postwar industrialisation, urbanisation, population growth, immigration, socio-economic change and dislocation (see Gaspard, 1995; Hainsworth, 1996). Bresson and Lionet (p. 402) relate how Le Pen was not present to experience the Stirbois' breakthrough. In fact, Le Pen had felt previously that Stirbois was spending too much time away from party headquarters in Paris, while at the time of the Dreux local by-election success the FN leader was on vacation—returning to find an unexpected success on his hands. Stirbois, especially, pushed the theme of immigration to the forefront of the FN's agenda

and it became the party's key issue in the 1980s and 1990s, culminating notably in the party's *50 Mesures concrètes* in 1991 and figuring centrally in the
extensive *300 Mesures pour la Renaissance de la France: Front National Programme de Gouvernement* (1993).

As Jonathan Marcus (1995, p. 100) explains, immigration is for the FN
'an omnibus issue', a matrix through which most other issues are situated:
unemployment, security, culture, public expenditure, Europe, education and
so on. The centrepiece of the FN's immigration discourse is the idea of 'the
national preference'. The basis behind this is that French nationals should enjoy clear priority in terms of employment opportunities, housing provision,
public subsidies, redundancy procedures, and so on. Payment of taxes, rights,
resident and work permits, social need or other factors are all deemed as secondary or non-existent criteria in these matters. The FN's national-populist
approach is summed up via the articulation of now familiar slogans such as
'France for the French' and 'France first'. In a similar vein, one of the party's
50 proposals on immigration calls for the introduction of a label: 'Made in
France by the French'.

The concept of a national preference has a long pedigree in France, notably characterising the writings of late nineteenth century national-populists.
According to Barrès, for instance, 'the ideal of the fatherland implies an inequality but to the detriment of outsiders' (see Sternhell, 1978, p. 70). As argued elsewhere (Hainsworth, 1992, p. 31), Barrès provided 'a demagogic and
populist exploitation of the insecurity factor based opportunistically on economic difficulties and the scape-goating of foreign labour in a deliberately
exclusionist manner'. In particular, Barrès' national chauvinist press, *La
Cocarde*, anticipates the pages of the FN's *National-Hebdo* outlet. Writing in
*La Cocarde* in 1894 (see Sternhell, 1978, p. 70), Barrès wrote: 'In France, the
French must come first, the foreigner second', an attitude replicated enthusias-
tically in Le Pen's *Les Français d'Abord* (1984) and FN theoretician Jean-
Yves Le Gallou's *La Préférence Nationale* (1985). The idea of a national preference was taken on board by other extreme right-wing movements of the 1920s
and 1930s as well as by 'new right' (*Nouvelle Droite*) advocates in recent decades. Thus, there is a conceptual continuity evident over a century or more of
extreme right thought.

However, over-concentration on the above political family may neglect
observing the prevalence of national preference politics on a broader scale.
Silverman (1992, pp. 79–80) illustrates, for instance, how the concept was put
into practice in France in the 1930s, including the forced repatriation of Polish
workers. Moreover, from the late 1960s onwards, again as Silverman illustrates, the ideological ground was prepared for the FN by the increasing offi-

cial tendency to link immigration with unemployment. According to Silverman (pp. 90–91), 'few statements were made which did not equate immigration with unemployment in some way. The link made between immigration and unemployment in the notorious slogan of the FN in early 1980s—'two million unemployed, two million immigrants'—was not invented by Le Pen, merely exploited by him'.

Indeed, prior to immigration becoming a favoured theme within the FN, the Gaullist Prime Minister Jacques Chirac in 1976 had linked immigration and unemployment in a manner which predates the movement's adoption of the national preference:

> A country which has 900,000 unemployed but more than two million immigrant workers is not a country in which the problem of jobs is insoluble. It requires a systematic revalorisation of the condition of manual workers in sectors which are being abandoned by French workers (quoted in Silverman, p. 90).

In this context, therefore, it was perhaps unsurprising to hear Chirac's subsequent Minister of the Interior, Charles Pasqua, express the view in 1988 that the FN shared 'the same preoccupations and values' as the mainstream right-wing parties, but that it expressed them in a different manner (quoted in Marcus, 1995, p. 144).

The concept of national preference, therefore, is adopted by the FN in order to restrict the rights and opportunities of those perceived as being outsiders to the nation. In his 1995 presidential campaign, Le Pen promised to bring in constitutional change by incorporating the national preference principle into the constitution of a new Sixth French Republic. The target for the FN, then, are immigrants and foreigners. However, not all immigrants are seen as unwanted, but only those deemed to be culturally different from and economically superfluous to France's socio-economic well-being. Immigrants from Christian, Latin, European countries are seen as assimilated or assimilable and as presenting little threat to France's national culture and identity.

In contrast, some immigrants or culturally different citizens are perceived as poorly assimilable. Thus, the FN's '50 Concrete Measures' on immigration— launched by Le Pen's then second in command, Bruno Mégret—aspire to be 'an alternative immigration policy', which advocates the return of third world immigrants to their country of origin. Particularly, though not exclusively, targeted in the FN's discourse are North African (Maghreb) immigrants and Muslims/Islamists. The emphasis is not accidental but is bound up with France's post-colonial legacy *vis-à-vis* Algeria especially and the nostalgic and *revanchist* sentiments within the FN. As one author (Gorjanicyn, 1994, p. 55) explains:

The legacy of colonialism and the Algerian War of Independence have had a part to play in shaping the political discourse and policies relating to North African immigrants. Former colonies, once of political and economic advantage to France, are now seen as causing the nation's 'immigration problems'. Furthermore, the issue of Algeria's independence which divided the French nation in the 1960s, and the horrors associated with the Algerian War of Independence, are still recent political memories.

Consequently, initially (and still) stigmatised as terrorists against French national integrity, North Africans are now also seen as Islamic fundamentalist (and still terrorist) cultural threats to French national identity. Islam, moreover, is portrayed as a fundamentally intolerant and dangerous anti-national creed which by implication must also undermine French identity, culture and homogeneity. North Africans are stereotyped as persons unable to integrate because of their cultural and religious differentialism. Labelled as 'the other', Northern Africans are thereby targeted for exclusion. The process of labelling the alleged non-integrative attributes of third world immigrants may be paralleled with the manner in which Protestants, Jews, Belgians, Italians, Poles and others have been stigmatised historically in France via previous nationalist exclusionist discourses based on non-assimilative premises.

North Africans and Muslims are the categories most negatively represented and stereotyped in FN literature, such as the (weekly) *National Hebdo*. Allegedly non-integrative immigrants are equated in a reductionist manner with all the real or imagined evils confronting the French nation: unemployment, urban problems, demographic decline, cultural dilution, falling educational standards, AIDS, excessive public expenditure, drugs, crime and terrorism. According to Wolfreys (1993, p. 423), 'an astonishing list of grievances' are pinned on North Africans. In short, whatever the problem, immigrants are portrayed in some manner as the cause (see also Cohen, 1992). The process of stereotyping is quite easily compounded via official state policies, which have racialised immigration since 1968 (for further see Silverman, 1992), and by media and popular representations. As regards the latter, Brigitte Bardot's autobiography, *Initiales B.B.*, praises Le Pen's stance against the 'invasion' of France by Islamic fundamentalists and regrets seeing the 'church belltowers of our abandoned villages' being replaced by mosques (quoted in *Herald Sun* (Australia), 25 September 1996).

A different perspective on integration is provided by Hargreaves, whose well-researched analysis concludes that 'in their cultural practices and aspirations, people of immigrant origin are increasingly inclined to embrace French values, seeking inclusion rather than exclusion' (Hargreaves, 1994, p. 84). Significantly, the principle of integration characterises the main pressure groups representing immigrant and anti-racist causes; notably *SOS Racisme* and *France Plus*. The latter's 1988 campaigning slogan, for instance, was *Être Français aujourd'hui et demain*. Hargreaves again (pp. 157–8) refers to 'mistaken but sincerely held beliefs concerning the population of immigrant origin', fed by negative images, second-hand information and the absence of contact. Discrimination, exclusion, superficial contacts and state policy and legislation are seen to be more powerful factors of (non) integration than immigrant cultural differences. Aubry and Duhamel too (1995, p. 150) point to the growing proportion of young Maghrebi males (50 per cent) and females (25 per cent) involved in 'mixed' marriages or cohabitations, whereas McKesson (1994, pp. 20–21) points to 'the powerful aggregate effect' on integration of such institutions as 'the school, workplace, the church, trade unions, military service, communal housing, mixed marriages and other forms of social contact'. Admittedly, some of these agencies may have lost potency and also may offer occasion for disintegrative processes but overall their impact is not inconsiderable. Hargreaves (p. 148) sees 'the biggest long-term obstacle to "integration" ... not in the cultural heritage of recent immigrants but in the barriers placed in their way by the French themselves'.

Difference nonetheless is elevated by the FN into a (pseudo) rationale—cultural differentialism—for rejecting, denying, excluding rights and individuals. As Taguieff (*Le Nouvel Observateur*, 28 November–4 December 1991) explains, direct racist language and crude biological references are usually avoided, but indirect racist discourse is apparent in the FN's representation of French national ethnic identity which is tantamount to 'cultural and differentialist neo-racism'. Le Pen sees nations more or less as races, whose cultural attributes are fixed and impermeable. Critics such as Taguieff (1986), therefore, define Le Pen's stance as differentialist and cultural racism.

Besides the cultural differentialist emphasis, the writings and discourse of Le Pen incorporated loose concepts of natural selection and, as Vaughan explains (Vaughan, 1987, p. 306), 'biological considerations are not very far from the core of the NF's propaganda, but they remain linked to assertions of cultural superiority' (see also Hainsworth, 1992, p. 52). Following the party's 'summer university' debates in 1996, Le Pen attracted considerable critical attention when in interviews he maintained that 'some races are more equal that others' (see *L'Express*, 19–26 September, 1996). From these ideological bases the party opposes the policy of integration.

Since the FN's declared alternative immigration policy refutes the concept of integration—which it sees as unworkable and (culturally) unwanted—the party proposes various measures which would serve to undermine integrative processes. On the one hand, therefore, the party contends that integration is not possible while, on the other, support is given to proposals which, if im-plemented, would exacerbate seriously integrative capacity. The core of the FN's immigration proposals is contained in the 50 Measures. While these are too lengthy to discuss here, a brief summary of the key ingredients will pro-vide a useful indication of the party's intentions. The party proposes to: stop all further non-European immigration to France, including curtailing family reunification; enforce the idea of national preference; introduce procedures to reopen all acquisitions of French nationality since 1974; restrict the construc-tion of mosques; abrogate protective legislation against racism and anti-Semitism; redefine French nationality via blood (*le droit du sang*) descent rather than place of birth (*le droit du sol*); reconvert immigrant housing facilities; further reduce naturalisation access; introduce tougher procedures for refu-gees and asylum seekers; introduce AIDS and other epidemic tests for non-European foreigners at the frontiers; and implement a more rigorous control over clandestine immigrants. Unsurprisingly, these proposals provoked much outcry and condemnation with some critics pointing to a return to the 1930s and to Vichy, and others to apartheid (see *Le Nouvel Observateur*, 28 November–4 December 1991).

## Nation

The FN's anti-immigrant policies reflect, of course, the party's imagining of the French nation. Nation, nationalism and identity are at the heart of the move-ment's discourse, with it claiming to be the political force which best repre-sents the French nation and people. The organisation's adopted name is a clear statement of intent to unite the nation. Le Pen's projection of the nation is illustrated too by the well-worn campaigning slogans referred to above— 'French first', 'France for the French'—which connote an essentialist inter-pretation leaving little scope for difference or alternative imaginings.

The nation for the FN is the essential framework which guarantees the identity and happiness of the French. It is a construct based eclectically on a common culture (language, race, religion, memories, roots, heritage, blood and soil). As Marcus (1995, p. 101) suggests: 'For Jean-Marie Le Pen, politics is nothing less than a Manichean struggle for the survival of the French nation and identity'. Furthermore, as Michel Winock explains, the FN serves 'up a closed, exclusive nationalism' (quoted in Marcus, 1995, p. 157). Taguieff (1986) also points to a closed, selective vision of French identity premised upon an exclusive, monocultural edifice incapable of evolution. According to Le Pen: 'We cannot share the heritage of France with anyone. Our heritage is our nationality transmitted by our ancestors' (quoted in Gorjanicyn, 1994, p. 52). French nationhood, for Le Pen, is not therefore an attribute that should be assumed or acquired lightly—off the cuff remarks about the ethnic make-up and 'unrepresentative' nature of France's 1996 national football squad confirmed this stance—but rather it is a quasi-sacred inheritance or a qualification earned in sacrifice for the nation, as with the pro-French, Algerian *harkis*.

Particularly castigated as threats to the nation are the doctrines and processes deemed to be anti-national and alien. These include such elements as universalism (*mondialisme*), American economic and cultural hegemony, European integration, unbridled free trade and communism—as well as the 'third world' immigration and Islam referred to above. As the self-proclaimed standard-bearer of the nation, the FN rejects the capacity or will of France's main political parties to redress so-called anti-national developments and perceived national deficiencies. Allegedly, 'the parties of the establishment have abdicated their responsibilities' (Front National, 1993, p. 13). At best, they offer quantitative, not the necessary qualitative solutions. The FN purports to represent 'a real alternative' to the routine alternation of the mainstream parties.

A striking feature of the FN's critique of other forces for selling the nation short is the lexicography utilised. Rival parties and pressure groups/movements (such as *SOS Racisme*) are labelled in the FN press as 'collaborators' in their approach to immigrants, who in turn are classified pointedly as the 'invaders' or 'colonisers' of France. The discourse echoes the spirit—and sometimes the letter—of late nineteenth century nationalist-populism (see Hainsworth, 1992, p. 31). Furthermore, the FN portrays itself as 'the new resistance', appeals to 'the resistance spirit' and claims the support of former *résistants* in the crusade to realise 'the national renaissance' (Front National, 1993, pp. 12–21). The thrust of this linguistic operation is to try to invert the language often used against the extreme right, in view of wartime associations with Pétain's Vichy regime, and to identify (however sincerely, tenuously or mischievously) with positive French national symbols. Political opponents are equated, too, with *l'abandon* (abandonment) of France via their policies—a word carrying strong, emotive connotations with the withdrawal of France from Algeria, a path opposed by many FN veterans including Le Pen.

An important recruit to the FN's nationalist and exclusionist agenda is the historic and myth-laden heroine, Joan of Arc. Marina Warner (1981) illustrates brilliantly how various claimants have drawn inspiration from the idealised Maid of Orleans, each stressing and appropriating the alleged inherent values personified which best suited their world view. Davies (1993) explains how the legacy and symbolism of Joan of Arc is utilised by the FN to promote its particular nation-based discourse. In recent years, Le Pen is seen to have closely identified with Joan of Arc, virtually privatising her memory and heritage. Le Pen's appropriation of the saint rests on the idealisation of her as the personification of France and cherished French values and the subsequent correlation of her with Le Pen/the FN. Both are deemed to represent the quest to purify France and drive away the alien invader, whether it be the fifteenth century English or the twentieth century third world immigrant. Identification of Le Pen with Joan of Arc also, by implication, transfers the qualities of the latter onto the former: leadership, moral guidance, heroism, purity of thought, warriordom, vision, self-sacrifice, martyrdom and so on.

The value of Joan of Arc, too, is that, by claiming her, the FN is able to construct a historic national continuum which dates back several centuries and minimises the notion that modern French nationalism takes its inspiration from the ideas which emerged from the French Revolution. While not expressly denied, the nationalist contribution of the Revolution is placed in the context of twenty centuries of nation-building with Christian and monarchist influences given greater emphasis than concepts of rights. Particularly anathema to the party are theories of universal rights—'a war machine against nationalism' according to Bruno Mégret (quoted in Marcus, 1995, p. 102)—since they represent the wider cosmopolitanism which, in Le Pen's view, runs counter to the construction of the nation ('blood and soil') as the true repository of legitimacy and belonging.

Unsurprisingly, Le Pen's interpretation of Joan of Arc is not uncontested. Patrick Marnham (*Independent,* 11 May 1988) has suggested that Le Pen's obsession with Joan of Arc is a means of 'living out his exaggerated fantasies'. Michel Winock challenges Joan of Arc's status as 'the patron saint of the extreme right' and wonders how the least tolerant Catholics—a reference to Catholic fundamentalists, reactionaries and counter revolutionaries—can pretend to claim this celebrated victim of Catholic intolerance (see Aubry and Duhamel, 1995, p. 131). Ex-Socialist Party *premier,* Michel Rocard shares Winock's view of Joan of Arc as a collective, non-exclusive symbol:

> The history of Joan of Arc is for all the people of France. And it forms a part of our collective identity ... This is why we will not permit it to become monopolised by nationalist and partisan minorities ... In the epoch of Joan, the word 'nation' had no real sense anyway ... She is even less able to speak for a people or a race, (nor) for a community welded by language (quoted in Davies, 1993, p. 15).

Nevertheless, the FN continues to commandeer Joan of Arc for *their* nationalist cause. For instance, the annual May commemorative parade dedicated to Joan of Arc is now monopolised by Le Pen and party campaigns are often announced with the saint's image as a legitimating backcloth. At the

1996 annual rally (ie. 1 May 1996), for instance, Le Pen used his customary address to denounce 'the wave of immigration which is going to submerge us after having ruined us'. The FN's leader warned of a 'civil war' provoked by 'massive immigration', a 'worrying phenomenon' which 'imposes upon us its customs, mores, religion' and 'steals from us our souls' (*Libération*, 2 May 1996). The previous year's event was marked by the racist drowning in the Seine, by FN fellow travellers, of Brahim Bouraam, a Moroccan. Although the perpetrators were not card-carrying members, they travelled to and from Paris for the May rally on an official party coach and were well enough known to the security wing of the FN. Unsurprisingly, the fatal incident raised questions about the nature of the relationship between the party and violence.

Certainly violence and illegality are not foreign to the FN—ranging from its ex-OAS (Secret Army Organisation) connections to its members' empathy with sabotage against clinics performing legal abortions. Undoubtedly, though, violent incidents embarrass the party and undermine the quest for acceptance and respectability. Noteworthy, therefore, was the cooperation given by the FN to the police in apprehending the attacker(s) of Brahim Bouraam. Also, Matonti's detailed analysis (Matonti, 1993, p. 137) of the party's training guide for militants reveals a movement anxious to move away from skinhead and beret/paramilitary associations. A strategy of terror or violent confrontation is not on the agenda. At the same time, it should be pointed out that party members and activists themselves (because of their affiliation) are sometimes the victims of aggression (see *La Lettre de Jean-Marie Le Pen*, No. 2075, November 1994).

According to Michel Wieviorka (*Libération*, 12 May 1995), it is erroneous to impute to the FN total blame for the violence associated with it. However, argues Wieviorka, the situation is complex and ambiguous, linking the FN to and distancing it from violence, simultaneously. It is not simply accidental that violence is attracted to the party. The racist and xenophobic discourse of the party stereotypes, and criminalises as unassimilable outsiders, immigrants and those perceived as different (such as French citizens of second and third generation North African origin) and nourishes racist aggressions. The negative public attitudes towards North Africans and Arabs, evident in the findings of official reports and surveys, owe something to the FN's representations—although, in view of the official racialisation and problematisation of immigration in recent decades (see Silverman, 1992), it would be reductionist and mistaken to draw simplistic equations between the FN and these attitudes. Nevertheless, two further factors need recalling: first, there is the willingness of the FN to utilise skinhead elements for security, bodyguard and internal policing work—Aubry and Duhamel (1995, p. 222) point to an ambiguous situation of connivance and rejection; second, there are the very real involvements of some party members in racist and violent attacks. Ultimately, therefore, we can agree with Wieviorka that violence can neither be reduced simply to FN causality nor completely disassociated from it.

In the final section, some brief interim assessment is made of the recent local government experience of the FN with a view to further understanding the policy orientations and practice of the party.

## Local

Recent attention has focussed upon the consequences of FN success in winning control of four towns in the party's South/South East of France area of strength. The movement's 1995 local election victories in Marignane, Orange and Toulon—followed by similar local by-election victory in Vitrolles in 1997—prompted the flowering or consolidation of various monitoring, campaign and rights associations which defined the geographical area as a likely 'Bermuda Triangle' in which rights might be undermined. The area has earned a reputation for clientelism and corruption associated with the previous right-wing incumbents. It was this which scuppered the possibilities in 1995 of creating an ad hoc mainstream coalition, based on 'republican discipline', which quite likely would have prevented the FN winning in a basically triangular contest (ie. left, right and extreme right). The above towns are seen widely—including by the FN—as laboratories wherein the party could demonstrate its aptitude for government (albeit local) while attempting to implement policy. Although it is premature to offer definitive verdict here, some initial observations are appropriate.

In office, the FN mayor of Toulon, Jean-Marie Le Chevallier, recalled that the concept of national preference was illegal and, in any case, had little relevance to most local government business. Also, it was important to distinguish between the general philosophy of the FN and his own local administration (*Libération,* 30 April 1996). Interestingly, Christiane Chombeau reports how local immigrants themselves in the area were practising national preference via their refusal to visit the town hall to request social entitlements. Regarding further immigration, however, Le Chevallier claimed to have received eighty-five requests for *certificats d'hébergement*, essential to permit entry to France. Using recent legislation (the 1993 Pasqua laws), the mayor refused all requests 'since it was not necessary to increase Toulon's foreign population' (quoted in *Le Monde*, 15 June 1996).

Generally, the FN mayors promised to cut local expenditure and balance the books. The process has involved cutting grants or facilities to some cultural and community associations involved with integrating immigrants. In Toulon, money to a local AIDS centre was also terminated on the grounds that it was seen to promote homosexuality, while in Orange, the human rights body, Amnesty International, lost the use of council rooms. On the other hand, local policing and security enjoyed increased funding, in line with party policy. Particularly favoured too have been various sports, leisure and tourist associations, most notably in Toulon and Orange, where close relatives (wives, nephew) of local FN mayors and their close supporters enjoyed control of them. Critics of these and other developments have complained of the dismantling (or appropriation) of local associative networks and their replacement by FN-controlled bodies, such as *Fraternité française* (a party relief organisation). Another recipient has been the local committee to commemorate Clovis' anniversary in 1996—with the national committee structure masterminded by Bernard Antony, de facto leader of the NF's Catholic fundamentalist wing (see Camus, 1992; *Libération*, 14 June 1996). Again, in Marignane, the FN mayor (Daniel Simonpieri) promised support to fund a local *Son et Lumière* spectacle dedicated to the glories of French Algeria—no doubt, to gratify the resident French Algerian population (*pieds noirs*). Indeed, it is in the cultural field where the FN's impact has been particularly marked. Noteworthy here are the incidents of local public library censorship in Orange.

In Orange, the FN mayor (Jacques Bompard) and his team stood accused of cultural censorship over library acquisitions. The reports of the practice led to the Minister of Culture (Philippe Douste-Blazy) ordering a special, top-level investigation which, in July 1996, found the local administration to be pursuing a policy of selection against works disapproved of (see *Le Monde*, 12 July 1996). Previously, *Alerte Orange*—a newly-formed local rights forum—had protested against the removal of *Le Monde* and *Libération* (that is, daily newspapers unsympathetic to the FN) and their replacement by *Présent*, the pro-FN daily. Among the books censored included ones on racism, rap music, regional Maghreb stories and those critical of the party. *Alerte Orange* also listed themes personally vetoed by the Mayor including works on the French Revolution, World War Two, Arab and African tales and those with 'big words' in the title (*Alerte Orange*, bi-monthly, No. 4, June–July 1996). The Minister of Culture warned against imposing *a priori* ideological orientations and against anti-pluralistic intolerance. Significantly, the official report claimed that the situation had parallels with 1987 when the Gaullist mayor of Montfermeil (Seine-Saint-Denis) had practised similar censorship—with Dreux in 1983 providing a further such example (see *Le Monde*, 6 January 1984).

Unsurprisingly, questions were raised in France about the abuse of public funds while a critical initiative emanating from the European Parliament warned against the library becoming a 'place of propaganda and intolerance': 'A party which selects the authors and subjects always ends up by setting the books on fire in nights of hate' (quoted in *Libération*, 12 July 1996).

## Conclusion

The National Front has emerged as an influential force in French politics. Legitimation via votes, alliances and appreciable public support for the ideas expressed (see Schain, 1987; Aubry and Duhamel, 1995; Marcus, 1995) has helped the party to popularise, to some significant extent, a discourse which stereotypes perceived outsiders through a process of cultural differentialist racism and selective interpretation of the nation, and works against integration, pluralism and tolerance. The party's agenda has been facilitated by the ideological groundwork prepared by more mainstream parties and channels as well as by the historic building of the nation-state in France (for further see Silverman, 1992). However, political rivals have contributed to unleashing a genie which they (and society) find difficult to contain. Out of office and considered dangerous by majority public opinion, the FN has nonetheless been able to influence the debate and legislation on immigration and rights. In office, locally, the party has been able, via cultural and budgetary choices, to impact upon the lives and facilities of local residents.[1]

It was only the recent division of the party into two rival organisations, based around Le Pen and Mégret, which called into question the ongoing strength of the party and the durability of its support base. With almost identical programs, the two parties target the same constituency, albeit with Mégret's claim to greater respectability and his proclivity towards alliances with the mainstream right.[2] While recent election results suggest that support for the party may have decreased, it is too early to judge whether this will lead to a long-term weakening of the party and the undermining of its distinctive contribution to French politics and society.[3]

## Notes

[1] While this chapter examines the local impact of the FN, it is also important to note that, in a handful of France's regions/regional councils, the party has a significant influence upon policy making and budgetary outcomes, where the mainstream right lacks a clear-cut elected majority and has to rely upon FN support.

[2] For a comprehensive chronology of the split, see the dossier at *Le Monde*'s website: <http://www.lemonde.fr/>

[3] Results in the June 1999 European Parliament elections gave Le Pen's *Front national* 5.7 per cent and 5 seats; with 3.3 per cent, Mégret's *Mouvement national* did not win a seat. This was a decrease from the 10.5 per cent gained by the (unified) FN in the 1994 elections, and, more markedly, from the near 15 per cent achieved in more recent French electoral contests. See *Le Monde*, 14 June 1999.

## References

Aubry, M. and Duhamel, O. (1995), *Petit dictionnaire pour lutter contre l'extrême droite*, Seuil, Paris.

Bresson, G. and Lionet, C. (1995), *Le Pen: Biographie*, Seuil, Paris.

Camus, J.-Y. (1992), 'Political Cultures within the Front National: The Emergence of a Counter-Ideology on the French Far-Right', *Patterns of Prejudice*, Vol. 26, Nos. 1 and 2, pp. 5–16.

Cohen, M. (1992), 'The French National Front and Immigration: the Appeal and the Challenge', *Mediterranean Quarterly*, Vol. 3, Part 2.

Davies, P. (1993), 'The Political Symbolism of Joan of Arc in Front National Discourse', *Politics*, Vol. 13, No. 2, October.

Front National (1993), *300 Mesures pour la renaissance de la France: Front National Programme de gouvernement*, Editions Nationales, Paris.

Front National (1991), *Immigration: 50 Mesures Concrètes*, FN pamphlet/ Front National, Marseille.

Gaspard, F. (1995), *A Small City in France*, Harvard University Press, Cambridge, Massachusetts and London.

Gorjanicyn, K. (1994), 'Race, Culture and Identity: The "Other" in French Political Discourse', in S. Alomes and M. Provis (eds), *A changing France in a changing world*, Institute for the Study of French Australian Relations, Monash University, Clayton, pp. 51–70.

Hainsworth, P. (1992), 'The Extreme Right in Post-War France: the emergence and success of the Front National', in P. Hainsworth (ed.), *The Extreme Right in Europe and the USA*, Pinter, London, pp. 29–60.

Hainsworth, P. (1996), 'At the Front', *West European Politics,* Vol. 19, No. 3, July, pp. 649–654.

Hargreaves, A. (1994), *Immigration, 'race' and ethnicity in contemporary France,* Routledge, London.

Le Gallou, J. Y. (1985), *La Préférence nationale*, Albin Michel, Paris.

Le Pen, J. M. (1994), *Les Français d'abord*, Carrère Michel Lafon, Paris.

Marcus, J. (1995), *The National Front and French Politics*, Macmillan, London.

Matonti, F. (1993), *'Le Front national forme ses cadres'*, Genèses, 10, January.

McKesson, J.A. (1994), 'Concepts and Realities in a Multiethnic France', *French Politics and Society*, Vol. 12, No. 1, Winter, pp. 16–38.

Schain, M. (1987), 'The National Front in France and the construction of political legitimacy', *West European Politics*, Vol. 10, No. 2, April, pp. 229–252.

Silverman, M. (1992), *Deconstructing the Nation: Immigration, Racism and Citizenship in Modern France*, Routledge, London.

Sternhell, Z. (1978), *La Droite révolutionnaire 1885-1914: les origines françaises du fascisme*, Seuil, Paris.

Taguieff, P. A. (1986), *'L'identité nationale saisie par les logiques de racisation. Aspects, figures et problèmes du racisme différentialiste'*, Mots, No. 12, March.

Vaughan, M. (1987), 'The Wrong Right in France', in E. Kolinsky (ed.), *Opposition in Western Europe*, Croom Helm, London, pp. 289–317.

Warner, M. (1983), *Joan of Arc: the Image of Female Heroism*, Penguin, Harmondsworth.

Wolfreys, J. (1993), 'An Iron Hand in a Velvet Glove: The Programme of the French National Front', *Parliamentary Affairs*, Vol. 46, No. 3, July, pp. 415–429.

## Newspapers/Newsletters/Weeklies

*Alerte Orange*
*Herald Sun (Australia)*
*Independent (London)*
*La Lettre de Jean-Marie Le Pen*
*L'Express*
*Le Monde*
*Le Nouvel Observateur*
*Libération*

# 5 Reflections on Minority Rights and the Liberal State in Central Europe

STEFAN AUER

One of the most serious challenges facing the post-communist societies of Central Europe is to find a way in which different ethnic groups can live together peacefully in a stable, liberal democratic order. For that to happen, the needs and aspirations of minority cultures must be reconciled with the interests of the majority. How, or whether, that can be achieved has puzzled political theorists from John Stuart Mill in the 19th century to the likes of Charles Taylor in our present day. How can political liberalism with its focus on individual freedom accommodate the political demands of groups and conceptualise a multicultural society free of culturally based oppression and domination? What sort of functions, if any, is a liberal state supposed to fulfill regarding national minorities? Should the state embrace and actively support ethnic diversity by acknowledging the special rights of the national minorities, or should it be indifferent, or even resistant, to any special demands?

John Stuart Mill argued that democracy is virtually impossible in a state populated by different nationalities. From this point of view, the best state is the one that has no minorities; if it does have some, as the next best option they should, if possible, be fully integrated into the dominant national culture. The integration of a national minority into the dominant culture can, according to Mill, be beneficial to its members if it allows them access to a civilisation that is more developed. Thus, for a Breton or a Basque, it is better to be fully accepted as a Frenchman, 'than to sulk on his own rocks, ... revolving in his own little mental orbit, without participation in the general movement of the world' (Mill, 1991, p. 431). If Mill's premises were to be accepted, it would be a legitimate task of a liberal state—at least in some cases—to promote integration and in that way actively encourage the nation-building process as this ultimately leads to a more stable democratic system.

John Stuart Mill, with his concerns about the political implications of national identities, is rather an exception amongst liberal theorists, who traditionally viewed the questions of belonging as something private that is beyond

69

the legitimate interest of the state. Liberals from John Locke to John Rawls derived the legitimacy of the state from a legal compact between free individual citizens that are thought of as bearers of some universal rights, rather than members of a particular national community (Czarnota, 1998, p. 9). Thus, even if the state is inadvertently conceptualised as national, it is ideally seen as ethnically neutral towards its citizens. A parallel could be drawn with the approach of a liberal state towards religious diversity. Even if some religious beliefs are arguably more propitious to liberal democracy than others (the Protestant religion, for example, with its stress on personal responsibility can be seen as more favourable to the cause of liberal democracy than Islam, which stresses the importance of a religious community), ideally the neutrality of a liberal state towards them must not be violated.[1] But is such an approach applicable to dealing with the national identities of citizens?

The fiction of ethnocultural neutrality prevented political theorists in the past from any meaningful conceptualisation of the relationship between the state and national culture(s). This has changed with the writings of liberal nationalists (Tamir, 1993; Miller, 1995) and communitarians (ie. Taylor, 1992; Kis, 1996; Kymlicka, 1995a, 1998).[2] Communitarian theories of multiculturalism are united in their criticism of a liberalism that underestimates the societal context that not only allows individuals to act as political beings, but also constitutes their identities. To that extent, theories of multiculturalism provide a good starting point for studying the political relevance of a multitude of national cultures within a society. Most communitarians believe that the state should actively endorse the politics of recognition and in that way do justice to the different identities of people inhabiting that state. The critics of communitarianism (Holmes, 1993; Hardin, 1995; Kukathas, 1995, 1998) warn, however, that active state support of diversity leads to more division and conflict within a society and thus ill serves the main aim of a liberal state, which is to maintain peace between various groups and individuals following their own conceptions of the good.

The aim of this chapter is to explore how theories of multiculturalism that originated in the West can apply to the question of minority rights in Central Europe. Thus, I will contrast Taylor's conception of the politics of recognition that calls for active state involvement in questions of cultural diversity with Kukathas' politics of indifference that warns of extending the powers and influence of a patronising state. I will then discuss different meanings of multiculturalism and demonstrate that concepts derived from migrant societies such as Australia cannot be directly transferred to Europe. After consideration of some examples from the Czech Republic and Slovakia and the situation of, among others, the Romany minority, the strengths and weaknesses of both approaches will be re-examined.

## The Politics of Recognition

To explore the possible ways of dealing with nationality within a framework of a liberal democratic state, it is useful to recall some recent studies of nationalism that do not shun the possible contradictions between the claims of liberal theory and the practical demands of national communities (whether they are in a majority or a minority). Yael Tamir convincingly argued that the proponents of liberalism have more in common with some proponents of nationalist projects than is usually assumed. Both liberals and nationalists concede the importance of seeing individuals in a social context. Tamir suggests that 'the liberal tradition with its respect for personal autonomy, reflection and choice, and the national tradition, with its emphasis on belonging, loyalty and solidarity, although generally seen as mutually exclusive, can indeed accommodate each other' (Tamir, 1993, p. 6). Tamir's liberal nationalism is polycentric, which means that it 'respects the other and sees each nation as enriching a common civilisation', unlike the ethnocentric nationalism, 'which sees one's own nation as superior to all others and seeks domination' (Tamir, 1995, p. 430). This conception is considerably more optimistic about the potential of nationalism for a modern liberal democracy, than most writers on nationalism allow for (eg. Hobsbawm, 1990). Liberal nationalism, that is foreigner-friendly and tolerant, creates the environment in which democratic order can develop and flourish, and this applies as much to the long established democracies in the West as it does to the newly developing post-communist societies in Central Europe.

Identities matter. If we agree with the premises on which the importance of liberal nationalism is based (that is, not only on its relevance to a liberal democratic society, but also for the well being of individuals), we cannot ignore the findings of communitarians who render identities important not only if they are national, or ethnic. Individual identities are partly constituted by the sense of belonging to different communities, be they racial, ethnic, cultural, or gender based. To treat individuals fairly, hence, necessitates a fair treatment of all these communities, since 'my own identity crucially depends on my dialogical relations with others' (Taylor, 1992, p. 34). Misrecognition is impermissible as it amounts to oppression. 'The projection of an inferior or demeaning image on another can actually distort and oppress, to the extent that the image is internalized' (Taylor, 1992, p. 36). Patriarchal societies, for example, perpetuate the inequality of genders by imposing on women a male sexist image of them that hinders their full emancipation long after more practical barriers have been removed.

As Charles Taylor stated, 'due recognition is not just a courtesy we owe people. It is a vital human need' (Taylor, 1992, p. 26). On these grounds affirmative actions sponsored by the state are justified.

> Where the politics of universal dignity fought for forms of nondiscrimination that were quite 'blind' to the ways in which citizens differ, the politics of difference often redefines nondiscrimination as requiring that we make these distinctions the basis of differential treatment (Taylor, 1992, p. 39).

In other words, in certain circumstances the state has to discriminate in order to be genuinely non-discriminatory. The practical consequence of this, in the context of national communities, is that a liberal state does not have to be culturally neutral and can actively follow a policy that favours some culture and a particular 'definition of the good life' (Taylor, 1992, p. 59). Taylor uses the example of the French speaking Canadians in Quebec to demonstrate that it can be legitimate to expect from the state that it does more in order to preserve a particular culture than a strictly neutral conception of a state would allow for. Taylor argues that the state has to protect cultural diversity not only for the people currently living within their (French minority) culture, but also for the future generations. 'Policies aimed at survival actively seek to *create* members of the community, for instance in their assuring that future generations continue to identify as French-speakers' (Taylor, 1992, p. 58). In that way, it is legitimate for the state in Quebec to demand from new migrants that they learn French rather than English, even if it violates their right to free choice. Another regulation outlawed commercial signage in any language other than French. Thus, 'restrictions have been placed on Quebeckers by their government, in the name of their collective goal of survival' (Taylor, 1992, p. 53).

As Michael Walzer highlighted, Taylor distinguishes between two different models of liberal societies (see Walzer in Taylor, 1992, pp. 99–103). Against the popular model of a strictly neutral liberal state that treats everyone equally without promoting any particular conception of a good life (espoused by Rawls, Dworkin and others), Taylor contrasts a different model of a liberal society, which is organised 'around a definition of a good life' and which follows 'strong collective goals' (Taylor, 1992, p. 59). The second model of a society is liberal, Taylor maintains, as long as it secures some fundamental rights and liberties for those who do not share its common goals. Thus, the English speaking 'minority' in Quebec would not be able to claim a right for all commercial signage being written in English, as this is not a fundamental right.

One has to distinguish the fundamental liberties, those that should never be infringed and therefore ought to be unassailably entrenched, on one hand, from privileges and immunities that are important, but that can be revoked or restricted for reasons of public policy—although one would need a strong reason to do this—on the other (Taylor, 1992, p. 59).

But how can the importance of 'privileges and immunities' be determined fairly as to avoid their misuse? In the case of French speaking Canadians, Taylor derives the urgency and legitimacy of their linguistic rights from the threat to the very survival of their culture. We do not need to worry too much about the feelings of English speaking Canadians in Quebec, since theirs is the culture of the ruling majority and therefore certainly not threatened in its very existence. But this is not a convincing argument. Liberals can and should realise the importance of a culture (as all the liberal nationalists do), but not for the sake of a particular culture as an abstract entity, but only as long as it benefits the individuals that are, after all, of primary concern for a truly liberal theory. Since there probably will always be *some individual* Quebeckers who are not interested in the survival of the French speaking culture in Canada, the state demands on them could be seen as an arbitrary imposition. Thus, when Taylor defends restrictions placed on Quebeckers 'in the name of *their* collective goal of survival' (my italics, Taylor,1992, p. 53), he actually departs from the liberal platform as he allows the interests of individuals to be overtaken by the demands of the community as a whole.

If Taylor's assumption about the intrinsic value of all cultures were correct, and if the survival of cultural diversity were the primary goal of politics of identity, one could even speculate (as Hardin did) about the necessity of 're-creating' long dead cultures. 'But many of those cultures were ill-suited to providing good lives to their members. Many of the cultures died from within, as individuals abandoned them for other opportunities' (Hardin, 1995, p. 67). As Kis rightly argued,

> interests attributed to the community are derived. We can say that a community has an interest in its preservation and the flourishing of its culture if it is also possible to say that the individuals making up the community have an interest in the preservation of their community and the flourishing of their culture (Kis, 1996).

It is, however, not clear from Kis' article who is to determine what the interests of these individuals are. In the real world, minorities are represented by some leaders who do not and cannot always fully reflect the interests of all the members.

Furthermore, Taylor's defence of the politics of recognition sounds appealing only when applied to a national minority. But the English speaking Canadians could be equally concerned about losing their identity as they are being culturally dominated by the United States. Can they, hence, restrict the linguistic rights of the French minority, or of the new migrants to Quebec on the grounds that they need to foster a unity badly needed vis-a-vis the challenge from the South? This is not just a theoretical construct. Consider the Slovak case. Were the moral claims of Slovaks to protection of their culture stronger when they inhabited larger states as a minority that had to defend itself against the potential or real dangers of assimilation, be it within the Austro-Hungarian empire, or within Czechoslovakia, than they are now, when they constitute a majority? If yes, why?

To answer this question, it is instructive to recall the modern history of nationalism in Central Europe that is notorious for turning majorities into minorities and vice versa. The requirements of modernisation of Austro-Hungary in the nineteenth century called for the introduction of one common vernacular throughout the whole empire. The Germanising policies of Joseph II were thus primarily inspired by the practical needs of industrialisation (as it happened, the elite spoke German). The attempts to introduce German as a universal language of the empire were met with fierce Hungarian resistance. In turn, the Hungarians, who managed to secure their rights for their own national culture and language against the Austrian dominance, tried to impose their own culture and language on the Slovaks, who reacted the same way as the Hungarians before them. Hungarian nationalism engendered by default the evolution of the Slovak nation, which in turn strove for independence (Schwarz, 1994). Thus, were the Hungarians right to follow their collective goal of cultural survival by imposing their culture on all the people living within their territory?

Similarly, the Czechs who saw their culture endangered by the surrounding Germanic influence sought to defend it by the creation of a united 'Czechoslovakian identity by way of incorporating the Slovaks into the Czech nation-group' (Bollerup and Christensen, 1997, p. 121). This had an ambivalent impact on the Slovak nation. Even though it is contested to what extent the Masaryk's conception of Czechoslovakism implied cultural unity, there can be little doubt that Slovaks were culturally and politically dominated in the first Czechoslovak Republic of 1918–38.[3] Still, the Slovaks being considered with the Czechs a part of the *státotvorní* people (the official constituent nationalities of the state) did certainly have more influence on the policies of the state than the other national minorities of the new Czechoslovak Republic, such as the Hungarians (Leff, 1997, pp. 24–29). Was it then right for the 'Czechoslovak nation', in the name of its struggle for survival, to ignore the demands for recognition of other minorities?

The 'struggle for survival' (incidentally this is the title of a nationalistic account of Slovak history, Kirschbaum, 1995) was later used in Slovakia not only for justification of the very existence of the independent Slovak state, but also to deny the Hungarians some basic minority rights, since they were, and by some still are, perceived historically as endangering the very survival of the Slovak nation. In fact, some of the most adventurous justifications of more restrictive policies towards the Hungarian minority during the third rule of Vladimír Meciar in Slovakia (1994–1998) were derived from irrational fears about the unabated threat of Hungarian dominance. Roman Hofbauer, a member of parliament for the then governing party—the 'Movement for a Democratic Slovakia'—and a senior journalist working for the *Slovenská Republika* argued in the issue of January 27, 1998, that the Slovak nation is threatened by genocide (sic) and must therefore be protected against both its enemies from abroad and traitors from within (Kamenec, 1998, p. 5). As a journalist supported by Meciar's government, Hofbauer was awarded the 1994 prize '*Cena Ludovíta Stúra*' following the nomination of the 'Association of Slovak Journalists' that had very close links with the ruling coalition (Schmögnerová, 1997, p. 203), which indicates that his views would then have been widely shared within the ruling elite.

The above examples do not imply that Charles Taylor would support any restrictions of minority rights in Austro-Hungary, or Czechoslovakia, let alone in present day Slovakia. Taylor's argument was voiced, after all, in support of minority rights. Moreover, the suggestion in some cases to override the will of individuals in Quebec was meant to apply to new migrants, whose demands have a different degree of urgency and legitimacy. But the logic underpinning Taylor's reasoning remains problematic. The suggestion that some collective goals can override the interests of an individual deserves scepticism. All the more reason to turn to consideration of a radically liberal alternative to communitarian projects, proposed by the Australian political philosopher Chandran Kukathas.

## The Politics of Indifference

Opposing Taylor's second type of liberalism, Kukathas boldly states that the most viable response of the liberal state to the growing demands for recognition is to ignore them. Confronted with the complex realities of multicultural societies, liberalism 'recommends doing nothing' (Kukathas, 1998, p. 687). Kukathas claims that the philosophy of liberalism does not have a problem with multiculturalism, because 'liberalism is itself, fundamentally, a theory of multiculturalism'. Liberalism's answer to the religious and cultural diversity inherent in modern societies has been the realisation that diversity should be accommodated and difference tolerated, but without an illusion that all the conflicting interests can ever be reconciled. As Kukathas states, 'division, conflict and competition would always be present in human society and the task of political institutions is to palliate a condition they cannot cure' (Kukathas, 1998, p. 690). As the conflicting demands of different groups are unavoidable, it is better for political institutions to try, as far as possible, to be indifferent to them, rather than putting them at the very centre of the political agenda. Thus, 'a positive delight in the diversity of human cultures, languages, and forms of life' (Nussbaum, 1996, p. 137) characteristic of virtually all the theorists of multiculturalism, can lead, ironically, to more conflict to the extent that the politics of recognition diminishes room for compromises. Something that becomes essential for personal identities cannot be easily compromised.

When the Protestants in Northern Ireland 'celebrate' their identity with marches commemorating a glorious event in their history, they inadvertently demean the identity of the Catholics, whose common reaction is to make the march impossible (even by using terrorist methods). This is not to say that some sort of politics of recognition is to be blamed for the persistent crisis in Northern Ireland; but it could be argued that a multiculturalism which cherishes differences could hardly prevent it. In contrast, Australia has managed potential religious conflict of the migrants from different parts of Ireland as well as from Britain by 'forgetting' about their dividing histories (Hirst, 1994, pp. 32–34).[4] Arguably, it was this historical politics of indifference that made the peaceful living together of different communities in Australia possible. Similar problems could arise from the differing views of Slovak and Hungarian national histories, when personalities and events that marked an important step in the history of the Hungarian fight for freedom and independence—such as Louis Kossuth and the revolution of 1848/1849—are for Slovaks associated rather with oppression. As the revolution eventually led to the reorganisation of the Austrian empire as the Dual Monarchy of Austria-Hungary in 1867, Hungarians acquired equal status with the German-Austrians. The demands of Slovaks, on the other hand, were ignored, and in fact the ensuing politics of 'magyarisation' that aimed to turn Slovaks into Hungarians resulted in the suppression of Slovak language and culture (Johnson, 1996, pp. 156–8). Thus, to stress and celebrate the importance of different histories in Central Europe can contribute paradoxically to more division than to mutual understanding. In that way, Kukathas' theory that argues for a minimalist liberal state which ignores the political relevance of ethnic identities could be seen validated. The question remains, however, whether Kukathas' proposition, which relies on the experience of a migrant country, offers a realistic option for Europe and for issues related to both resident or intergenerational minorities and recent immigrants.

## Two Types of Multiculturalism

The politics of indifference can only be equated with multiculturalism, however, when multiculturalism is just another word for tolerance of ethnic differences. Thus, we should distinguish between *soft* multiculturalism that allows for and is even supportive of an overarching identity (defined by common language and some basic commitments to the ideals of a liberal state) that unites people of different ethnic backgrounds, and *hard* multiculturalism that implies that all the cultures and ethnic groups within a society are equal and should therefore be actively encouraged to fully realise their particular ethnic identities.[5]

Consequently, in the second version of multiculturalism there is no space for an overarching identity as this would inadvertently privilege one group (say Anglo-Celtic) over others. As Hirst convincingly argued, the success of multiculturalism in Australia can be attributed to the application of its soft version (Hirst, 1994).[6] While the new migrants were not expected to give up fully their ethnic and cultural identities, they did have to accept some basic Australian values and they were expected to learn English if they were to succeed in their new country.

This experience cannot, however, be easily 'exported' to Europe, where the situation is radically different. As Kymlicka rightly pointed out, the moral claims for preservation of migrants' identities are different from claims of people living in the countries of their birth who constitute national minorities (Kymlicka, 1995a, 1998).[7] The partial loss of one's culture is mostly a painful experience, but migrants are usually better prepared to accept this. Ideally, they made a voluntary trade off and renounced the 'culturally comfortable' living within their familiar environment for better opportunities in a new country. This is not to say that, in the case of Australia, the state actively demands that the new migrants forget about their ethnic and cultural identities; the assumption is rather that they can be successfully accommodated within a very broad context of an Australian culture. Soft multiculturalism creates space for migrant cultures to negotiate the conditions of settling down. Instead of forced integration, a benign state makes the adaptation to the new environment easier by formally acknowledging the equality of all cultures.

In the context of Central Europe, however, soft multiculturalism that ultimately leads to assimilation (even if it takes generations) hardly offers an adequate solution for a peaceful co-existence of national minorities. Even though there are historic instances in Europe of states being relatively successful in incorporating some ethnic minorities into the dominant nation (like Basques and Bretons in France), in our times 'the attempts to suppress minority nationalism have been abandoned as unworkable and indeed counter-productive' (Kymlicka, 1998). In fact to the extent that assimilation policies were successful in the past, they were usually only made possible thanks to an unacceptable extent of coercion. Presently, there is a growing consensus that any practices leading to forceful integration or homogenisation are morally reprehensible. Unlike migrants, the members of national minorities have not actively chosen to live in a country that is dominated by a different culture, but were born into it. Therefore, they should not suffer permanent marginalisation that would follow from state policies based on ignoring the differences. Hungarians in Slovakia, for example, cannot reasonably be expected to subordinate the importance of their ethnicity and culture to some higher good of the country as a whole. Even if political stability is easier to maintain with a population that shares a common culture and the public administration is more effective when conducted exclusively in one official and dominant vernacular, the Slovak state cannot aim at full assimilation of a large minority that would lead to its cultural marginalisation (or even cultural extinction).

Thus, a harder version of multiculturalism is needed in the Central European context that does not only allow for a minority culture simply to exist, but actively provides for some of its basic needs. The state must, for example, fully accept its responsibility for education with languages of instruction mirroring the cultural diversity of the country. Moreover, depending on the size of the minority in question, the state should help to sustain the vibrant cultural life of the ethnic communities by providing assistance for newspapers, public broadcasting, theatre and the like. Inevitably, ethnic communities compete with other groups for limited resources that are available for redistribution, and ultimately not all claims can be fulfilled. This is yet another reason why it is crucial that ethnic communities secure adequate political representation which can articulate and persuasively follow its interests.

Surprisingly, apart from the extreme right Slovak National party, no one in the newly independent Slovakia actually questioned the obligation of the state to spend money on ethnic minorities. Certainly, the extent and quality of state support for minority cultures was contested; however not even the former prime minister Meciar, who was rightly criticised for his authoritarian style of government and some extreme nationalistic tendencies in his policies, questioned the basic obligation. Yet, on the other hand, Meciar's government (1994-1998) found ways of perverting the purpose of affirmative policies, so that they primarily served the particular political interests of his party, ignoring the needs of the minority in question. In one telling instance, the government cultural fund 'Pro Slovakia' allocated a substantial subsidy for the creation of a Hungarian supplement to an extreme nationalistic Slovak newspaper *Slovenská Republika* that was closely affiliated to Meciar's 'Movement for a Democratic Slovakia' (Bútora, 1998, p. 40). The likelihood of any Slovak Hungarians ever reading this propaganda was negligible, but the government fulfilled two goals at once. First, it bettered the financial situation of its 'own' newspaper, and second, this being a 'truly democratic government', it was able to argue that it was taking its responsibility for supporting minorities seriously.

Thus far I have argued that a multiculturalism based on ignoring differences is not a plausible option in Central Europe. Kymlicka's concept of multicultural citizenship which acknowledges and accommodates the ethnocultural diversity of the people is more convincing than any politics of indifference. But the critique voiced by Kukathas clearly shows the limits of an active politics of recognition, and points to some serious practical problems which cannot be ignored. The implication of Taylor's assertion that denial or negligence of identity amounts to an act of oppression is that people who feel that their identities (not necessarily limited to race/ethnicity) are not fully recognised have strong moral claims to make.[8] In that situation it would not make sense for them to negotiate 'a little bit less oppression', and in that sense it could easily turn political processes into a zero sum game in which one side always has to lose. As oppression is morally reprehensible, it would not make sense morally to expect a slave to negotiate 'better conditions of slavery'. It must be abolished altogether.

Furthermore, the state can never fully secure undistorted recognition of various differing identities. The Czech and Slovak languages, for example, are so deeply imbued with racism against Romanies, that much more than some formal political changes will be needed to secure their full equality. Significantly, when the leader of the Czech extreme right Republican Party, Sládek, defended himself against accusations from Romanies who alleged that he made offensive remarks about the Czech President Václav Havel and his wife by claiming that they were lying, he relied simply on the meaning of '*cikán*' that denotes in Czech both a 'Gypsy' as well as a 'liar', or to lie.[9] '*Cikáni cikáni*', meaning Gypsies are lying, appears to be a tautology that does not need any further substantiation. Clearly, Sládek's extreme right Republican Party could and should have been prevented from using slogans in the Czech election campaign of 1998 that utilised the racist implications of the term *Cikáni*. Hence, the state must step in where it can to avoid excesses, such as open racial vilification that certainly constitutes a serious offence. But not even a police state could fully eliminate a word and its implications in its daily use. This change can only come about as a result of a slow process from within a civil society. The culture of tolerance has to develop and cannot be imposed on the people by the state, even though the state can help actively in promoting it. Havel's repeated interference on behalf of Romanies was a good example of this.

Apart from Havel, however, the Czech state institutions failed in dealing with the above mentioned incident between Sládek and the two Romany brothers Tancos, who physically attacked him. Ironically, the brothers Tancoˆs were charged with racially motivated violence against an individual and a group of people, as they denounced Sládek as '*bílá svine*' (white pig). Thus, laws that were clearly created for the protection of minorities were in this instance interpreted in a way that assisted the defence of a politician, who had for seven years programmatically incited racial hatred and violence against Romany minority (Camrda, 1998). It required a radical step by the Czech President, who made use of his power by granting the brothers clemency, to restore a sense of justice. As the proper procedures of the rule of law were obstructed by his quick decision, however, the sense of legality suffered. Many observers criticised Václav Havel for over-stretching his competencies (eg. Sustrová, 1998). Yet, with his controversial decision, the Czech President was able to take a clear stance against racism that arguably contributed to the failure of the Czech Republican party to secure seats in parliament in the June 1998 election.[10]

## Liberal Censorship?

With respect to racial vilification, a conflict arises between the imperative of protecting vulnerable minorities and the concern with protection of freedom of speech. An argument could be made that some sort of censorship is not only reconcilable with the basic principles of liberalism, but even required in order to protect the very liberal democratic order that makes freedom of speech possible. Onora O'Neill utilises the Kantian conception of liberalism to show that in certain circumstances restrictions are needed to allow for efficient and undistorted public deliberations. Immanuel Kant, in his famous essay 'What is Enlightenment?', made the distinction between the public use of reason that 'must always be free' and the private use of reason that may 'often be very narrowly restricted' (Kant, 1983, p. 42). Before dismissing this idea as yet another instance of German proclivity for illiberal thoughts, one has to make clear that Kant's understanding of the 'private use of reason' differs significantly from our current usage. Whenever a person employs his reason relying on authorities other than that of reason itself (like some institutions, or prejudices), one makes a private use of it, as opposed to the public use that is employed in 'communications which presuppose no external authority'. Thus, it is not the nature of the audience in a discourse that decides whether it is private or public, but rather the quality of the intellectual exchange. The public use of reason is, then, vital for enlightenment, or in political terms, a functioning deliberative democracy.

Onora O'Neill's defence of censorship adds another important argument in favour of an efficient politics of difference as espoused by Taylor:

> There are no good reasons for tolerating any private uses of reason which damage public use of reason. For example, communications and expressions which denigrate or mock or bully others, or more generally fail to respect them, may make it harder or impossible to think for themselves, so following the maxim of enlightenment. Communications and expressions which foment divisions between persons and groups may make it harder to follow the maxim of enlarged thought. Hence some forms of censorship and restrictions of private use of reason may be acceptable (indeed required) when (but only when) they are needed to foster or sustain capacities for communication with the world at large. Kantian liberalism can provide reason for specific restraint and censorship where their absence would lead to forms of defamation or harassment that damage capacities for agency or for recognition of others' agency (O'Neill, 1987, p. 547).

Even if Kantian liberalism appears attractive, since it inhibits any expressions of intolerance at the very beginning of some undesired discourse, the problem is that it presupposes some enlightened leader (like Frederick the Great of Prussia in the case of Immanuel Kant), or some sort of 'philosopher king' (like Václav Havel). For who is to decide what constitutes in Kant's terminology 'a private use of reason'? Even if rationality is universal, it is not easy to find a universal agreement as to what constitutes a truly rational discourse. In many cases, it is a more realistic expectation to see claims based on unfounded prejudices discharged by simply exposing their irrationality in the public realm. Immanuel Kant, who wrote his essays in conditions favourable for a free exchange of ideas, had himself experienced that to rely on an enlightened ruler is simply not enough. As soon as Frederick the Great was replaced by the less open minded ruler Frederick William II, Kant was no longer able to enjoy freedom from censorship (Scruton, 1997, p. 14). This does not invalidate the need for some form of liberal censorship, but once again it shows the extent to which the state can protect minorities against any form of racial vilification.

## Feasibility versus Desirability

The consequent politics of recognition in which the state would take full responsibility for due acknowledgement of often conflicting identities is, as we have seen, hardly a practical proposition when dealing with cultural diversity. But it still could be argued, at least from the point of view of an individual who can ignore the practical implications of such a policy, that such policies are, in any case, desirable. This depends ultimately, however, on individual preferences. Only for the people who value the acknowledgement of their identities more than other goods, which can be in conflict with this requirement, does the politics of recognition remain morally valid whatever its practical implications. For in some cases a choice has to be made between incommensurable options. One has to decide whether living within a closely knit 'culturally comfortable' community is more important than some other goals, like professional advancement, or artistic independence[11] that can only be fulfilled within a broader society.

Any meaningful conception of minority rights will include some elements of affirmative action, which means that the state will inevitably interfere in the value system of a cultural minority. When the state, for example, takes responsibility for education it cannot but promote some sort of values. The idea that at least primary education is obligatory for all citizens is based on the rationale that only in that way can some basic equality of opportunities be maintained. This is supported *inter alia* by the European Convention on Human Rights (Article 2 of the First Protocol) which explicitly states that 'no person shall be denied the right to education' (Poulter, 1987, p. 600). Moreover the liberal thinkers like John Stuart Mill highlighted the importance of education for the stability of the liberal democratic order that—at least in the long run—relies on well informed and thus well educated citizens.

For minority cultures, such as Romanics, which '[do] not value schooling, the parents believing they can educate a child satisfactorily through informal instruction in the ways of their culture' (Kukathas, 1995, p. 248), compulsory schooling can be perceived as an undesired imposition of a patronising state. 'Our' instinct would tell us that it is surely in the interest of the Romany children to receive the best possible education, even allowing for some significant differences that would accommodate the specifics of their culture—at least some subjects, for example, should be taught in Romanes. The underlying assumption is, however, that 'our' life-style (typically based on education and wealth acquired through a successful career) is more valuable than the lifestyle of Romanies. If that is the case, the whole project of a multicultural liberal state is self-defeating as, in the process of assisting a minority culture, it undermines the very culture it aims to protect. As Kukathas states, 'there is no more reason to insist that gypsy [sic] parents offer their children 'rational choice' of life-style through public education than there is to require that other parents offer their children the opportunity to become gypsies' (Kukathas, 1995, p. 248).

In both models, the cases of discrimination seem to be unavoidable. Kukathas' politics of indifference is discriminatory because it precludes the individual members of Romany culture from an opportunity to fully partici-pate in the dominant culture, by practically denying them access to an institu-tionalised education system. The politics of difference, on the other hand, which would provide Romany children with some form of institutional education, allows a patronising state to promote values foreign to the actual culture, even if the content and form of education takes into account Romany culture. Which conception, then, is more just? Both are open to the accusation of being racist. The state makes itself either guilty of implementing a policy based on ideas of cultural supremacy (in the case of institutional education imposed on Romany children), or it fails in its pronounced adherence to individual rights that cer-tainly include the right to proper education. It will be rightly said that the state is able to accommodate differences by, for example, taking seriously the exist-ence of the Romany language. Nevertheless, the question is not whether the Romany children should be taught in Romanes language, but whether they should go to school at all!

As we have seen, infringement of cultural autonomy is in some cases a result of the liberal welfare state pursuing social justice. The idea that the state has some responsibility for a downward distribution of wealth is presently hardly contested (with the notable exception of Nozick). In the pre-modern times, when democracy was restricted to people with property, this problem could not have been significant. People were free to live within their communal cul-ture, but were also 'free' to remain marginalised. Indeed, Edmund Burke de-fended the economic injustice of the *ancien régime* by espousing the idea of an 'equality of happiness'. All lives are inherently valuable regardless of the ma-terial conditions. People should hence, according to Burke, be taught to seek

the happiness that is to be found by virtue in all conditions; in which consists the *true moral equality of mankind*, and not in that monstrous fiction, which by in-spiring false ideas and vain expectations into men destined to travel in the ob-scure walk of labourious life, serves only to aggravate and imbitter that real in-equality; and which the order of civil life establishes as much for the benefit of those whom it must leave in a humble state, as those whom it is able to a condi-tion more splendid, but not more happy (my italics, Burke, 1968, p. 124).

This is not to suggest that in order to meet the demands of cultural recognition, we should return to pre-modern times, or revive Burkean conservatism. Nor does it mean that the politics of recognition is *always* in conflict with welfare politics. But it is instructive to remember that pressure to homogenise the populations of larger states arose with the process of modernisation (vividly described by Gellner, 1983). The first instance of systematic oppression of Romanies goes back to the assimilation policies of Maria Teresia, who was one of the most energetic modernisers of Central Europe. It is not surprising that the communist rulers, being even more ruthless modernisers, continued her endeavour. We know now that these and similar policies are both morally indefensible and politically not feasible. The nationalist dream of a perfect cultural unity has never materialised. The question is how a genuine cultural diversity can be accommodated in our 'post-socialist' times (to use the words of Nancy Fraser[12]) without endangering but rather supporting the liberal-democratic order.

## The Redistribution–Recognition Dilemma

Nancy Fraser has identified a dilemma of modern liberal welfare states that are concerned both with the politics of recognition as well as the politics of social justice. While the demands for recognition are commonly addressed by some form of affirmative action that leads to valorisation of group specific differences, the ultimate goal of social improvements is to abolish any group specific differences (Fraser, 1997). When for example, Romanies are discriminated against on the labour market because of their ethnicity and/or 'race', social justice would require overcoming this unfavourable differentiation. As Fraser put it (writing about the discrimination of Afro-Americans):

> Eliminating 'race'-specific exploitation, marginalization, and deprivation requires abolishing the racial division of labour—both the racial division between exploitable and superfluous labour and the racial division within paid labour. The logic of remedy is like the logic with respect to class: it is to put race out of business as such (Fraser, 1997, pp. 21–22).

Policies against racism are, according to Fraser, trapped in a dilemma. They must at once 'pursue political-economic remedies that would undermine 'racial' differentiation, while also pursuing cultural-valuational remedies that valorise the specificity of despised collectivities' (Fraser, 1997, p. 23). Thus, in certain circumstances, struggles for recognition of diverse identities are in opposition to struggles for a just distribution of material benefits. Affirmative action directed towards disadvantaged groups can actually lead to backlash misrecognition, as the groups that are in need of assistance are made visible and therefore easier to attack by the people who are unwilling to accept their rights.

Fraser believes, however, that the contradiction between the imperatives of social justice and the demands for recognition can and should be overcome. For that to happen, conventional affirmative multiculturalism and social policies that aim 'at correcting inequitable outcomes of social arrangements without disturbing the underlying framework that generates them' must be replaced with a more radical approach that is transformative in that it aims at 'restructuring the underlying generative framework' (Fraser, 1997, p. 23). Transformative remedies would redress disrespect of disadvantaged groups by 'destabilizing existing group identities and differentiations', and thus they 'would not only raise the self-esteem of members of currently disrespected groups; they would change *everyone's* sense of self' (Fraser, 1997, p. 24). 'The long-term goal of deconstructive antiracism is a culture in which hierarchical racial dichotomies are replaced by networks of multiple intersecting differences that are demassified and shifting' (Fraser, 1997, p. 31). In the economic realm, the remedies would also be directed towards a thorough restructuring of underlying causes of unequal distribution, rather than simply relying on half-hearted remedies of the liberal welfare state. Here again, while the former remedies seek to undermine class differentiation, the latter more traditional remedies create 'strongly cathected, antagonistic group differentiations' (Fraser, 1997, p. 25) and in that way perpetuate the structural injustice.

Leaving aside the economic and political viability of the proposed socialist transformation (that aiming at 'deep restructuring of the relations of production' (Fraser, 1997, p. 27) very much resembles a communist revolution), Fraser's remedies are not very convincing even in the context of race and ethnicity. If the 'selves' were malleable to the extent that Fraser assumes, then the whole project of a multicultural society based on recognising differences would not be needed, as it would be simpler to turn people into 'deconstructed' cosmopolitan citizens of the world, for whom the notion of cultural identity would be obsolete anyway. Thus Fraser, having rightly identified potential tension between the politics of recognition and the politics of the welfare state, obscures the problem by proposing a solution that is both inconsistent and unrealistic. The problems with affirmation of differences are, however, real.

## Conclusion

The presentation of these examples should not suggest that the state should fully withdraw from interference with minorities and ignore its responsibility for their well-being. This constitutes a politics of indifference which does not solve the problems raised by ethnocultural difference within states. Similarly, the fact that the existence of a welfare state makes its misuse possible is not, in itself, an argument against any welfare politics whatsoever. But we are well advised by Kukathas and others that we should be realistic about and often suspicious of the state, and not expect any definite solutions to all the problems derived from the living together of different cultures. Ultimately, Kukathas is right to say that a liberal state can only ameliorate conflicts rather than abolish them all together, but, I would argue, he is wrong to insist on a consequent politics of indifference.

To sum up, rather than proposing some simple solutions, I have tried to identify some of the inherent contradictions of dealing with ethnic and cultural diversity. I do not argue that because of these contradictions a liberal state should withdraw from issues of ethnicity. Both affirmative action and minority rights are needed. But no rights are absolute and even minority rights have to be weighed against other legitimate considerations, such as stability of a democratic order, or individual equality of opportunity. The critics of the politics of recognition provide a useful corrective to some projects of communitarians who tend to raise expectations no state can ever fulfill. It may well be argued that in many circumstances the modern centralised state is partly the problem, rather than the solution. The more competencies given to the institutions of the state, the more they are open to misuse. It is of little use to try to overlook the problems that arise from the cohabitation of different ethnicities—as some theorists of multiculturalism try to do. If different people can and do live in harmony, then we do not need political theories to celebrate that. But to strike the right balance between unity and diversity, and between individual and collective rights, requires careful consideration of intricate and often ultimately insoluble problems. When demands (say) for social justice are incommensurable with demands for cultural recognition, a choice has to be made that excludes other options. In making these choices, the western political theories are helpful in Central Europe only as long as they are critically applied according to the specific social, political and historical context.

# Notes

1  The implementation of this ideal can, however, be very difficult. The promotion of religious tolerance goes against any fundamentalist religious belief systems for which the assumption is central that *their* and *only their* belief is correct. When children, for example, are exposed to a variety of religious doctrines, they can come to doubt the doctrine promoted by their parents and in that way a religiously tolerant state inevitably undermines some religious communities. (For a legal case in the United States, in which some fundamentalists and evangelical religious families saw their religious freedom violated by the existing state school system see Macedo, 1995).

2  I am aware of the fact that this term is being contested. As far as communitarianism denotes a concept that is in opposition to liberalism, neither Kymlicka nor Taylor can be thus labelled, since they both tried to accommodate insights of the communitarians *within* the liberal theory. But to the extent that they shifted the focus of theorising from individuals to groups they certainly did adopt some basic tenets of communitarians. In fact, it can be argued that at least occasionally they leave the platform of political liberalism whenever they put the interests of groups above the interests of individuals. (See for example the critique of Kymlicka in Laitin, 1998, pp. 221–236, especially p. 232).

3  Tomás Garrigue Masaryk (1850-1937) was the founder and the first president of the Czechoslovak Republic between 1918-35.

4  This has been an ongoing process fed from within a civil society that was facilitated by the Australian state. As Hirst documented, after a violent confrontation between Catholics and Protestants in Melbourne 1846, 'the colony's mini-parliament immediately passed a law banning processions held to commemorate festivals, anniversaries, or political events related to any religious or political differences between Her Majesty's subjects' (Hirst, 1991, p. 23). 'Matters which were known to be divisive had to be kept at a distance or subject to strict local quarantine' (Hirst, 1991, p. 25). 'The poisonous cycle of demonstration and counter-demonstration by which Northern Ireland keeps alive its troubled past was nipped in the bud. But all the color gone from the streets! A disappointing outcome according to true multiculturalists who appear to believe that no social differences can be damaging, no matter how acute or passionately held they are' (Hirst, 1991, p. 23). Obviously, a policy based on 'ignoring' conflicts was easier to implement in Australia than in Ireland, as the migrants had naturally weaker allegiances to their homelands than people who have never left their country of origin. For that reason Irish Australians were better able to accept any restrictions than their compatriots in Ireland.

5  The distinction between the 'soft' and 'hard' versions of multiculturalism is ideal-typical. Policies in the real world can usually be located somewhere in-between. While the former Australian Prime Minister Paul Keating, for example, inclined more towards 'hard' multiculturalism (see Sheehan, 1998), his liberal successor, John Howard supported rather 'softer' multiculturalism. As he stated, 'if multiculturalism means that there should be respect for everybody's own indi-

vidual identity then I'm totally supportive. If it means you're promoting the diversity ahead of the unity then I put a couple of question marks over it' (The *Australian*, September 19–20, 1998).

6    Jerzy Zubrzycki, who was a spiritual father of the Australian policy of multiculturalism, stated explicitly that 'because some minority values are totally inconsistent with fundamental values of the dominant Australian culture [...], it *would be nonsense to say that multiculturalism means that every culture is equally valued and equally legitimate*' (my italics, in Hirst, 1994, p. 29). In other words, whenever a conflict arises between different values espoused by various migrant groups, the Australian values override the values of migrant cultures.

7    Kymlicka's distinction is plausible, but not without dangers. The competing claims on territories of the ethnic communities of the former Yugoslavia are, after all, based on their historic right to live on a certain piece of land. Similarly, Slovak extreme nationalists try to invalidate claims of Hungarians for more cultural autonomy, or minority rights, by referring to a thousand years of history of Slavic inhabitation of Slovakia. In that sense Slovak nationalists consider themselves more 'indigenous' than the Hungarian tribes. 'Are the Slovaks [who allegedly inherited their territory from their Slavic forebears] in any way better than Hungarians only because they came earlier?' asked Slovak historian Eduard Krekovic rhetorically, questioning the ethical validity of political arguments based on different readings of histories (Krekovic, 1998, p. 6).

8    I would argue that this claim could, however, turn grotesque if applied too widely.

9    This happened a few weeks before the 1998 elections in a popular television program 'Kotel' in *TV NOVA*, 20 May, 1998 (see also Sulc, 1998).

10    This is not to suggest that this sort of incident could only happen in the Czech Republic. For numerous cases of state institutions failing to counter racism (or even themselves being racist) against the Romany minorities in Slovakia see, for example, a report by the European Roma Rights Center, *Time of the Skinheads: Denial and Exclusion of Roma in Slovakia* (1997).

11    In order to challenge the presumption of communitarians that individual identities are constituted by the surrounding cultures, Waldron contrasted the open-ended cultural identity of Salman Rushdie (or the lack of it) to clearly defined identities that are deeply rooted in some closed communities. Rushdie, a 'cosmopolitan' who is in his own way proud of his 'mongrel' self, having gone through the 'experience of uprooting, disjuncture and metamorphosis' follows his conception of a good life that is, according to Waldron, certainly not inferior to a conception based more on a communal culture (Kymlicka, 1995b, p. 93). If that is the case, then some claims of communitarians, that communal cultures are vital for the development of identities, are seriously undermined.

12    Fraser uses the term post-socialist condition to describe the tendency of ever more left-wing intellectuals in America after the 1989 revolutions in Central and Eastern Europe to focus more on the politics of recognition while neglecting (the often related) problems that stem from social injustice in societies (Fraser, 1997).

# References

Bollerup, S.R. and Christensen, C.D. (1997), *Nationalism in Eastern Europe: Causes and Consequences of the National Revivals and Conflicts in Late-Twentieth-Century Eastern Europe*, Macmillan, Basingstoke.

Burke, E. (1968), *Reflections on the Revolution in France*, Penguin, Harmondsworth.

Bútora, M. and Skladony, T. (eds) (1998), *Slovakia 1996-1997: A Global Report on the State of Society*, Institute for Public Affairs, Bratislava.

Camrda, J. (1998), 'Co je a co není rasov'y motiv', *Lidové noviny*, 20 May, 1998, p. 11.

Czarnota, A. (1998), 'Constitutionalism, Nationalism and Law', paper presented at the AASCPCS/ANZSA 1998 International Conference on Communist and Post-communist Societies, Melbourne, July 7–10.

Fraser, N. (1997), *Justice Interruptus*, Routledge, New York.

Gellner, E. (1983), *Nations and Nationalism*, Blackwell, Oxford.

Hardin, R. (1995), *One for All*, Princeton University Press, Princeton.

Hirst, J. (1991), 'Australia's Absurd History: A Critique of Multiculturalism', *Quadrant*, March, pp. 20–27.

Hirst, J. (1994), 'National Pride and Multiculturalism', *Quadrant*, November 1994, pp. 29–34.

Hobsbawm, E. (1990), *Nations and Nationalism since 1780: Programme, Myth, Reality*, Cambridge University Press, Cambridge.

Holmes, S. (1993), *The Anatomy of Antiliberalism*, Harvard University Press, Cambridge, Massachusetts.

Johnson, L.R. (1996), *Central Europe: Enemies, Neighbours, Friends*, Oxford University Press, Oxford.

Kamenec, I. (1998), 'Stereotypy v slovenskych dejinách a v slovenskej historiografii', *OS*, March, pp. 3–5.

Kant, I. (1983), *Perpetual peace and other essays*, Hackett, Indianapolis, Cambridge.

Kirschbaum, S.J. (1995), *A History of Slovakia: The Struggle for Survival*, St. Martin's Press, New York.

Kis, J. (1996), 'Beyond the Nation State', *Social Research*, Vol. 63, Spring, pp. 191–245.

Krekovic, E. (1998), 'Etnogenéza, archeológia a nacionalizmus', *OS*, January, pp. 5–6.

Kukathas, C. (1995), 'Are There Any Cultural Rights?', in W. Kymlicka (ed.), *The Rights of Minority Cultures*, Oxford University Press, Oxford, pp. 228 255.

Kukathas, C. (1997), 'Liberalism, Multiculturalism and Oppression', in A. Vincent (ed.), *Political Theory*, Cambridge University Press, Cambridge, pp. 132–153.

Kukathas, C. (1998), 'Liberalism and Multiculturalism: The Politics of Indifference', *Political Theory*, Vol. 26, No. 5, October, pp. 686–699.

Kymlicka, W. (1990), *Contemporary Political Philosophy*, Clarendon Press, Oxford.

Kymlicka, W. (1995a), *Multicultural Citizenship*, Clarendon Press, Oxford.

Kymlicka, W. (ed.) (1995b), *The Rights of Minority Cultures*, Oxford University Press, Oxford.

Kymlicka, W. (1998), 'Ethnic Relations and Western Political Theory', in M. Opalski (ed.), *Managing Diversity in Plural Societies: Minorities, Migration and Nation-Building in Post-Communist Europe*, Forum Eastern Europe, Ottawa, pp. 275–322.

Laitin, D. (1998), 'Liberal Theory and the Nation', *Political Theory*, Vol. 26, No. 2, April, pp. 221–236.

Leff, C.S. (1997), *The Czech and Slovak Republics: Nation Versus State*, Westview, Boulder.

Macedo, S. (1995), 'Multiculturalism for the Religious Right? Defending Liberal Civic Education', *Journal of Philosophy of Education*, Vol. 29, No. 2.

Mann, A.B. (1992), 'The Formation of the Ethnic Identity of Romany in Slovakia', in J. Plichtová (ed.), *Minorities Politics*, Czechoslovak Committee of the European Cultural Foundation, Bratislava, pp. 260–265.

Mill, J.S. (1991), *On Liberty and Other Essays*, Oxford University Press, Oxford.

Miller, D. (1993), 'In Defence of Nationality', *Journal of Applied Philosophy*, Vol. 10, No. 1, pp. 3–16.

Miller, D. (1995), *On Nationality*, Clarendon Press, Oxford.

Nussbaum, M. (1996), *For Love of Country: Debating the Limits of Patriotism*, Beacon Press, Boston.

O'Neill, O. (1986), 'The Public Use of Reason', *Political Theory*, Vol. 14, No. 4, November, pp. 523–551.

Poulter, S. (1987), 'Ethnic Minority Customs: English Law and Human Rights', *International and Comparative Law Quarterly*, Vol. 36, July, pp. 589–615.

Rawls, J. (1971), *A Theory of Justice*, Harvard University Press, Cambridge, Massachusetts.

Schmögnerová, B. (1997), *Cúvanie napred*, Nadácia Ladislava Novomeského, Bratislava.

Schwarz, K P. (1993), *Tschechen und Slowaken: Der lange Weg zur friedlichen Trennung*, Europaverlag, Wien, Zürich.

Scruton, R. (1997), 'Kant', in *German Philosophers: Kant, Hegel, Schöpenhauer, Nietzsche*, Oxford University Press, Oxford, pp. 1–104.

Sheehan, P. (1998), *Among the barbarians*, Random House, Milsons Point, N.S.W.

Sulc, F. (1998), 'Kotel plny hruzy', *Lidové noviny*, 22 May, p. 10.

Sustrová, P. (1998), 'Prezident a státotvornost', *Lidové noviny*, 14 May, p. 10.

Tamir, Y. (1993), *Liberal Nationalism*, Princeton University Press, Princeton.

Tamir, Y. (1995), 'The Enigma of Nationalism', *World Politics*, Vol.47, April, pp. 418–440.

Taylor, C. (1992), *Multiculturalism and 'The Politics of Recognition'*, Princeton University Press, Princeton.

# 6 Rights, Institutions and Culture after Communism

MARTIN KRYGIER

In a book on rights in Europe, post-communist Europe offers more questions than answers. One large, overarching, question is: Are the rights that are acknowledged, and to a considerable degree institutionalised in the West likely to thrive in the post-communist Centre and East? In the euphoria which followed the unheralded collapse of communism from 1989, the question which many found it appropriate to ask, was 'why not?'. In subsequent years, in certain fraught post-communist countries, it has become common to hear the question 'why?'.[1] Moreover, the questions asked and the answers given were rarely direct and unmediated responses to the evidence on the ground. They commonly emanated from deep-lying assumptions about the possibility of deliberate transformations in social, political and cultural matters. Indeed, these assumptions lie so deep that one can find them deployed in answer to an astonishing range of questions: about prospects for rights, democracy, constitutionalism, market economy, middle classes, the Protestant ethic; and really whatever it is that some want to import to the region and others deny can be successfully imported. So what follows is a sketch of these assumptions and a critique of some implications that have been drawn from them. It is an abbreviated version of observations I have made elsewhere on discussions of constitutionalism and the rule of law.[2] But readers are free to apply it to virtually any major institutional innovation that some favour for the region, and others do not. For the curious fact is that the arguments commonly remain the same, although the subjects are various.

What are the prospects for legally protected civil and political rights after communism? What would one need to know to hazard a guess? In the state of the world and the state of the art, our answers to these and similar questions must necessarily be tentative, incomplete and controversial. One reason for that is simple ignorance. But the variety of these stories stems not only from the many ways in which we are ignorant. It flows equally from the different things we believe we know, which may not be so. What people regard as significant in and for post-communism often tends to betray as much about their intellectual, or even just personal, biography as it instructs us about the matters with which they deal.

91

I want to bring two such biases to the surface and examine them. Both are prevalent, and in pure form they have directly contradictory implications. The first is common among optimistic reformers, and its natural object is institutions. The second is found among—usually sadder but they might say wiser—pessimists. Its orientation is cultural. So first I will speak of institutional optimism, and second of cultural pessimism.

Those with an institutional bias spend a great deal of time discussing the best form that laws, constitutions and institutions should take. Typically such forms are modelled on others considered to have worked well somewhere else or are advocated on theoretical grounds. Constitutions, parliamentary arrangements, presidents, privatisation, rules of property, bills of rights, and so on. Those of a more cultural turn of mind are often sceptical of such institutional experimentation, at least when the institutions are new or foreign. If institutions are alien to the cultures onto which they are grafted, this approach suggests, the grafts are unlikely to take. In post-communist societies, moreover, institutions of the rule of law *are* typically alien, and, so culturalists often assume, many of the existing political and legal cultures are not likely to be receptive to solutions of the first, institutional, kind. Uncongenial national traditions and/or the experience of communism are often pointed to here. I will take each approach in turn.

## Institutional Optimism

Thinking about institutions, it is tempting to think about law. Indeed lawyers find the temptation irresistible. And so, legal and constitutional measures—to constitutionalise the polity, to protect rights, to facilitate or legitimate business activities and proscribe illegitimate ones, and much else—are plentiful, in post-communist Europe and elsewhere, and the literature on them is not small. That in itself is not a bad thing. But it is not clear how good a thing it is. In what circumstances do constitutions and other measures have any bite; in what circumstances are they worthless? What is it about the instruments and institutions themselves that makes for good consequences, what for bad? What beyond these instruments and institutions is necessary for a written constitution to be a working one? Are such conditions sufficient, and if so, is there any need for constitutions? Perhaps they will be unnecessary where social and political conditions are propitious and useless where they are absent. We do not have rich answers to these questions, but in post-communist Europe we have plenty of legal and social experiments which bear on them.

Some post-communist actors—both among elites and in sections of the society—hope that law will come to have a particular role and significance in their societies; a role and significance that it did not have under communism nor, in many countries in the region, before communism either. They hope that it might take root as a relatively impersonal, independent and institutionalised practice and medium for the exercise and restraint of power; one which might contribute to channelling, but also to setting limits on the power of citizens and states, including powerful citizens and powerful states. That is how things work, they believe, in 'normal' countries. These people hope, in other words, that not just law but the *rule of law* might be introduced, in societies which have long lacked it or never had it. What should be done to promote these ambitions and what chances do they have?

A lot of attention has been devoted to the drafting and passing of rights-bearing constitutions. Many people think this is central and devote much attention to theoretical and practical arguments in favour of, or against, particular constitutional arrangements. Yet some countries do well with unsightly constitutions, while others seem to get nowhere with works of high constitutional art. It is obvious that even a perfectly designed constitution can never be either self-interpreting or self-enforcing. It needs institutions and it needs something far less palpable but just as important—what might be called a spirit of constitutionalism—and we have no recipes for producing that. More broadly, we lack recipes for the effective protection of human rights wherever they have long gone unprotected. But we do not lack chefs.

Institutionalist menus primarily feature laws and institutions, rather than societies and cultures. They are particularly congenial to lawyers. It is natural for them to think that law and lawyers are of great importance, particularly when it is their own laws which so many people seem to wish to emulate these days. And there is no shortage of legal 'experts' who have been enlisted as advisers by post-communist governments. If, say, the criminal code of Atlanta Georgia seems to work well, why not hire an Atlanta lawyer to write a code for Tbilisi Georgia? Stranger things have happened.

As practised by lawyers, the simple universalism of this first approach is often fairly unreflective. Laws are often treated as kinds of technical equipment, social machinery, which can be transported and plugged in wherever the need for them arises. That laws 'in action' might also be—and depend upon—complex cultural accretions lies outside most lawyers' expertise (and, often, their range of interest). But there can also be sophisticated reasons to ignore local peculiarities. Economists assume rational economic actors, not Russians or communists: *homo economicus,* not *homo sovieticus.* This is not necessarily because economists are parochial or ignorant, but because their manner of theorising does not start from empirical particulars. Asking what any rational actor would do in the circumstances, they focus on clearing the space and designing incentive structures to enable such actors to do what one thinks they should do. Overall, and if circumstances allow, ordinary people are expected to do likewise. Many theorists of constitutionalism and public choice are accustomed to think similarly. Their underlying social theory is individualist, their mode of procedure is rationalist, and their ambitions are literally unbounded. To do this sort of work well, it certainly helps to be clever, and many of those who do it certainly are. It is not necessary, however, to know very much about the societies on which you bestow your advice, and many do not.

The fruits of such approaches are mixed. At their best, they can allow richly informed theoretical discussion, of practices and institutions of real and demonstrated value, to be brought to bear on important problems. They can also aid in the transplantation of institutions, values, and traditions of thought which are worthy, highly valued, and might stimulate thoughtfulness in difficult conditions. Since a key problem of communist societies was intellectual isolation, this is all to the good.

More prosaically, perhaps, good legal craftsmanship is more than likely indispensable both for effective laws and for the development of a culture of legality. It is intrinsically a useful thing to propagate in societies where it is thinly spread around. There has been a lot of serious thought about such matters in liberal democratic societies, and it would be silly not to draw on it. And some transplants work—like the Polish Ombudsman and the Hungarian Constitutional Court. Why, then, reinvent the wheel or insist that Polish or Hungarian wheelwrights have nothing to learn from foreign ones? Yet the effectiveness even of particular, special-purpose laws depends on a lot besides the laws themselves. Even more so, constitutionalism and the rule of law. Although more thought has been given to the export of specific laws and institutions than to what might be necessary to make them count, if no one is listening it does not matter too much what the law is saying. And if one is concerned with why people listen and why laws count, then one will have to look outside the law itself. Since, moreover, there are differences both within and between societies in this regard, one might need to learn not just about people or societies in general, but about particular features of particular societies.

## Cultural Pessimism

Post-communist societies, it is often said, *lack* important cultural prerequisites possessed by societies which their leaders seek to emulate, and *possess* cultural legacies incompatible with such ambitions. In particular this approach emphasises aspects of social and political culture, purportedly necessary for liberal achievements, and missing from the history of the region.

It has become increasingly evident that not every value advocated for the region is valued in the region, even when—as with 'rights', for example—the label is widely used.[3] 'Human rights', so we are often told, 'are historically and ideologically the property of the liberal democracies of the west ... they enshrine values which are universal neither in time nor in place. They are in essence the Enlightenment's values of possessive individualism' (Gray, 1993, 1995; Sedley, 1995). Moreover, means of institutionalising such values allegedly travel even less well than the values themselves. All sorts of 'hard facts'[4] can be assembled to show, for example, why post-communist soil is particularly inhospitable to grafts of constitutionalism, democracy, or whatever else it is from the West that seems desirable in, but absent from, the East.

Very often these hard facts amount simply to the absence of aspects of Western culture which are taken to have contributed to what the West has. Thus, by comparison with western Europe and its offshoots, many post-communist countries lack traditions of legality, democracy and tolerance. Middle classes were rarely well developed. So too capitalism (and Protestantism). They are poor, and in relation to the great centres and engines of modernity, they have always been peripheral. The political orders of many, for long periods, were despotic or at least non-democratic. The eastern countries among them belong not to Latin Christendom and the law-centred civilisation that it spawned, but rather to Orthodox and—to a lesser extent—Islamic civilisations, where law and the rule of law played less prominent roles. To the extent that law counted, it did so primarily as an instrument of central command, and less—if at all—as a medium of communication and defence among citizens and between citizens and the state. And whatever the countries of the region might once have been, for the 40 to 70 years preceding the collapse of communism, they experienced communism. That experience and the 'bloc culture'[5] it generated, many allege, is good for nothing, certainly nothing so liberal as the rule of law.

Such lines of thought are reinforced by the increasing modishness of cultural and 'civilisational' explanations of social behaviour, which is becoming evident in many disciplinary contexts. Samuel Huntington finds the world divided into seven or eight civilisational blocs, most of them millennia old, and only one of them— the West—hospitable to the rule of law.[6] Apart from what he says about post-communism, which will be discussed below, he endorses the now widespread talk of 'Asian values', which, it appears, are very old, good for business but bad for liberal democracy. And even if one wanted to adopt them (as some Australian politicians appear to, for example), they—like other civilisational characteristics—are not for sale.

Robert Putnam (1993) distinguishes between those regions of Italy which possess 'civic' culture and many good things that flow from that, and those which do not, and suffer. The sad lesson for reformers is that he finds these differences going back about a thousand years. He does not rule out the possibility of useful institutional reform, but he does emphasise the time it takes, and he does rather take the edge off it. As he extrapolates for the post-communist region:

> Many of the formerly Communist societies had weak civic traditions before the advent of Communism, and totalitarian rule abused even that limited stock of social capital. Without norms of reciprocity and networks of civic engagement, the Hobbesian outcome of the Mezzogiorno—amoral familism, clientelism, lawlessness, ineffective government, and economic stagnation—seems likelier than successful democratization and economic development. Palermo may represent the future of Moscow. The civic community has deep historical roots. This is a depressing observation for those who view institutional reform as a strategy for political change (Putnam, 1993, p. 183).

What are constitutionalists to make of all this? There is no doubt that cultural inheritances often do reproduce themselves and mould the frames of thought and action of their heirs. One's thoughts, values, symbols, are enveloped and to a large extent constituted by the given. Such cultural traditions are not mere instruments which can be taken up or put aside at will; the existence of such traditions and one's participation in them is a precondition for the renovation of elements of them and for the invention and construction of others. No one starts from scratch.

This is generally true and it is true of the rule of law. Where institutions and rules of restraint are strong, a large part of that strength typically flows—not directly or solely from the institutions and rules themselves—but from the traditions in which they were formed and from the culture which they themselves generated and which grows around and encrusts them, coming to form and shape the routine expectations of participants and observers.

Moreover, the wider social efficacy of official law requires, not merely that elites observe and seek to enforce it, but also that it enter into the norma-

tive structures which nourish, guide, inform, and coordinate the actions of ordinary people; people who do not merely comply resentfully when they feel
they might otherwise be punished, but who comply happily (enough) even
when they are confident they will not be. And for the rule of law to *count*,
rather than simply to be announced or decreed, people must *care* about what
the law says—the rules themselves must be taken seriously, and the institutions must come to matter. They must enter into the psychological economy of
everyday life. None of this can be simply decreed.

If institutions are to endure and take on strength, then, they owe their
solidity to things deeper than the bare existence of appropriate rules, to
understandings and expectations—many of them borne by and grounded in
cultural traditions, within which the rules take on meaning and significance.
These understandings, expectations and traditions, in turn, gain strength from
their often invisible pervasiveness. Where thickly institutionalised constraints
*do* exist—indeed typically where they do their best work—they are often not
noticed, for they are internalised by both the powerful and those with less power,
as the normal ways to behave. Limits are not tested because people cannot
*imagine* that they should be. Without all this, all the more when a state's and
society's traditions are *hostile* to restraint of power by law, one lacks a great
deal. These are hard facts indeed.

However, cultural sensitivity is not the same thing as cultural determinism. The former might encourage 'piecemeal social engineering'[7] which—in
the face of some institutionalist enthusiasms—would be salutary. The latter is
likelier merely to encourage despair. And when, as often in recent debates,
culture is invoked as a kind of prime 'unmoved mover' of the social world,
there are reasons to share Hermann Goering's reaction to the term, though they
are not his reasons. Not to evade the cultural point, but perhaps to sharpen it,
certain distinctions should be kept in mind.

First of all, it pays to distinguish different sorts of cultural explanations
from each other, since they emphasise different things and often point in different directions. The main candidates appear to be: aspects of culture common to the *civilisation* to which a society belongs, those which stem from
national or regional traditions, and those which flow from the communist regimes which dominated in the area until very recently.

The currently most-discussed representative of the first alternative is
Samuel Huntington's work, *The Clash of Civilizations and the Remaking of
World Order*. Huntington emphasises *civilisational* differences which allegedly are the primary sources of allegiance and division in the globe, which are
rooted most deeply in religion and are millennia old. While he is primarily
concerned with international relations, his comments about civilisation and

culture suggest that they go all the way down. Among the 'central characteristics of the West, those which distinguish it from other civilisations', is the rule of law. On this basis, it appears that one can ignore the pre-communist authoritarian regimes that ruled for much of the history of Poland and Hungary, and that distinguished them from inter-war Czechoslovakia. One need not worry too much that all three suffered under forty years of communist rule either, since all three belong to Western Christian civilisation. They should therefore be able to manage constitutionalism and the rule of law, though neither is a feature of their recent experience. Whether one of these countries might do better than another does not appear from this approach, nor is it clear why either should do better than Croatia. All three countries, however, must be presumed to have more chance than Romania and Serbia (Orthodox) and Bosnia (Islamic) which, given their civilisational disqualifications, need not even try.

Some culturalists, more modest in their ambitions, deal merely with central and eastern Europe rather than the planet. Even here, however, their analyses diverge dramatically. The two most popular candidates in cultural explanations of regional affairs are old national or regional traditions, on the one hand, and the cultural consequences of communism, on the other. Of course, there almost certainly are significant residues from both, and the latter might have reinforced the former, but their implications differ. If analyses of the first sort are correct, then discussion of these countries as 'post-communist' misses the deeper cultural point.

Thus, writers on Yugoslavia often portray communism as little more than a giant glacier enveloping the seething tribes within. It managed to keep them frozen still for a time, but on melting down exposed them in all their ancient vileness, tragically alive and refreshed once more. Writing of less apocalyptic matters, Jerzy Jedlicki (1989) reminds us, in a brief but nuanced discussion of '... The Unbearable Burden of History' in Eastern Europe that this is not the first time that many East Europeans have sought to 'return to Europe'. He seems to suggest that they were never really there in the first place, but since the eighteenth century have nonetheless repeatedly indulged in dreams of 'return'. He suggests that many of the reasons for their backwardness continue to weigh on the countries of the region. Prospects that the most recent attempts to 'return' might succeed, while not closed, are not enormously promising: 'There is no linear development in East European history, but rather a Sisyphus-like labor of ups and downs, of building and wrecking, where little depends on one's own ingenuity and perseverance'(Jedlicki, 1989, p. 40).

Sacrificing nuance for rhetorical power, John Gray explains that:

in throwing off the universalist institutions that supposedly nurtured *Homo Sovieticus*, the post-Soviet peoples have not thereby adopted the Western liberal self-image of universal rights-bearers, or buyers and sellers in a global market. Instead, they have returned to their pre-Soviet particularisms, ethnic and religious—to specific cultural traditions that, except in Bohemia, are hardly those of Western liberal democracy ... not, manifestly, an ending of history, but rather its resumption on decidedly traditionalist lines—of ethnic and religious conflicts, irredentist claims, strategic calculations, and secret diplomacies. This return to the historical realities of European political life will remain incomprehensible, so long as those realities are viewed through the spectacles of ephemeral Enlightenment ideologies. We will not, for example, understand current developments in Poland if our model for them is the transitory nightmare of Marxian Communism; we will gain insight into them if we grasp them as further variations on historical themes ... that are millennial (Gray, 1993, p. 27).

So much for all those Poles who treated the label 'post-communist' seriously, and imagined that forty years of communism had made some mark on their country. According to Gray, that is simple Enlightenment folly. With this revelation come both bad and good news. The bad news appears to be that it was all a ghastly mistake, worse still a Western mistake (though it came to Poland from the East). The good news is that it will have no enduring effects, since it was just a 'transitory nightmare' dreamt up in the West, and therefore not Polish at all. That will be particularly welcome news to those in the third group of culturalists, such as Sztompka, who attribute much of Polish and other post-communist 'civilisational incompetence' to the 'bloc culture' which all communist countries shared and which stemmed directly from the imposed communist political order and the social adjustments it generated. Subjects of communism, Sztompka (1993, p. 90) argues, developed a number of 'civilisationally incompetent' cultural traits, which he elaborates in terms of a series of dichotomies that he takes to be exaggerated in post-bloc societies, and the first pole of which, so to speak, is characteristically favoured there: '(a) private vs. public, (b) past vs. future; (c) fate vs. human agency; (d) negative vs. positive freedom; (e) mythology vs. realism, (f) West vs East, (g) usefulness vs. truth'.[8] Sztompka argues that the culture of civilisational competence is indispensable for the workings of civilised institutions, and post-communist societies are not rich in it. Although he does not argue that nothing can be done or that culture is unalterable, he insists that it lies far deeper than institutions, is rarely the product of design, and takes far longer than institutional structures to change. Similar views about 'post-communist' cultural residues are widespread in the region and among scholars of it.

Thus, according to many scholars seeking to decipher the phenomenon of post-Communism, there was a distinctive and deep pattern to and legacy of the social impact of Leninist regimes. It was most apparent in the lack of a routinely and normatively regulated public sphere Jowitt (1991, p. 293).[9] The consequences of this were clear in regard to law. Law existed, at times in bulk, but primarily, and professedly, as a subordinate—indeed servile—branch of political, administrative, and at times quasi-theocratic power.[10] The role of law was conceived of in almost exclusively instrumental terms, sometimes as a repressive instrument of social control, sometimes as an executive instrument of centrally determined goals, values and decisions; never as an independent check on governmental power. Communist rulers saw the law as a flexible statement of subjects' duties rather than of their rights; still less of duties with which state institutions themselves should comply. In any event, whatever the law said, the Party might decree otherwise and the law would bend. Citizens also did not expect the law to vindicate their rights or to restrain state officials, still less party officials. Nor were they often persuaded that their own legal duties amounted to moral ones.

To the extent that such bloc-wide problems and a post-communist culture exist, then even Huntington's Western Christian post-communists will be afflicted with them, and it is hard to see immediately what can differentiate post-communist Poland from post-communist Serbia. More surprisingly still, if one were to concentrate on bloc culture above all, perhaps the Czech Republic—which had a heavy dose of it—should be expected to do worse than the former Yugoslavia, where it lay less heavily on the ground. But that is not how it looks at the moment.

Apart from the fact that each of these cultural perspectives—civilisational, national-historical, post-communist—differs from the others in the depth of archaeological excavation that is encouraged, there are two similarities between them all, and two differences also worth noting. The first similarity is that they all are congenitally prone to a methodological fallacy that Stephen Holmes has identified among many students of Russia: '*they confused analogy with causality*. Their thesis was, put crudely, that the world is the way it is because it reminds us of the way it used to be' (Holmes, 1995, p. 6). Second, and partly because history makes so many stories available, cultural explanations have a seductive promiscuity about them. Thus, at this *fin de siècle* moment, the analogies that most authors favour serve to confirm disappointed expectations, since there are many such expectations about. But when—not so long ago—expectations were overwhelmed with equally unexpected, but apparently triumphant developments, culture was equally available to help out.

Notwithstanding these overarching similarities among different cultural pessimists, it is important to attend to the particular layers of culture that are invoked. Different forms of cultural explanation generate quite significant differences in analysis and predictions about particular countries in the region. Is a country's present a recycling of the immediate communist past, the mediate national past, or the civilisational framework which has shaped the land since time immemorial? Though it might be all three, it makes a very great difference what one emphasises.

Moreover, devotees of rights and the rule of law might draw significantly differing levels of cheer and gloom from the variety of cultural determinisms currently on offer. Poles and Czechs will be happy enough with Huntington, for he emphasises their civilisational, and apparently ineradicable, Europeanness. They will, however, draw apart on Gray's advice that Poles (and virtually everyone else in the region), lacking Bohemia's democratic experience, should try something else. This may not even please those Czechs persuaded by Gray's form of cultural archaeology, since their experience—21 years between two world wars—might be adjudged too recent and brief to count for much. But if it *does* count for anything, that might suggest the following question: if the Czechs could do it then, why can no one else do it now? The answer might come from Sztompka's emphasis on common bloc culture, which puts Czechs back in the same listing boat with the whole region. Worse still, since Czechoslovakia suffered an altogether harsher imposition of that culture than, say, Poland, the tables might be turned. Who lies deeper, then, and who is more present in his effects: Masaryk or Husak? Hard to say.

It is a major and underexplored question about traditions of every sort: what is it that distinguishes those residues of the past which mould successive presents, whether recognised or not, and those which sink without presently effective traces? One reason that the question is so hard to answer is that presently effective culture and cultural templates are not *only* historical residues. Often they are retrospective reconfigurations or even creations rather than the deep unalterable patterns and codes that they might seem to be. Is the past of which a tradition speaks really inherited from the past, and particularly the past it alleges, or is it a more or less retrospectively imagined and selected, perhaps invented 'past'? Has it seeped into social context without entering consciousness, its authority made manifest rather than acknowledged, or is it dependent on the existence of particular reflective contemporary attachments and evaluative commitments? Is it really transmitted from when it says by whom it says, or is it merely believed to be? If it is so transmitted, why should that matter more than a good story—whether or not it is true—that many people believe? Until we have confident answers to questions such as these, we should be a bit discriminating in attributing too much to culture or civilisation or tradition, *tout court*.

A related point can be made. Cultural pessimism, and more broadly cultural and civilisational determinism, tend to slight the patently *dialectical* nature of participation in culture. It is the *interweaving* of inheritance and present response that makes cultural traditions as tangled and absorbing as they are. Inheritance is not sovereign, responses are not autonomous. The one—like language—provides contexts and resources for action and thought, often as important as they are unseen; the other—like speech—embroiders, improvises and innovates within these contexts, with these resources, often in unprecedented ways. Cultural traditions are ambiguous in their implications, open to interpretation and reinterpretation, there are many of them, and they often conflict. They condition, but they do not necessarily determine, and they in any case never can rule out novelty. Versions of the past are continually being refashioned for present purposes. In all complex and enduring traditions, there is constant interplay between inherited layers which pervade and—often unrecognised—mould the present, and the constant renewals and reshapings of the purported past in which authorised interpreters and guardians of the tradition indulge, and must indulge.

It is an obvious mistake, then, to think of participation in culture as a purely subjective matter, since it rarely begins with single individuals and, as culture, can never *end* with them. However, it is a less obvious, but often just as egregious, error to assume *in advance* that novelty is foreclosed by uncongenial inheritance. A dialectical understanding of culture and tradition gives *more* significance, not less, to the ingenuity, skill, craftsmanship, virtuosity of current actors. It does not render these talents pointless.

Moreover, even assuming that cultural scripts are unambiguous and their boundaries clear—which is a heroic assumption in present, perhaps any, times—current interpretations of a culture's past are often influenced by other things—some of them cultural too—which are drawn from outside the particular culture in which an interpreter is thought to stand. But then, if such interpretations are influential, the culture can come to accommodate much that is external, and might seem alien, to its origins. This is not to say that every graft will take. Much will depend on its prestige, the skill, energy and power of its promoters (and opponents), its intrinsic character, its adaptability to the interests of important social groups, as well as on the degree of clash between it and endogenously developed cultural values. But cultural syncretism is not new in the history of civilisations, and it has often spawned cultural and institutional novelties which nothing in the host culture allowed one to predict. New things, after all, do happen, some grafts take, and people learn. Poland, for example, never had an Ombudsman; nor Hungary a Constitutional Court. They do now and both are effective institutions.

Cultural explanations often rely on metaphors of depth and shallowness, to distinguish between phenomena of greater and lesser significance. Such metaphors, and the distinctions they suggest, should be treated with respect but also with caution. In particular, we should be cautious about eliding depth with age and shallowness with youth. On the one hand, such metaphors clearly point to important differences. We are all aware of aspects of cultures and social structures which seem characteristic and durable over long periods, and which change slowly; and others which are ephemeral and change or vanish fast. It makes sense to speak of the former as deeply embedded and the latter as shallowly planted. But there are dangers in reifying such helpful metaphors. If not all of cultural history is presently effective, then it must follow that old is not necessarily deep, or at least that it might as well be 'deeply buried' and presently ineffectual as 'deeply embedded' and ineradicable in its effects. Nor is new necessarily superficial: capitalism is new in South Korea and Taiwan, but its effects appear deep enough. It is hard to imagine them being quickly washed away. A written constitution was new in the United States, and the world, in 1787, but it stayed around, becoming a deeply significant aspect of American, and not only American, political and legal culture. But if that is the case, what do we learn when we are told that despotism is old in eastern Europe and the attempt to foster the rule of law is new? If that is all we know, then not a lot.

Cultural determinisms are liable to be embarrassed by novelty, not only in practice as we all are, but in principle. Just as such explanations often surface when rationalist optimists are disappointed, so they tend to generate an intellectually overreaching *theoretical* pessimism, where that is rarely warranted. It accounted for social scientists' failure to anticipate the collapse of despotisms in Spain, Portugal, Latin America and communist Europe. In each case, as in many cases where pessimism is plausible, there were many reasons for it but not enough to foreclose more optimistic possibilities. In each case, however, many observers took such pessimism as sufficient reason to rule out such possibilities and discourage those who strove for them. As di Palma has brilliantly demonstrated, '[h]ard facts do not mean necessity' (di Palma, 1990, p. 8). And as he goes on to demonstrate in rich and arresting detail, '[w]hatever the historical trends, whatever the hard facts, the importance of human action in a difficult transition should not be underestimated' (di Palma, p. 9).

Finally, and at the very least, this Babel of explanations suggests that, even if at what might be called the ontological level, cultural explanation is onto something important, we have no adequate theoretical basis to dissuade anyone from trying something new, at least not merely on the ground that it *is* new. Here our problem is as much epistemological as metaphysical. It is undoubtedly true that many aspects of culture often lie deep within and some do not, and that some are sticky and relatively resistant to change, and others less so. It is less obvious that, at present, anyone has any clear way of telling which is which and how much. Retrospective cultural explanations are often illuminating, but not in telling us what to do next.

For even if one is aware of cultural obstacles, what should one do about them? Hard facts are even less clear as guides to action than they are as explanations of conditions of action. It is one—important—thing to point out that everything that happens in societies is significantly 'path dependent' (Stark, 1992, p. 17): what a society is, has, and does depends crucially on what it was, had and did. It is something else simply to repeat the proverbial Irish answer to a request for directions: 'I wouldn't start from here'.

Should one infer from hard facts that nothing is worth trying? Or that one should try harder? It is a hard choice and it makes a difference. One might, of course, be persuaded to try something else, and that is always worth considering. But such consideration must be grounded in local knowledge, and it must go beyond both 'can-do' optimism and what might be called 'can't-do' pessimism. It needs to be informed by real and particularised understanding of what remains significantly present from the past, and thought about what can be done in the light of it, rather than by generalised cliches about what allegedly happened at some time or times in that past.[11]

## Conclusion

It is a brand of pessimism which can slide into racism, peremptorily to rule out families of nations from participation in valuable institutional and cultural possibilities, such as legally guaranteed civil and political rights, on the grounds that they are not used to them. Condescension and marginalisation are softer forms of the same phenomenon. On the other hand, only if culture and communism count for nothing will it be easy to understand what might be done in Poland, say, without understanding Poland. Or simply by understanding America. Yet many of the universalist assumptions and ambitions of post-communist institutional transformers are built on explicit or, more usually, implicit denials of the possibility that there are *fundamental* social and cultural particularities anywhere. Such denials might be justified, but they are hardly self-evident. For if communism produced societies that were truly *sui generis*, as some writers have alleged, then the fact that this is the first post-communist transition in history is a deep fact. If, however, pre-existing historical particularities and traditions have reasserted themselves on the rubble of communism, then those who would seek to understand the present and future will need to know something about these particulars from the past.

At various times, dissidents under communism described the situation in their countries as hopeless and serious, hopeless but not serious, and sometimes—when dizzy with success—wonderful but not hopeless. There are contemporary, post-communist parallels to each of these tragi-comic diagnoses. For what it is worth, my own guess about the matters I have been discussing is: serious but not hopeless, and certainly not hopeless in principle. For while there is no overwhelming reason to believe that constitutionalism and the rule of law will be successfully established in the region, it needs to be stressed that there is equally no overwhelming reason to believe that they will not.

## Notes

1.   For discussions of these questions, see M. Krygier and A. Czarnota (1996).

2.   This chapter began as a talk to the conference from which this book derives. A considerably extended version of what follows has appeared as 'Is there Constitutionalism after Communism?' (Krygier, 1996-97) reprinted as 'Institutional Optimism, Cultural Pessimism and the Rule of Law' in Krygier and Czarnota (1999). The present text is an abbreviated version of that article.

3.   See Sajo (1996).

4.   See di Palma (1990). Di Palma's first chapter, 'Rethinking Some Hard Facts' discusses many of the reasons adduced for pessimism about the possibility of democratic transitions in post-dictatorial states. The rest of his book is a brilliant demonstration that hard facts should not necessarily be assumed to be insuperable facts.

5.   I borrow the term from Sztompka (1993, p. 85).

6.   See most recently Huntington (1996).

7.   The phrase, of course, is Karl Popper's (1966). He contrasts it with 'Utopian social engineering'.

8.   See also Sztompka (1991, 1995).

9.   For similar characterisations, see Clark and Wildavsky (1990), Sztompka (1991) and Podgorecki (1994).

10.   I have sought to place this conception of law within a more general frame in Krygier (1992, especially at p. 245).

11.   Such cliches have played no small part in western diplomacy in the war in Bosnia-Herzegovina. As a result, specific aims of particular actors have been glossed over on the basis of half-understood cliches about 'ancient ethnic hatreds' for which, it appears, no one alive is responsible and about which, conveniently for some, nothing can now be done. See Malcolm (1995, p. 3).

# References

Clark, J. and Wildavsky, A. (1990), *The Moral Collapse of Communism: Poland as a Cautionary Tale*, Institute of Contemporary Studies, San Francisco.

Gray, J. (1993), 'From Post-Communism to Civil Society: The Re-emergence of the Western Model', *Social Philosophy and Policy*, Vol. 10, No. 2, pp. 26–50.

Gray, J. (1995), *Enlightenment's Wake,* Routledge, London.

Holmes, S. (1995), *Cultural Legacies or State Collapse? Probing the Post Communist Dilemma*, Public Lecture No. 3, Institute for Advanced Study, Collegium, Budapest.

Huntington, S.P. (1996), *The Clash of Civilizations and the Remaking of World Order*, Simon and Schuster, New York.

Jedlicki, J. (1990), 'The Revolution of 1989: The Unbearable Burden of History', *Problems of Communism,* Vol. 39, July-August, pp. 39–45.

Jowitt, K. (1991), *New World Disorder: The Leninist Distinction*, University of California Press, Berkeley.

Krygier, M. (1992), 'Legal Traditions and their Virtue', in G. Skapska (ed.), *Prawo w zmieniajacym sie spoleczenstwie,* [Law in a Changing Society], Jagiellonian University, Cracow.

Krygier, M. (1996-97), 'Institutional Optimism, Cultural Pessimism and the Rule of Law', *International Journal of Sociology*, Vol. 26, No. 4, Winter, pp. 17–47; reprinted as 'Institutional Optimism, Cultural Pessimism and the Rule of Law', in M. Krygier and A. Czarnota (eds) (1999), *The Rule of Law after Communism. Problems and Prospects in East-Central Europe*, Ashgate, Aldershot.

Krygier, M. and Czarnota, A. (1996), 'Rights, Civil Society, and Post-Communist Society', in A. Sajo (ed.), *Western Rights? Post-Communist Application*, Kluwer, Law International, Amsterdam, pp. 101–38.

Malcolm, N. (1995), 'Bosnia and the West. A Study in Failure', *The National Interest*, No. 39, Spring, pp. 3–14.

di Palma, G. (1990), *To Craft Democracies: An Essay on Democratic Transitions*, University of California Press, Berkeley.

Podgorecki, A. (1994), *Polish Society,* Praeger, Westport, Connecticut.

Popper, K. (1996), *The Open Society and its Enemies*, 5th revised edition, Routledge and Kegan Paul, London.

Putnam, R. (1993), *Making Democracy Work. Civic Traditions in Modern Italy*, Princeton University Press, Princeton, New Jersey.

Sajo, A. (ed.) (1996), *Western Rights? Post-Communist Application,* Kluwer Law International, Amsterdam.

Sedley, The Hon. Sir Stephen (1995), 'Human Rights: a Twenty-First Century Agenda', *Public Law*, pp. 386–400.

Stark, D. (1992), 'Path Dependence and Privatization Strategies in East Central Europe', *East European Politics and Societies*, Vol. 6, No. 1, pp. 17–54.

Sztompka, P. (1993), 'Civilizational Incompetence: The Trap of Post-Communist Societies', *Zeitschrift für Soziologie,* Vol. 22, No. 2, pp. 85–95.

Sztompka, P. (1991), 'The Intangibles and Imponderables of the Transition to Democracy', *Studies in Comparative Communism*, Vol. 24, No. 3, pp. 295–311.

Sztompka, P. (1995), 'Looking Back: the year 1989 as a Cultural and Civilizational Break', paper presented at the Annual Conference of the European Sociological Association (ESA), August, Budapest.

# 7 Economic Rights in Contemporary Europe

DONALD MACLAREN

The industrialised countries, including those of western Europe, experienced a so-called 'golden age' of economic growth and prosperity between the years 1950 to 1973. Economic fluctuations were small by comparison with those of the inter-war period and inflation, in comparison with the 1970s, was socially tolerable. The economic institutions which had been put in place following the Bretton Woods conference of 1944, namely, the IMF for international monetary matters and the GATT for international trade in goods, helped to coordinate government policies in the international economy. Domestically, many governments followed Keynesian macroeconomic policies which were aimed largely at controlling aggregate demand and, through it, maintaining full employment of labour. Governments had entered into a social contract: providing full employment and, to varying degrees, comprehensive social welfare.

The golden age was one of economic tranquillity and relative certainty. Over the period, the annual average growth rate of GDP per capita in twelve European countries was 3.8 per cent (Crafts and Toniolo, 1996).[1] That figure should be contrasted with the corresponding figure for the period 1913 to 1950 of 1.0 per cent and that for the period 1973 to 1992 of 1.7 per cent. The years 1950 to 1973 were clearly unusually good years for reasons which are not yet fully understood. Today, not only is the rate of economic growth lower than that during the period 1950–1973, but so too are people's expectations of the economic future. The perception in most industrialised countries is that there is: growing income inequality; reduced public expenditure and taxation; greater job insecurity and unemployment, with 'downsizing' in both the private and public sectors; greater volatility and uncertainty; and, contemporaneously, a reduction in the provision of social welfare. There is also a perception that these changes are for the worse and that they have coincided with globalisation, with increased openness, a freer rein for market forces and with the uptake by politicians of right-wing economic ideas which support minimalist government. There is no doubt that globalisation, which has been brought about by highly mobile international capital, has undermined the ability of governments to separate domestic and international policies and to maintain the efficacy of each. However, whether globalisation *per se* can account for these perceived flaws in today's economic environment, is open to doubt.[2]

The remainder of the chapter is structured as follows. The way in which economists consider economic rights is explained in the second section. Some statistical background material is presented in the third section in order to highlight the extent to which economic conditions have changed since 1970 and to illustrate why there is growing concern in Europe about the sustainability of the long-cherished social welfare system. In the fourth section there is a brief review of some of the explanations advanced to help explain the events behind the statistics. And finally, an attempt is made to draw some conclusions about whether the economic rights which were enjoyed in Europe during the golden age can be re-established and to speculate on whether they will be.

## Economic Rights

In economic theory there are no economic rights *per se*. Households (Consumers) are assumed to maximise utility subject to an income constraint. Firms are assumed to maximise profits subject to the resources available to them as supplied by households. Markets comprise the aggregation of households and of firms as these two groups create the demand for and the supply of products and factors of production. Under a set of specific assumptions, households and firms interacting through markets will generate outcomes which cannot be improved upon in the sense of economic efficiency. There is no role for government in achieving efficiency. However, such outcomes need not accord with society's sense of equity or fairness. Hence, there is an income redistributive role here for government. Moreover, it can be shown under the assumptions already alluded to above that the twin objectives of efficiency and equity can be separated and, hence, pursued independently. This means that an outcome that is both efficient and fair can be achieved: the first through free markets and the second through government intervention. What concerns many citizens today is that governments which deregulate appear to have decided to leave market forces to achieve efficiency but have ignored the income distributional consequences of so doing.

Unfortunately, in theory and in practice the assumptions necessary to achieve this utopian outcome do not pertain. There exist several forms of market failures. These failures, such as unemployment of labour, occur for a number of reasons and the conclusion is that, without government intervention to correct them, free markets will not produce efficient, let alone equitable, outcomes. The basic and important contribution of Keynes to macroeconomic policy and to social welfare was that he recognised the labour market might find an equilibrium at less than full employment. Therefore, there will be some households in which income is non-existent in the absence of transfer payments. However, if government were to intervene in the economy by stimulating aggregate demand, then output and the demand for labour would increase, unemployment would fall, and the incomes of those previously unemployed would rise. Society would be better off.

Such intervention was viewed as desirable by most economists for almost four decades until the early 1970s. However, the advent of stagflation at that time—that is, zero growth of output together with inflation—undermined the Keynesian prescription and prompted the development of new macroeconomic theories based on the microeconomic foundations outlined above for free markets. In the United States particularly, some economists began to argue that government failure was inevitable and that it was likely to be just as serious, if not more so, than market failure. This quantitatively unsubstantiated idea caught the imagination of conservative politicians and led to the re-birth of the concept of minimalist government.

However, despite the rhetoric of the Thatcher government in its early years in office that one of its aims was to reduce public expenditure as a proportion of GDP, during that period the proportion actually increased. The subsequent influence of the minimalist government model on economic policies in the United States and Britain has been considerable, although the outcomes may have been different, and in the view of some, for example Hutton (1995), Kapstein (1996) and Solow (1996, p. 172), damaging in terms of social welfare. For example, in the case of the United Kingdom, income inequality has increased as a result of reductions in the top marginal rates of income tax for the rich and reductions in welfare payments to the disadvantaged. Moreover, the real value of these benefits has been eroded by their being index linked to prices rather than to wages. Poverty has increased with the percentage of those classified as poor doubling between 1975 and 1985 to 12 per cent and most of that increase due directly to changes in policy (Bean and Crafts, 1996, p. 152). Between 1979 and 1994 there was a threefold increase in homelessness (to 200,000) (Hutton, 1995, p. 210). This increase may be explained by a combination of the disadvantaged losing from real reductions in welfare benefits, the privatisation of part of the stock of public housing but, most of all, from the rise in unemployment which occurred over this period (see Figure 7.2).

In many European countries, the tendency to abandon the economy to market forces has been resisted for much longer than it was in either the United States or Britain. Nevertheless, the European social model, which was established in the early postwar years to achieve the equity goal, is now under considerable stress.[3] That stress is seen at its most stark in the context of the unemployment statistics and the apparent inability or unwillingness of European governments to identify policies which will reduce it to more socially acceptable levels. One proposed solution is the dismantling of that very social model in order to make the labour market work in a way which will encourage, rather than discourage, employment, particularly of the unskilled.

## Some Statistical Background

During the golden age, the main target of domestic macroeconomic policy was the maintenance of full employment. But during the 1970s, following the first oil shock in 1973, inflation became the target. It has remained so for the past two decades. Monetary policy has become the principal instrument used to achieve this objective in the absence of any desire by governments to tighten fiscal policy through increased taxation.

The consequences for unemployment are evident in the statistics. The overall trends in unemployment over the period from 1970 to 1996 have been upwards in the United States, the European Union and Japan since 1970, although in the case of the United States, the trend has been downwards from its peak of almost 10 per cent in 1983 (Figure 7.1). For the EU, the situation looks bleak, the rate of unemployment having risen relentlessly from 2.4 per cent in 1970 to 11.1 per cent in 1995, considerably higher than that of its main competitors. However, what these aggregate figures mask is the much higher rates of unemployment for youth. In the EU (15 Member States), for those under 25 years of age, the unemployment figure was 21.4 per cent in 1995 (Eurostat, 1996). A comparison of EU with United States data is not meaningful because of the substantial differences in the proportions of youth in tertiary study in these two economies. It is now well established that the rates of unemployment are higher amongst the young and the unskilled, and that the proportion of the workforce in employment which is involuntary part-time, is increasing. In other words, unemployment is structural rather than cyclical and, therefore, there is no guarantee that unemployment will once again fall to the levels experienced in the 1960s.

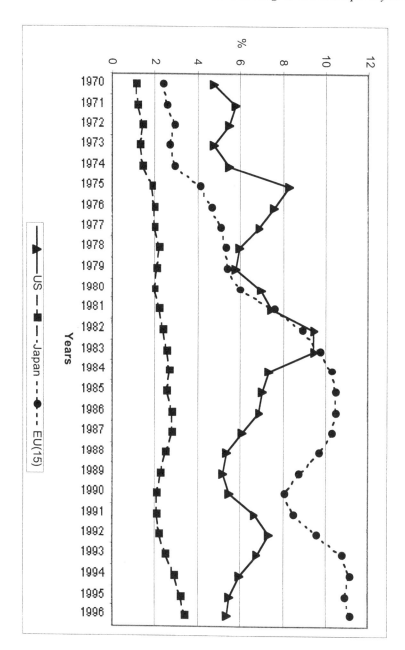

**Figure 7.1   Unemployment as a Percentage of the Total Labour Force**

*Source:*      *OECD (1997)  Labour Force Statistics 1976-1996, Paris*

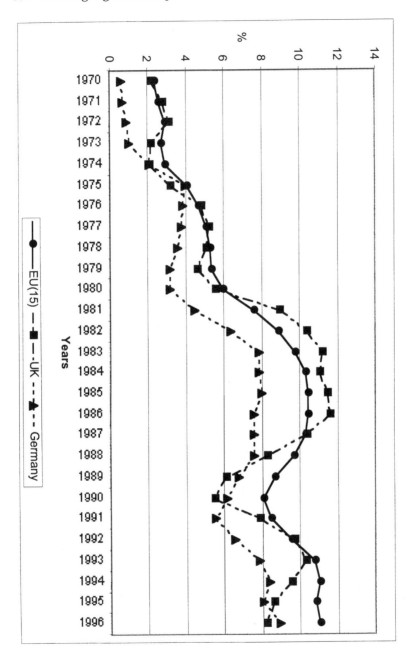

**Figure 7.2 Some European Unemployment Rates**

*Source:*     *OECD (1997) Labour Force Statistics 1976-1996, Paris*

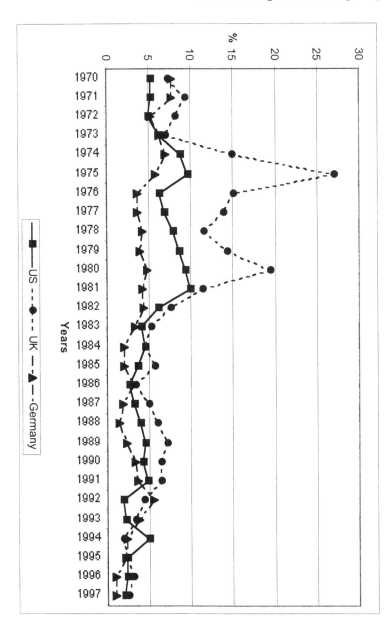

**Figure 7.3  GDP Deflator***

* percentage change from the previous year

*Source:*     *IMF (1998) International Financial Statistics Yearbook 1998, Vol. LI,
Washington DC. The data for Germany for the period 1970 to 1979 are
from the 1995 Yearbook*

Within the EU, although the rates of unemployment in Germany have been below the EU (15 Member States) average, there is now growing concern that they are converging on that average (Figure 2). In the United Kingdom, rates have also been below the EU(15) average except during the 1980s, a period during which the government was vigorously pursuing a policy of labour market deregulation which was designed to reduce unemployment.

The effect of the first oil shock on inflation in Britain was quite dramatic, the rate rising from 7 per cent in 1973 to 15 per cent in 1974 and to 27 per cent in 1975 (Figure 7.3). Not all of these increases were due directly to the rise in the price of oil, some were due to macroeconomic mismanagement but it took a whole decade for the rate of inflation to fall to a socially tolerable level. Even then, the rates for Germany and the United States were lower still, as they had been since 1973. By 1995, the rate of inflation in each of these countries had converged to 2 per cent, although by 1997 in Germany, it had fallen further to only 1 per cent. It would appear that the undeniable benefits of low inflation may have been purchased at the expense of unemployment (the Phillips curve effect). However, controlling inflation is only one of several potential explanations for increased unemployment, lower rates of income growth and lower levels of social welfare. Some of these will now be outlined.

## Potential Explanations for Increased Unemployment

Economic growth is dependent upon resources, technology, demand and the functioning of markets. In a recent survey of the empirical evidence from Europe in support of the various explanations for the golden age and the markedly lower rates of growth over the past two decades, few firm conclusions were drawn (Crafts and Toniolo, 1996). It follows that if increases in employment are dependent upon economic growth, and the processes that drive growth are not understood, then the appropriate policies to enhance growth and, thereby, employment, cannot be identified with certainty.

In interpreting the European experience of economic growth, a number of explanations were investigated by Crafts and Toniolo (1996) and the following conclusions drawn. First, while total factor productivity in the twelve European countries listed above (see note 1) was higher during the golden age than in the earlier or later periods, the question remains as to why this was the case.[4] Second, even if there is a causal relationship between growth and technological change, it is not clear what drives technological change. In the early models of economic growth, there was no explanation; in the new growth models developed since the mid 1980s, much store is placed on physical and human capital, and on savings and investment. And third, it is conceded even by free marketeers that governments can and should influence the accumulation of capital and provide an environment conducive to research and development (R&D) and the adoption of new technologies.

Another relationship of equal controversy is the one between unemployment and the provision of social welfare.[5] There are the two components in the debate: first, there are rigidities in the labour market, such as minimum wage laws and various payroll taxes, which prevent supply and demand from equilibrating at full employment; and second, there is the belief that unemployment benefits act as a disincentive for the recipients to seek employment. Put in these terms, the policy prescription seems obvious, namely, make labour markets more flexible and reduce welfare payments. However, the reality is at once both more complex and more subtle. The effect of labour market deregulation has been to widen wage inequality. In 1995, a male worker in the United Kingdom at the 10th percentile of earnings earned 55 per cent of the median wage, the corresponding figure for France was 62 per cent, for Germany (in 1993) it was 73 per cent and for Sweden (in 1993) it was 75 per cent (*The Economist*, 20 July 1996). Over the past decade, this percentage has fallen in the United Kingdom and Sweden, has remained constant in France but has risen in Germany. If flexibility of labour markets creates greater inequality and if flexibility leads to lower rates of unemployment, then cross-country studies should substantiate the link. The OECD was not able to uncover one (*The Economist*, 17 August 1996). As the data for the United Kingdom tend to show (Figure 7.2), labour market reforms are not a sufficient condition for reduced unemployment. One explanation is the interrelationship between flexibility of the labour market and unemployment benefits. In countries which have gone for flexibility (such as the United States and the United Kingdom), steps have been taken to ensure that an incentive structure has been put in place to encourage recipients to move from welfare to employment. But if, at the margin, there are no jobs, then such incentives are repressive and unfair. The empirical evidence is that the unemployed would prefer a job even at a wage below that provided by a welfare payment.

Another explanation for the inability of the industrialised world to create sufficient employment has to do with changes in the international economy. Technological change in conjunction with international capital mobility and increased competition from the developing and newly industrialising countries, have reduced the demand for low-skilled labour in the industrialised countries. With downward inflexibility of wages, the quantity of employment has to adjust rather than the price.[6]

In the case of the European Union, there is a further and more recent explanation for high unemployment, namely, the criteria for the establishment of Economic and Monetary Union. These criteria make it very difficult for many governments concurrently to target unemployment and still achieve the criteria, notwithstanding the financial support proposed in the Cohesion Plan of the Maastricht Treaty for infrastructure projects (Trans-European Networks) (Pinder, 1992, p. 167). These criteria relate to inflation, long-term interest rates, exchange rates within the European Exchange Rate Mechanism, and government budget deficits (Pinder, 1992, p. 228). All criteria are related to price stability, not to employment. In the view of Dornbusch, the EMU will only add to unemployment, not only as governments attempt to achieve the criteria for its establishment, but also once it is in place because of the constraints placed on divergent economies by fixed exchange rates. 'If there was ever a bad idea, EMU is it' (Dornbusch, 1996, p. 124).

## Conclusions

The economic rights expected by citizens in a 'good' society are under threat in Europe.[7] Full employment is no longer a goal of macroeconomic policy and the provision of high levels of social welfare is viewed as a cause of the problem of increasing structural unemployment. The real explanations for the demise of the social contract and the end of the golden age are complex and as yet not properly understood by economists. At the same time, citizens are beginning to recognise that their elected representatives no longer have control over their (citizens') economic well-being and social security.

Within the European Union, the drive towards federalism is ceding greater authority to the EU's institutions and in the economic sphere, ultimately to a largely unaccountable European Central Bank, the main aim of which is price stability (Brouwer *et al.*, 1994, p. 128). At the same time, both national governments and EU institutions are constrained in defining and implementing economic policies by the greater integration and openness of the international economy, as well as by possible eastward enlargement. If citizens believe that their politicians no longer exercise economic control over unemployment and social welfare, then by what means, if any, can economic rights be guaranteed? There is no simple answer to this question. The ideas of the mainstream in economics do change over time and just as minimalist government with its tax and expenditure cutting and emphasis on market forces have flowed, so will they ebb. It is very probable that they will be replaced by a re-emphasis on economic growth, on lower unemployment rates, on social welfare, and on a better understanding of the role of government in bringing about these outcomes. However, whilst the mainstream ideas may change, their translation into policy outcomes depends upon the policy making process, including the functioning of political and bureaucratic institutions. In the European Union, the lack of a powerful European Parliament, together with the conservative policy-making institutions of the Commission and the Council, may well mean that the implementation of imaginative policies which could bring about a 'good' society will not eventuate.

## Notes

1. These countries are Austria, Belgium, Denmark, Finland, France, Germany, Italy, The Netherlands, Norway, Sweden, Switzerland and the United Kingdom.

2. For a spirited debate on this topic, see Kapstein (1996) and Krugman *et al.* (1996) and for a thorough analysis and some thoughtful policy proposals, see Lawrence *et al.* (1996).

3. Grahl and Teague (1996, p. 2) define the European social model as a combination of comprehensive welfare systems and strongly institutionalised and politicised forms of industrial relations.

4. Using the annual average percentage change in GDP/person-hour as a measure of changes in total factor productivity, the figures were 1.9 per cent for the period 1913–1950, 4.7 per cent for 1950–1973 and 2.7 per cent for 1973–1992 (Crafts and Toniolo, 1996, Table 1.1).

5. For an extended discussion of this issue in the context of Europe, see Soete (1994) and for a review of the empirical evidence, see *The Economist* (20 July and 17 August 1996).

6. For a fascinating discussion of this issue, see Chapter 3 of Hinshaw (1996).

7. Galbraith has stated that: 'The discomfort and social disarray from unemployment and economic deprivation must always be in mind, as, also, the measures for their mitigation. The good society does not allow some of its people to feel useless, superfluous and deprived' (cited in the Foreword of Brouwer *et al.*, 1994).

## References

Bean, C. and Crafts, N. (1996), 'British economic growth since 1945: relative economic decline ... and renaissance?', in N. Crafts and G. Toniolo (eds), *Economic Growth in Europe since 1945*, Cambridge University Press in conjunction with the Centre for Economic Policy Research, Cambridge.

Brouwer, F., Lintner, V. and Newman, M. (eds) (1994), *Economic Policy Making and the European Union*, Federal Trust for Education and Research, London.

Crafts, N. and Toniolo, G. (eds) (1996), *Economic Growth in Europe since 1945*, Cambridge University Press in conjunction with the Centre for Economic Policy Research, Cambridge.

Dornbusch, R. (1996), 'Euro Fantasies', *Foreign Affairs*, Vol. 75, No. 6, September/October, pp. 110–124.

Eurostat (1996), *Unemployment*, Office for Official Publications of the European Communities, Luxembourg.

Grahl, J. and Teague, P. (1996), *Is the European Social Model Fragmenting?*, Paper No. 351, Economics Department, Queen Mary and Westfield College, University of London, London.

Hinshaw, R. (ed.) (1996), *The World Economy in Transition: What Leading Economists Think*, Edward Elgar, Cheltenham.

Hutton, W. (1995), *The State We're In*, Jonathan Cape, London.

IMF (1998), *International Financial Statistics Yearbook 1998*, Vol. LI, IMF, Washington DC.

Kapstein, E.B. (1996), 'Workers and the World Economy', *Foreign Affairs*, Vol. 75, No. 3, May/June, pp. 16–37.

Krugman, P., Lawrence, R.B., Barnes, H., Donahue, T. and Forbes, S. (1996), 'Workers and Economists: The Global Economy Has Left Keynes In Its Train', *Foreign Affairs*, Vol. 75, No. 4, July/August, pp. 164–179.

Lawrence, R.Z., Bress, A. and Takatoshi, I. (1996), *A Vision for the World Economy*, The Brookings Institution, Washington DC.

OECD (1997), Labour Force Statistics 1976–1996, OECD, Paris.

Pinder, J. (1992), *European Community: The Building of a Union*, Oxford University Press, Oxford.

Soete, L. (1994), 'European Integration and Strategies for Employment', in F. Brouwer, V. Lintner and M. Newman (eds), *Economic Policy Making and the European Union*, Federal Trust for Education and Research, London.

Solow, R.M. (1996), 'Is All That European Unemployment Necessary?', in R. Hinshaw (ed.), *The World Economy in Transition: What Leading Economists Think*, Edward Elgar, Cheltenham.

*The Economist* (1996), 'Jobs and wages revisited', 17 August, p. 66.

*The Economist* (1996), 'Moving up, moving out', 20 July, p. 7.

# 8  Towards a Wider Europe: Eastern Europe's Rocky Road into the European Union

HARALD SANDER

Soon after the fall of the iron curtain it became evident that the Central and Eastern European Countries' (CEECs) 'return into Europe' will eventually lead to membership in the European Union (EU), the world's largest trading bloc.[1] The EU's motives for integrating the CEECs into a 'wider Europe' are predominantly, although not exclusively, of a political nature: delivering on promises made during the Cold War, securing peace and stability, locking-in democratic and market-oriented reform in the transition countries, and—not to forget—keeping migration in check. For the CEECs membership in the European Union would not only politically restore their European identity and provide them with an implicit security guarantee, but it is also expected to yield huge economic benefits. Since trading blocs, by definition, discriminate against non-members, getting free access to the world's largest regional market is a strong motive. Market access could, however, also be provided through free trade agreements. But EU membership promises to offer more: a catalyst role in economic and democratic reform, complete elimination of remaining trade obstacles, full labour and capital mobility, representation in the EU decision making process, and, last but not least, access to the EU's agricultural and structural funds.

Although EU accession was not promised openly in the early 1990s, 'Europe Agreements', also known as 'Association Agreements' (AAs), were concluded with an increasing number of CEECs from late 1991 onward. In June 1993 the European Council meeting in Copenhagen first established that those countries which had signed *Europe Agreements* with the EU could be eligible for membership, and all ten CEECs with AAs discussed here had applied for EU membership by 1996. The implied 'right to join the EU' is, however, a qualified one. Next to the broad conditions of being European, democratic, and having a market economy system, three qualifications deserve to be mentioned: the prospective candidates need to prepare themselves for the rights and obligations of membership; adoption of the whole body of rules and regulations of the European Union known as the *acquis communautaire,* and provisions on the Union's 'absorptive capacity'.[2] The prospective candidates' access to EU funds that comes with membership could therefore act as an important obstacle to membership. CEECs are currently so poor and so reliant on agriculture that applying the existing EU rules on distributing agricultural, structural and cohesion funds could be beyond the limits of what the EU taxpayers, or governments, might find acceptable. Poorer EU members may fear funds diversion and could subsequently veto and/or press for postponing Eastern enlargement. But not only financial considerations may delay accession. Other areas of concern are voting issues in the EU decision-making process and EU member countries' worries about the economic adjustment costs of potential industrial relocations that may come with the integration process. In short, what is desirable from a political and *long-term* economic point of view may conflict with short-term economic interests of the incumbents.

On July 16, 1997, the European Commission published *Agenda 2000*—an outline of reform to prepare itself (among others) for the enlargement process, which at the time of writing is still under discussion. The EU also has now also published 'opinions on each of the applications for membership' ('*avis*') that make the accession criteria more explicit. On the basis of these *avis* the EU has started membership talks with five CEECs, namely, the Czech Republic, Hungary, Poland, Slovenia and Estonia in 1998. An optimistic view would not expect EU membership for (at least some) of these most advanced CEECs before the year 2002,[3] while others may follow later, probably only by 2010 or even later. Given such long transition periods, in particular for the less advanced countries, not only are the potential implications of EU enlargement as such important, but also—and probably even more so—the impact of the transitional arrangements on the accession candidates.

The road into the European Union has been built, but it is still a rocky one. The next section details shortly the main elements of the 'Brussels mechanics' of the accession process. It is followed by a discussion of the expected costs and benefits of an EU enlargement. It will be argued that while in the shorter term the economic net benefits would be mainly on the side of the CEECs, in the longer term the net gains for the incumbent EU countries could be tremendous, but would not come without risk. The subsequent section analyses the features and shortcomings of the current accession system. In particular, it stresses that the current system of AAs does contain some problems—provisions for contingent protectionism and a so-called hub-and-spoke architecture—that can lead to trade and investment diversion, particularly to the detriment of the less advanced CEECs and may thus run counter to the ultimate goal of producing 'EU maturity' in some transition countries. The conclusion discusses some proposals for 'paving the road' into a wider Europe.

## The Architecture of the Integration Process

In December 1991 the European Union signed the first Association Agreements with Poland and Hungary. Bulgaria and Romania followed in the first half of 1993. In June 1993 at the EU's Copenhagen summit the European leaders made explicit that countries with a Europe Agreement may eventually qualify for future membership.[4] After this 'qualified promise' the freshly divorced Czech and Slovak Republics signed their separate agreements and later also the Baltic States applied for and finally signed separate AAs. The latest agreement was initiated in mid-1995 with the former Yugoslav Republic of Slovenia and finally signed in mid-1996.[5] By mid-1996, 10 AAs had been signed with CEECs and all of them had applied for EU membership.

Three important features of AAs should be highlighted. First, all AAs differ in detail according to the country involved. Second, an AA offers more than a free trade agreement. In the area of political relations it introduces a political dialogue between the individual country and the EU that covers most areas of the Union's policy. An AA also asks an CEEC to commit itself to introduce rules and laws similar to that of the EU, especially in the fields of competition policy, property rights, and cultural cooperation. In the area of economic relations, a typical AA establishes free trade in industrial goods and some provisions for preferences in the fields of agricultural trade, trade in services, labour mobility, and national treatment issues. However, AAs do not establish free market access. Substantial entry barriers—at least in the beginning (to be phased-out by 2001)—remain in sensitive product areas, such as agriculture, textiles, steel and coal. Even more importantly, they do not exclude the use of contingent protection on the side of the EU, such as anti-dumping and safeguard measures. The third important feature is that the EU's relations with the CEECs are characterised by a system of AAs that constitutes a so-called hub-and-spoke system. The EU acts as the single market hub of the system with the deepest degree of integration. The (remaining) European Free Trade Association (EFTA) countries do have a far-reaching free trade agreement with the EU that virtually provides full access to the single market (the European Economic Area-EEA). In the next group of spokes are those countries with AAs. Spokes positioned further outward are countries with a free trade agreement like Israel and countries that have special preferential trade relation with the EU such as the Lomé countries. As will be argued later, such a hub-and-spoke system can favour the hub at the expense of the spokes.

In December 1994, the EU's summit in Essen devised a framework of regular contacts ('structured relations'), including the preparation of a White Paper that sets out a program for the applicants for meeting the obligations of the single market. Essentially, the White Paper is meant to 'assist associated countries in preparing themselves for operating under the requirements of the EU's internal market'. The implementation of the White Paper and the Europe Agreements are two out of four elements of the pre-accession strategy. The other two supplementary elements are a 'structured dialogue' and the Phare (Assistance) Program. The EU, however, has maintained that '... alignment with the internal market is to be distinguished from accession to the Union which will involve acceptance of the *acquis communautaire* as a whole'.[6] Together with *Agenda 2000* the EU Commission has now made membership criteria more explicit as it is laid down in the 'Commission Opinion on Application for Membership of the European Union'. The criteria comprise political and economic criteria and relate to the ability of the candidate to assume the obligations of membership as well as to the administrative capacity to apply the *acquis* (see Table 8.1).

**Table 8.1   Criteria for EU Membership**

| |
|---|
| 1.  Political Criteria |
|     – Democracy and Rule of Law |
|     – Human Rights and the Protection of Minorities |
| 2.  Economic Criteria |
|     – The Existence of a Functioning Market Economy |
|     – The Capacity to Cope with Competitive Pressures and Market Forces |
| 3.  Ability to Assume the Obligations of Membership |
| 4.  Administrative Capacity to Apply the Acquis |

*Source:*     *Adapted from:* European Commission (1997), *Agenda 2000, Commission's Opinion on Application for Membership of the European Union.*

On the basis of these reports, the EU decided to begin negotiations with the five most advanced CEECs in 1998. While no clear time framework is visible, the expectations are that the first candidates may enter not before 2002, while some of the least advanced candidates may have to wait considerably longer, possibly until 2010 or even later. For the accession phase the EU has now launched a 'reinforced pre-accession strategy', that comprises so-called 'Accession Partnerships'. It should, however, become clear that joining the European Union is very different from quasi-hemispheric regional integration elsewhere. The CEECs' 'return into Europe' means it is not only joining and widening an existing regional bloc, but it is essentially jumping on an ever faster moving train of a Union that seeks to deepen its economic and political integration. The steps forward from a 'common market' towards the 1992 project of the 'single market' and the 1999 introduction of European Monetary Union are emblematic of this. Joining the Union means accepting the idea of a continuous deepening of integration which is widely regarded as a part of the *acquis* (Wagner and Fritz, 1998). Widening the EU thus requires a balancing of both deepening and widening strategies to the benefit of incumbents, new entrants, and those in the waiting line.

## The Costs and Benefits of a Wider Europe

### *A Short Note on Regional Integration Economics*

Joining a regional club is in fashion. The former European Community enlarged towards the South in the 1980s and most recently integrated three former EFTA countries. In the Western Hemisphere, the former US-Canada Free Trade Agreement was joined by Mexico and became the North American Free Trade Agreement (NAFTA). A hemispheric-wide 'Free Trade Area of the Americas' is under discussion. In East Asia, cooperation among the ASEAN countries has been somewhat intensified by means of the ASEAN Free Trade Area (AFTA), and cross-Pacific cooperation has been put on the agenda of APEC. Among all regional blocs the European Union stands out in both sheer size and degree of integration. In 1996 the EU countries were responsible for 39.1 per cent of world merchandise trade, of which 61.5 per cent was conducted inside the EU (World Bank, 1998).

Economists tend to doubt the efficiency of regional clubs and fear that they could do more harm than good when giving preferential treatment to members of the club, but not to outsiders. They argue that this may create trade among the member countries by lowering or abolishing internal trade barriers, but may also divert imports from more efficient non-members and replacing such imports by more expensive products from a member country. If such trade diversion effects exceed the trade creation effects, regionally-limited trade liberalisation can be worse than no liberalisation at all. In general, the probability that a trading bloc will be a net trade creator is higher the more the integrating region constitutes a natural trading bloc, that is, an economic space where market forces would establish a high level of de facto regional integration in absence of such an integration scheme. Generally speaking, a regional integration process is therefore expected to be the more successful the closer the following four criteria are met: (1)

a similar level of per capita GNP, (2) similar or compatible trade regimes, (3) geographic proximity, and (4) political commitment to regional organisation (Schott, 1991, p. 2). Too divergent development levels could make poorer members feel that their industrialisation strategies could be undermined by the influx of manufactured imports from their technologically more advanced industrialised partners, while the richer members may feel threatened by the low-wage competitor. Working out compensation schemes in such cases could constitute an insurmountable obstacle (Wonnacott and Lutz, 1989). Similarly, if countries with low and high tariff levels form a free trade area, establishing uniform tariffs implies an unequal distribution of tariff cut concessions. Because of transportation costs, but also because of cultural closeness, proximity is a key factor for success. Finally, political commitment is necessary for safeguarding the durability of a free trade area, mainly because elements of national sovereignty have to be handed over to a supranational body.

From these criteria it is obvious that per capita income differences are amongst the most important risk factors in Eastern enlargement. Per capita income differentials are as wide as 1:22 between the richest and poorest potential members of an enlarged union—as opposed to the relation of 1:3.6 within the EU.[7] But this is a static point of view that has to be qualified by at least four arguments. First, 'catch-up' income growth in the CEECs may bring income convergence in the nearer future; second, a more dynamic approach to the subject will insist that the economies of scale provided by a bigger market will be able to 'produce' least cost suppliers inside the trading club, thus reducing the risk of forming a trade diverting union; third, technological catch-up in CEECs—in particular with the help of foreign direct investments—can help to extend the share of intra-industry trade as it is already and increasingly becoming visible,[8] and, last but not least, the so-called 'non-traditional benefits' of 'locking-in' economic and political reform may simply dwarf the costs envisaged in trade-creation trade-diversion frameworks.

## Western Motives: High Politics, Low Politics and Economics

Eastern enlargement from the European Union's point of view has been primarily a matter of 'high politics'. When it comes to delivery on the promises, however, the actual procedures are often governed by reasoning about the costs of accession and the corresponding 'low politics' of serving special interest groups. Embracing this constellation, Baldwin (1994, 1995) has suggested that enlargement could be significantly postponed because the CEECs are so poor and so agricultural that the costs for the EU's structural and cohesion funds as well as for the common agricultural policy (CAP) would be too high. Without going here into the budgetary details, it should be recalled that—according to Baldwin (1995)—integrating only the four Visegrád countries by the year 2000 would cost some 58 billion ECU on agricultural and structural subsidies, equalling some 60 per cent of the EU's projected budget for the year 2000. This would either require higher contributions to the EU's budget, which would be very unpopular with EU voters, or the higher costs would have to be financed by cutting back expenditure on farmers and the current poorer incumbents.[9] Baldwin (1995, p. 478) concluded that '… as a matter of self defence, coalitions of farmers and poor regions are likely to veto an Eastern enlargement until CEECs get much richer and much less agricultural. This could take two decades'.

The Baldwin calculations have been revised, widely discussed, and a huge body of literature has been produced since then, giving various estimates of the budgetary costs of enlargement. It is clear, however, that such calculations merely illustrate the size of the problem and can hardly give any evidence of the expected consequences unless it is clear what adjusting procedures the EU will take to reform its structural and agricultural policies in a way that enlargement will not discomfort the incumbents too much. 'Agenda 2000' has become the code-name for the controversial reform instrument the EU intends to use to prepare itself for enlargement. Unsurprisingly, Agenda 2000 must change the rules for distributing structural and agricultural funds in such a way that the potential spending on new members is below the level for which they would be eligible under the current system. Thus the reform agenda comprises: first, a reform of the CAP (also a necessity also due to the results of the Uruguay Round of the last GATT talks) and second, a restriction on the distribution of structural funds to the new members. Under the old rules, new members would be eligible for structural funds as high as ten to twenty per cent of their respective GDP and this aid is supposed to be matched by the same amount coming from the recipients' own funds. This could imply tremendous absorption problems. Italy, for example, spends only three-quarters of the money allocated to it. Therefore it is now most likely that a cap on regional funds' allocation will be set in terms of percentages of the recipients' GDP. The range being discussed is currently around four to five per cent of GDP. Furthermore, 'waiting' and 'designing' economic regions where economic growth could lead to a growing-out of 'Objective 1' status by the time of accession (probably the Prague and Budapest region) could be instrumental in limiting the financial burden.[10] While under such conditions Agenda 2000, as well as a number of researchers (eg. Martin, 1998), are optimistic that the costs will be within reasonable limits, enlargement nevertheless will require much from the incumbents who seem to have become increasingly cost-benefit oriented as far as their EU 'membership fees' are concerned. Thus at the time of writing the 'absorptive capacity' of the Union appears to be the major obstacle for a speedy accession of most advanced CEECs. Accession will, to a large extent, depend on the Union's ability to reform itself in time.

In contrast to the various budgetary scenarios, the economics of EU enlargement are more difficult to assess. In general, one may expect some relatively small economic benefits in the short term and a potential for higher benefits in the longer term. Starting with the short-term economic impact, an Eastern enlargement by adding the CEEC10 to the EU would bring some additional 105 million people into the Union, an increase of 28.4 per cent. In terms of economic activity or market size—the average CEEC10 citizens' income is less than 12 per cent of the average EU incumbents' income—it would add only a meagre 3.4 per cent to EU's total GDP.[11] These small gains in market size could, however, stand against the adjustment costs (structural and regional unemployment) following an increased market access for CEECs, especially in sensitive sectors where they do have comparative advantages, such as agriculture, coal, steel, and labour-intensive manufactures, thus potentially hurting some of EU's more traditional industries, especially in the poorer countries of the Union. This, however, is a static picture.

First, fears of intensified competition from the CEECs in sensitive sectors should not be overestimated. CEECs exports of such goods do often not compete with EU producers but with products from extra-regional sources. Moreover, CEEC exports are often complementary to EU production and competitiveness of EU producers could also be increased by using lower cost input goods from CEECs. Finally, various studies show that intra-industry trade rather than inter-industry trade is the most dynamic force in EU-CEEC trade.[12]

Second, looking forward and assuming that CEEC10 would eventually attain a per capita income comparable to that of a poorer EU country, enlargement would increase the economic activity of Union by some 17 per cent. But the exact impact on EU income is more difficult to access, a reason why many analyses start with the trade impact that can be estimated more easily by means of so-called gravity equations. Gravity equations assume that trade among a pair of countries is more intense the closer the physical distance and the higher the income of both economies are.[13] An early estimate provided by Baldwin (1994, pp. 80–119) has been used to project the potential trade pattern with the CEECs. Three factors are important. First, by opening-up Eastern European countries in 1989/90, formerly suppressed trade will be redirected into a 'natural direction', given the physical distances and pre-determined income levels of the trading partners. Baldwin's calculations point to a doubling of EU's exports to the CEECs as compared to the 1989 level, from 18.2 billion US dollars to 36 billion dollars, which approximates very closely the figure reached in 1994.[14] The second factor is income growth, both within the EU and income catch-up (or lack of it) in the CEECs. If CEECs manage to converge with the poorer EU countries' income level this would imply that the CEECs could in the long-run account for 5 to 10 per cent of most European countries' exports. For some countries (Austria, Finland, Greece, Italy, and Sweden) the figure is above 20 per cent (Baldwin, 1995, p. 476). The third factor is EU membership that would give trade another boost. Baldwin's gravity equation implies that trade among members would be 70 per cent higher as compared to the no-membership case, a result that is indicative, but should probably not been taken too literally.[15]

Third, while potential gains for exporters are tremendous in the longer term, it is, however, by no means clear from this finding that EU incumbents' welfare will be enhanced. Quantitative analyses of the welfare consequences of trade integration have been provided by 'computable general equilibrium models' (CGEs) in other cases, notably for assessing NAFTA, the EC 1992 project and the recent GATT round.[16] Unfortunately, because of lack of reliable historical data there are no CGE results available for Eastern enlargement. However, CGE results in other cases, notably NAFTA, point to the fact that the potential gains for the smaller country are often a multiple of those of the larger countries. One reason is simply the relative size of the markets: extending the free trade area towards Mexico affects only a small share of US exports which—in turn—command only a relatively small share in the United States' GDP. Furthermore, the US also had initially much lower trade barriers towards both Mexico and the rest of the world, and given the large internal US market it seem reasonable to assume that economies of scale have already been exploited before NAFTA. The economic gains of Eastern enlargement continue therefore to appear small.

Fourth, and on a more speculative base, however, the potential impact on the economic geography within Europe could be tremendous. Huge gains could result from economising regional production patterns along the lines suggested by the 'flying geese' pattern of foreign direct investment in East Asia, ie. the successive relocation of labour-intensive production processes according to a pecking order of lower wage countries with differing real wage levels, possibly involving frequent relocation as development successes lead to real wage increases (Sander, 1995). Inasmuch this would push up wages in the region, it could create, on the one hand, the larger Eastern market many are waiting for. On the other hand, a more diversified EU could provide a huge potential to increase productivity and competitiveness of major European industries. While some of those gains may come at the expense of extra-regional low-wage countries such as those in East and Southeast Asia, to some extent this may also threaten Southern Europe and low-skilled workers throughout the existing Union. A recent general equilibrium model study by Francois (1998) suggests some, albeit not dramatically, positive overall effects on the EU by means of 'pro-competitive effects', ie. effects related to induced exit and entry in industries, potential shifts in production costs and increased competitive pressure on domestic producers. According to this study, sectoral downsizing would be concentrated in the textile sector and to a much lesser extent in chemicals and steel, while the machinery and equipment sector would gain from the increased demand from the CEECs. However, and without driving this issue too far,[17] one might therefore conclude that there are higher potential gains in the long run that may come with a potential risk of threatening cohesion within the Union, a problem that may command strong policy action by the Union (the latter issue is, however, beyond the scope of this chapter).

## *The CEECs' Expectations towards the EU*

On a general level one can distinguish three major expectations of the CEECs towards EU membership: (1) accession as an objective in itself: the historic 'return to the Europe' they have (arguably) traditionally belonged to, including the political issues of security and securing democracy; (2) the catalyst and the role model function that the EU lends to the CEECs in the transition process; and (3) EU membership's potential role in promoting national development and wealth. I will comment on the last two points.

It is obvious that in the transition process towards a market economy system it is of utmost importance to establish the legal and institutional framework necessary for a functioning market economy: a system of property rights, a civil law, competition rules, the whole regulatory system, including that for establishing a two-tier banking system, and so forth. Given the region's political goal of returning to Europe, as well as the early promises concerning future EU membership, EU legislation and regulation became a role model for the build-up of CEECs' legislative and regulatory systems. With the device of a pre-accession strategy and the production of the White Paper, the European Commission has established a guide for CEECs to prepare themselves 'for operating under the requirements of the European Union's internal market' (as it is put officially in order to distinguish it from a guide to accession which would involve acceptance of the *acquis communautaire* as a whole).

For transition countries, following the White Paper's guidance is a necessary—although not sufficient—step to take before entering the EU. On the positive side, it must be recognised that a regulatory system can be imported off-the-shelf. Moreover, for the 'approximation of legislation' the Union is providing technical and financial assistance through its so-called Phare program. On the other side, the EU's internal market legislation and regulation requirements go much beyond what is necessary for running a market economy. One can therefore identify three areas of concern:

- adapting to a range of complicated EU legislation absorbs a lot of qualified personnel in administrative operations;
- not all EU legislation may be functional at this point of the transformation process; and
- adoption of the EU regulatory framework at a pre-membership stage implies 'regulation without representation' (Rollo, 1995) which can lead to concerns about an 'imperial harmonisation' (Lawrence, Bressand and Ito, 1996; Lorenz, 1996).

Given the high acceptance of the ultimate goal of joining the EU within the population of the CEEC10—which is in the range of 90 per cent according to some surveys[18]—no effective opposition to EU membership exists in the political sphere. This has led some analysts to argue that CEECs have not taken as strong a negotiating position as they could have (Richter, 1996), arguably also because of the enormous potential economic benefits expected. From the previous discussion of the economic impact on the EU, it is obvious that:

- the potential for trade expansion is tremendous and speeded up by all three sources: by redirecting suppressed trade flows into the natural direction, by income catch-up processes, also contributing to a higher share of intra-industry trade, and by gaining a preferential margin by becoming a Union member;
- joining the Union provides a safe haven because members will not be subject to contingent protectionism and may, in time, enjoy protection by such measures;
- income and welfare effects can be considerable for the smaller countries as CGE models have proved in the NAFTA case;
- expected financial aid from the EU makes regional integration more attractive than global integration which has not always been successful in integrating very poor countries in the presence of complementary trade pattern;
- the region could gain enormously from an emerging new division of labour. It has been argued that the future real wage developments may be one of the most important factors in determining the economic geography

in a wider Europe (Oman, 1994, p. 65). The region may partly divert investment from incumbent Europe, specifically the poorer part of it, but it may also attract investment from outside the region. The more potential investment will contribute to rising wages, the more likely it is that the change of economic geography will be less painless for the incumbents as it will increase the size of the Eastern market. It is essentially the interaction between the real wages as an investment incentive and its demand-creating potential that will shape the future structure of the European economic geography, thus leaving room for both possibilities, that (some) CEECs remain low wage countries or that they experience a big push in development.[19]

The simulation study by Francois (1998) suggests that overall, EU-CEEC integration will increase the CEECs' real income by some 22 per cent of a benchmark GDP. Most of these effects are due to induced accumulation and pro-competitive effects rather than static allocation effects (which account only for one per cent of the benchmark GDP). As far as sectoral restructuring is concerned, unsurprisingly a contraction of CEEC heavy industry and a move into lighter industries such as textiles, chemicals, and other manufactures are the expected results.

Joining the club, however, is not without risk. A first and more traditional argument dwells on the trade diversion potential in highly protected areas, specifically agriculture. A second problem is the readiness of local producers to 'cope with competitive pressures and market forces' after dismantling the economy (as the membership criteria in *Agenda 2000* state). A third issue points to the risks related to the high demands a deeper European Union puts on applicants, implying a 'big step problem' (Baldwin, 1995) as the whole gamut of regulations necessary for a 'single market' will have to be adopted in one giant step (an issue discussed under the *Agenda 2000* membership criterion 'ability to assume the obligation of membership'). A fourth issue, and a special variety of the third one, is that with the arrival of the European Monetary Union in 1999, countries that meet the so-called Maastricht criteria *must* become members of the single currency bloc. Equally, those who do not meet the criteria at entrance may feel pressure to reach for 'Maastricht convergence'. Either way, this could imply that applicant countries may run into the dangers of pursuing an overly restrictive monetary and fiscal policy—and/or fix their exchange rates at levels that are not compatible with full employment and competitiveness. Ultimately that could either also lead to currency crises if remaining outside the EMU, or if inside, to an increase in unemployment.[20]

## Rocky Roads into the European Union

The CEECs' expected gains from membership are high, probably sometimes even set too high. But it is not only for this reason that some analysts suggest that Eastern Europe should not solely focus its economic strategies on the European Union (eg. Brada, 1994). The receding entry date—in particular for the less advanced second and third tier CEECs—and also the shortcomings of the accession architecture have provoked increasing dissatisfaction in the region with some of the AA provisions (Inotai, 1995; Richter, 1996). In the following section, I argue that early catch-up scenarios were too optimistic and need to be updated. This update suggests that some countries may have to wait for a substantial period of time before EU accession may take place. This makes it necessary to examine more closely the shortcomings of the transitional agreements.

*Income Convergence—The Simple Arithmetics of the Long Way into Prosperity*

Catching-up in terms of income (as a proxy also for wage convergence) in a reasonable amount of time—at least with the poorer members of the EU—may be looked at as one criterion for EU maturity, whether because poorer applicants cause higher financial costs to the EU's cohesion funds, whether because poorer new members would divert such funds from incumbents, or whether because of the perceived threat from opening the door too wide to low-wage competitors. Against this background various researchers engaged in back-of-the-envelope calculations of catch-up scenarios. An early attempt undertaken by the author in 1992 (published in 1993) has shown that the initial hope of the transforming countries to join the EU by the end of the century has proved overly ambitious, since at that time annual and steady growth rates of 6 to 13 percentage points above the growth rates attained by the target reference group (consisting of Portugal and Greece) would have been required.

Such calculations give, however, a somewhat unreliable picture. One reason is that the 1990 income level overestimated the productive capacity of the CEECs—and the progress of the transformation made clear that 'creative destruction' of the state sector continued to outpace the growth of the upcoming, but still small, private sector. A second reason is that recurrent currency devaluation reduced the US-Dollar value of the CEEC's per capita income further.[21] A re-doing of the earlier exercise shows that—even when 2010 is made the target year (instead of 2000)—catching-up to the poor EU country average may now require an unrealistic 10 per cent excess of CEECs per capita income growth rates over that of the reference group. Or to put it differently, even when growing with a very optimistic (former) 'Southeast-Asian' growth rate of 5 percentage points above the poor EU's average, it will take the CEECs three decades to break even (Table 8.2).[22]

Table 8.2   **Catch-Up Scenarios for Central and Eastern European Countries**

| | GDP Per Capita 1994 (Poor EU = 100) | | Required Growth Rate Difference for Catching Up with Poor EU[b] by 2010 | | Years Required to Catch Up with Poor EU[b] Assuming a 5% Growth Differential | |
|---|---|---|---|---|---|---|
| | in US $ | in PPP $[a] | in US $ | in PPP $[a] | In US $ | in PPP $[a] |
| Czech R. | 27 | 69 | 8.5 | 2.4 | 27 | 8 |
| Hungary | 32 | 47 | 7.3 | 4.9 | 23 | 16 |
| Poland | 20 | 42 | 10.5 | 5.5 | 33 | 18 |
| Slovakia. | 19 | 48 | 10.9 | 6.5 | 34 | 15 |
| **CEEC4** | **23** | **48** | **9.6** | **4.7** | **30** | **·15** |
| Slovenia | 59 | 48 | 3.3 | 4.7 | 11 | 15 |
| **CEEC5** | **24** | **48** | **9.2** | **4.7** | **29** | **15** |
| Bulgaria | 11 | 34 | 15.1 | 7.0 | 46 | 22 |
| Romania | 11 | 31 | 15.0 | 7.5 | 46 | 24 |
| Estonia | 24 | 35 | 9.4 | 6.8 | 33 | 17 |
| Latvia | 20 | 25 | 10.7 | 9.1 | 33 | 29 |
| Lithuania | 11 | 25 | 14.5 | 8.9 | 45 | 28 |
| **CEEC10** | **20** | **42** | **10.7** | **5.6** | **33** | **18** |

*Source:*   Own calculation from GNP per capita data provided by the World Bank's *World Development Report, 1996*. The data for the different CEEC groupings have been calculated as population-weighted averages using World Bank mid-1994 population data.

[a]   PPP-$: Purchasing Power Parity Dollars are World Bank extrapolations from 1993 ICP estimates, except for Slovak Republic which are 1990 extrapolation from 1990 ICP estimates.

[b]   Poor EU is defined as the population-weighted average of the per capita GNPs of Greece, Portugal, Spain, and Ireland. The obtained numbers for 1994 are 11,850 US-$ and 12,987 PPP-$, respectively.

A different approach for convergence scenarios (that circumvent the exchange rate issue) is to base them on income data measured in purchasing power parity dollars (PPP-$). Earlier results provided by Sander (1993) came, however, with the attached warning that PPP-$ data—especially for late re-formers—can be equally flawed. For example, Bulgaria's PPP per capita in-come was estimated at 7,900 PPP-$ in 1990, but only at 1,250 PPP-$ in 1994. The reason is not simply the decline in economic activity, but predominantly the impact of price liberalisations on living standards.[23] In 1990-91 late re-formers tend to 'look better' than the early birds of transition, a problem that has now lost some significance, lending more reliability to the exercise. The figures provided in Table 8.2 suggest that convergence is a real possibility, but that it still takes much more time and effort than initially thought. Ten to 15 years would be the expected convergence time for the most advanced transi-tion countries, provided they will manage to grow at a (former) 'Southeast-Asian pace'. However, this may not be too unrealistic for three reasons. First, most adjustments in exchange rates and internal relative prices have already taken place, making the current data a more reliable source. Second, since we are measuring in purchasing power the non-tradable sector's expansion, espe-cially the service sector (including an eventually 'surfacing' informal sector) may be able to boost the statistically measured activity. Third, relatively low US-$ incomes may eventually lead to a surge in labour-oriented foreign direct investments leading to some combination of rising wages and relatively appre-ciating currencies. Nonetheless, the accession period for the least developed transition countries continues to appear lengthy, pointing to the necessity of providing them with supportive intermediate arrangements.

## Pitfalls in Associating

Association Agreements are essentially free trade arrangements (FTAs) with a couple of additional provisions. At least five crucial issues have attracted the attention of researchers and politicians alike: (1) the fact that duty-free trade as defined in the AAs does not exclude contingent protectionism, (2) the issue of asymmetric trade liberalisation and control over trade policy instruments in the CEECs, (3) the intrinsic problems of free trade areas such as rules of ori-gins which have to be evaluated against custom union solutions, and (4) the problem of overlapping FTAs, also known as hub-and-spoke bilateralism and said to tend to favour the hub and the expense of the spokes. All this may have an impact (5) on the foreign direct investment position of transition countries with potential long term consequences.

*Contingent Protectionism* The AAs do not rule out contingent protectionism. In fact, many CEECs seem rather disappointed by the extent to which the EU has made use of 'voluntary export restraints', non-tariff protectionism in sensitive sectors such as agriculture, textiles, coal and steel, as well as the Union's use of other non-tariff trade policy instruments such as safeguards (to a lesser extent) and anti-dumping measures (to a larger extent).[24] The crucial issues here are, first, that quotas and anti-dumping duties may have suppressed exports below what could have been obtained, and, second, that the contingent character of the protectionism in itself is a problem as it acts as a disincentive to foreign direct investment.

Since 1989/90 especially, the Central European countries managed to reorient their trade massively towards Europe. Within a few years the European Union become the most important trading partner for these countries (see Table 8.3). Since such figures are close to what can be considered as normal levels according to gravity equation estimates, it must be questioned to what extent these developments have been being spurred by the AAs as such. Observers from CEECs, such as Inotai and Kiss (1996), have argued that much of the surprisingly fast re-orientation of trade has not been caused by the provisions of the AAs, but rather by the preferential status granted to CEECs under the General System of Preferences (GSP). The authors have noted that in the area of sensitive products CEECs could not or only slightly increase their market share in EU markets; and in agriculture the bilateral trade balances of the CEECs remained in deficit, despite the countries' obvious comparative advantages in this sector. Other studies, such as Brenton and DiMauro (1998), found 'no compelling evidence that actual imports by the EU of sensitive products from CEECs are significantly depressed relative to the imports of such products from other supplies and relative to total imports'. Following Hoekman and Djankov (1996) one should, however, note that 're-direction' of exports should not simply be understood as 'diverted' CMEA goods. According to these authors, such 're-directions' account at most for 20 per cent of the export volume. Rather, export growth has been mostly spurred by new or substantially upgraded or differentiated products. In this respect, intra-industry trade as well as vertical integration are becoming increasingly important for which again foreign direct investments are a major driving force.

While some of the remaining barriers in industrial trade will be phased out by 2001—with the notable exclusion of agriculture—the threat of contingent protectionism remains, and will continue to retard domestic as well as foreign investment as long as membership is not clearly visible. Subsequently, protectionist sentiments in the CEECs have been increasing.

**Table 8.3    Merchandise Exports of Central and Eastern European Countries**

|  | Average Annual Growth Rate 1990-1994 (in per cent) | Exports 1994 (value in billion dollars) | Exports to EU 1994 (value in billion dollars) | Share of Export to EU 1994 (in per cent) |
|---|---|---|---|---|
| Czech R. | 8 | 12.0 | 7.6 | 63.3 |
| Hungary | 2 | 10.7 | 5.9 | 55.1 |
| Poland | 5 | 17.3 | 10.8 | 62.4 |
| Slovakia | 8 | 4.2 | 2.2 | 52.4 |
| Bulgaria | -6 | 4.0 | 1.6 | 40.0 |
| Romania | 6 | 6.2 | 3.0 | 48.4 |

*Source:*    World Trade Organization, *International Trade: Trends and Statistics*, Geneva, 1995.

*Note:* Export data for Czech Republic and Slovenia exclude trade between the two countries.

*Asymmetric Liberalisation* In the early days of transformation, most transition countries used trade liberalisation as an instrument of stabilisation policy. Price liberalisation took place when most companies were not yet privatised and/or not facing any serious domestic competition. Typically, to keep newly liberalised prices in check, a radical opening of domestic markets towards external competition was devised. Two instruments were used, maxi-devaluations and a drastic reduction of trade barriers (Sander, 1993). While even World Bank economists reckoned that 'one should not make the best the enemy of the good' (Lawrence Summers), trade barriers have in some cases been so drastically reduced that, in the case of Poland, for example, the EU in 1992 internally considered the low tariffs on agricultural goods as a potential obstacle for future membership. This 'over-liberalisation' heritage (Inotai and Kiss, 1996) of the early transformation days, has been supplemented by the results of the Uruguay Round of the GATT. While industrial countries agreed to a 38 per cent tariff reduction on average, thus bringing down the average tariff level for industrial goods to 3.9 per cent, transformation countries will reduce those tariffs by 30 per cent resulting in a 6 per cent level of average tariffs. Given that CEECs will neither have the market nor the bargaining power to make extensive use of the means of the new protectionism, Inotai and Kiss (1996) argue that the effective protection of transition countries' industries is lower than that in industrial countries and shows definitely the lowest level of protection given the region's level of GDP and development. It is interesting to contrast this view with the initial argument made by the EU that the AAs represent an asymmetrical opening of the EU market towards the East. The potential problem involved here is that some industries that may be in need of infant-industry protection or—in the case of restructuring of state-owned enterprises—'senile-industry' protection, may not be able to be nurtured, protected or rescued, respectively.

*Free Trade Areas Versus Custom Unions* Free trade areas (FTAs) differ from custom unions (CUs) essentially by allowing for trade policy autonomy, while CUs require an uniform external tariff. The trade policy autonomy—and the possible use of it for industrial policy purposes—that CEECs maintain in principle (but probably not in practice) comes at a price: since there is no single external tariff, 'rules of origin' are needed to avoid imports from third countries at too low a tariff. Such rules are often very complex and difficult to administer. Baldwin and Venables (1995, p. 1635) note for example, that the basic provisions of the Polish-EC Free Trade Arrangement take up 13 pages, while the rules of origin amount to over 60 pages. Moreover, enforcing such rules can be very costly. In the case of EFTA they have been estimated at 3 per cent of the value of intra-EFTA and EFTA-EU trade (Herin, 1986). If this figure holds for CEECs, back-of-the-envelope calculations suggest enforcement costs of about one per cent of the Visegrád countries' GDP.

The loss of trade policy autonomy in CUs can be seen as an important reason why most regional integration arrangements are FTAs and not CUs (Baldwin and Venables 1995, p. 1635). In the case of the CEECs it has however been shown that such trade policy autonomy is limited. Then, would not a custom union with the EU be a better solution? A CU would not only abolish the rules of origin problem, it probably would also make it more difficult to apply contingent protectionist measures. A CU would also require the progressive adoption of EU regulations, which leads to the particular problem of 'regulation without representation' which led Rollo (1995, p. 470) to conclude that the CEECs '... will find it difficult to identify resting places between association and full membership which are sustainable because of the loss of sovereignty'. A further issue is whether a CU should serve as a 'resting place' or as an intermediate step towards the ultimate goal of EU membership.

*Hub-and-Spoke Bilateralism* The current system of economic integration of the CEECs in Europe by means of FTAs and AAs, respectively, has been characterised as a hub-and-spoke system, with the EU being the hub and the CEECs the spokes. Hub-and-spoke systems have recently become prominent measures by larger trading blocs to arrange their external trade affairs. Not only is the EU increasingly using it, but also NAFTA. Such arrangements have been criticised for favouring the hub at the expense of the spokes. The critique rests on the fact that hub-and-spoke arrangements do not address the issue of remaining trade barriers among the spokes. Consider, for example, one transition country being the least cost supplier of beef and the other transition country being the least cost supplier of steel. Given remaining barriers in intra-CEEC trade, the EU may be able to export steel to best beef producer and beef to best steel producer. That is, the transition countries will suffer from trade diversion while the hub will have access to both least cost suppliers and will only experience the advantages of trade creation.

However, this is not to say that a hub will always gain from such an arrangement, since it may obtain its bigger slice from a smaller income pie (Wonnacott, 1996, p. 64). Spokes, however, will always lose from such an arrangement since they are facing discrimination in all other spoke markets. Given the current relatively small market sizes of the CEEC spokes, it may be argued that such discrimination may be quantitatively of less importance, but there are at least three arguments against playing down the dangers of a hub-and-spoke bilateralism in the case of Eastern Europe:

- It is not only the actual size of spoke-spoke trade that is important, but also its future potential (Wonnacott, 1996).

- The spokes are not only discriminated in the other spoke's markets, but individual spokes may also face discrimination in the hub market since not all bilateral FTAs or AAs are identical and typically do not rule out contingent protectionism. This holds also when agreements with new spokes are signed-up. The welfare effect on the incumbent spokes depends on whether the new spokes get more favourable treatment and whether their goods are substitutes, thus leading to a preference erosion. (Baldwin and Venables, 1995; Wonnacott, 1996).

- The spokes may suffer from investment diversion. If trade costs (transportation costs, tariffs, etc.) are important and firms are operating under conditions of imperfect competition, they will tend to locate production in the hub in order to be closer to the market. The hub market is usually the largest one. Location in a low-wage spoke may be then less profitable than location in the high-wage hub if hub-spoke trading costs overcompensate the labour cost advantage (Krugman, 1991a; Baldwin, 1994).

In sum, the hub-and-spoke system makes the Eastern spokes smaller than they need be. Or in Baldwin's words: '... signing bilateral deals with the hub, without signing deals with the spokes, is self-inflicted peripherality' (1994,

p. 134). While in principle the diversion that occurs through hub-and-spoke systems could be mitigated by signing free trade deals among the spokes, such a solution may be difficult to reach in practice. First, it is doubtful to what extent the political economy within an individual spoke country would on balance welcome competition from other spokes, in particular when spokes are specialised in similar areas and/or are making extensive use of 'exchange rate protectionism'. Second, since AAs often differ tremendously from country to country, asymmetries in the perceived granting of 'concessions' to other spokes could also contribute to a rejection of this idea for political economy reasons. And, third, it may not be possible to solve all problems introduced by complex hub-and-spoke systems by simple means of trade liberalisation among spokes (Wonnacott, 1996). A recent empirical study by Brenton and DiMaura (1998) suggests that a more open market access for sensitive products from some CEECs is likely to have a greater impact upon the exports of other CEECs than upon the exports and output of existing members of the EU. The authors therefore suggest that '…a key element of the approach of the Commission to the next enlargement should be to ensure that the chosen policy of differentiation among countries in Central and Eastern Europe does not lead to discrimination between them in their access to the EU market'. In other words, while the countries in the first accession wave may soon be part of the hub, 'spoke peripherality' continues to remain an important issue for the remaining CEECs.

*Foreign Direct Investment Deterrence* In the early days of transition much hope has been put on a huge inflow of foreign direct investment. In most cases, however, the influx remained behind expectations, with the notable exception of Hungary and, more recently, Poland, the Czech Republic and—when compared to the size of the country—Estonia (Table 8.4). Moreover, many investment inflows, especially in the first years, were market-oriented investments, taking advantage of the privatisation process.[25] It should, however, be noted that the heavy involvement of foreign companies in the privatisation process (rather than in greenfield investment) has increasingly been causing fears of a backlash against foreign direct investment ('selling of the crown jewels', 'deindustrialisation', etc, see UNCTAD, 1995, pp. 155–156). Consequently, when the privatisation process slowed down in 1996 this was also reflected in FDI inflows (UNCTAD, 1997). This situation is now gradually changing, especially in the most advanced countries that are increasingly taking part in integrated international production systems. But still, FDI inflows are concentrated on a few beneficiaries and in most cases fall short of what Southern European countries experienced when they joined the European Union in the 1980s. Mexico and especially Malaysia that heavily involve themselves in integrated international production may also serve here as a comparison. Table 8.5 shows the FDI stock in relation to GDP for the various countries. It should, however, kept in mind, that the time for accumulating foreign capital stock has been comparatively much shorter for CEECs.

**Table 8.4    Net Flow of Foreign Direct Investment into Eastern Europe 1990-1996**

(in million dollars)

| | 1990 | 1991 | 1992 | 1993 | 1994 | 1995 | 1996 | Cumulated Inflows 1990-96 | Average annual FDI inflow per capita ($)[1] | FDI flow/ GDP 1994 (per cent) |
|---|---|---|---|---|---|---|---|---|---|---|
| Czech R. | 120 | 511 | 947 | 654 | 878 | 2568 | 1200 | 6878 | 94 | 2.5 |
| Slovakia | 18 | 82 | 100 | 199 | 203 | 183 | 150 | 935 | 31 | 1.7 |
| Hungary | 311 | 1462 | 1479 | 2350 | 1144 | 4519 | 1982 | 13247 | 183 | 2.8 |
| Poland | 10 | 291 | 678 | 1715 | 1875 | 3659 | 5196 | 13424 | 50 | 2.1 |
| Slovenia | -2 | 41 | 113 | 112 | 87 | n.a. | n.a. | 351 | 35 | 0.6 |
| Estonia | n.a. | n.a. | 82 | 162 | 215 | 202 | 138 | 799 | 102 | 9.1 |
| Latvia | n.a. | n.a. | 29 | 45 | 214 | 180 | 292 | 760 | 57 | 6.2 |
| Lithuania | n.a. | n.a. | 10 | 30 | 31 | 73 | 152 | 296 | 60 | 1.1 |
| Bulgaria | 4 | 56 | 42 | 55 | 105 | 90 | 150 | 502 | 8 | 1.1 |
| Romania | -18 | 40 | 77 | 94 | 341 | 419 | 624 | 1577 | 10 | 1.2 |

*Source:*    United Nations Economic Commission for Europe, *The Economic Bulletin for Europe*, Vol. 47, 1995, Table 4.2.5.; UNCTAD, *World Investment Report 1997*, Annex table B.1; own calculations

*Note:*    1990-92 data for the Czech Republic and Slovakia are from UNECE, 1993 onward data are UNCTAD.

n.a.: not available

[1] 1990-1996, Slovenia 1990-94, Estonia, Latvia and Lithuania: 1993-96

**Table 8.5    Foreign Direct Investment Inward Stock as Per Cent of GDP**

|            | 1980 | 1990 | 1995 |
|------------|------|------|------|
| Portugal   | 4.4  | 7.6  | 7.4  |
| Spain      | 2.4  | 13.3 | 17.6 |
| Mexico     | 4.2  | 10.2 | 25.6 |
| Malaysia   | 24.8 | 33.0 | 52.1 |
| Czech R.   | ..   | ..   | 8.7  |
| Slovakia   | ..   | ..   | 3.4  |
| Hungary    | ..   | 6.3  | 31.5 |
| Poland     | ..   | 0.5  | 7.2  |
| Estonia    | ..   | ..   | 17.6 |
| Latvia     | ..   | ..   | 10.5 |
| Lithuania  | ..   | ..   | 2.4  |
| Bulgaria   | ..   | ..   | 0.8  |
| Romania    | ..   | ..   | 3.2  |

*Source:*    UNCTAD, *World Investment Report 1997*, Geneva.

The data show that particularly the less advanced transition countries may experience investment deterrence. The sluggish reform process can be made responsible for this. But this cannot explain the low performance in total, since those countries are also the ones with the lowest wage rates. And even when political and regulatory instability is brought into consideration, the diversion argument may retain some credit since labour-oriented investments are essentially export-oriented ones which are sensitive to trading costs. And trading costs are being pushed upward by contingent and non-tariff protectionism as well as by hub-and-spoke mechanisms alike.

If and when foreign direct investment is being deterred, this will also deter the emergence of a more rationalised regional division of labour that would require more free trade on a regional basis. This reflects the need for establishing regionally integrated production networks, as has become increasingly important in Southeast Asia (UNCTAD, 1994; Sander, 1995, 1999; Zysman and Schwartz, 1998). Furthermore, it can be argued that in presence of strong learning effects, as well as by means of strong backward and forward linkages, regions that get a head start may be able to lock-in or even create comparative advantages over time (Murphy, Shleifer and Vishny, 1989; Krugman, 1991a, 1995). Baldwin (1994) has argued therefore that in line with new location theory, hub-and-spoke bilateralism could give the hub a head start in the process of reshaping the European economic geography. While the

Baldwin argument has been originally applied in the EU-CEEC context, it may soon increasingly gain relevance with respect to the differential treatment of CEECs. This possibility of FDI diversion makes it important to establish a non-discriminatory accession system.

## Conclusions: Paving the Roads into the European Union

It is now clear that the CEECs 'return into Europe' will not come as an integration of a block of, say, ten countries at one point of time. Rather, some of the most advanced countries might join (eventually even individually) the EU around the year 2002. Less advanced countries will have to wait much longer. Two questions will therefore shape the debate on Eastern enlargement of the EU: how to reduce the waiting time and how to make the waiting time more comfortable for applicants?

With regard to the first issue, 'variable geometry' thoughts have been circulating in academic as well as political circles, especially addressing the issue of restricting the financial impact of Eastern enlargement on the EU budget. It should however be noted, that involuntary as well as 'voluntary' (ie. accepted) discrimination of Easterners could be counter-productive. As Baldwin (1995, p. 478) has put it '... unpleasantness is unavoidable, if second-class ticket holders can vote on what first-class passengers will have for dinner', but excluding new members from voting would be no membership that deserves the name. Non-discriminatory measures are therefore called for. The crucial issue is whether EU membership should come with several qualifications, thus introducing counter-productive second-class membership, or whether several levels of integration approaches plus a clearly defined graduation mechanism will be installed, as, for example, suggested by Pisani-Ferry (1997), probably allowing for transitional periods. With regard to the most advanced group of applicants, as of today, the ability of the EU to prepare itself for enlargement appears to be the crucial factor in determining the timing of the first enlargement round.

With regard to the second issue and in particular with a view to late joiners, the shortcomings of the current systems of AAs need to be addressed, especially the issues of the remaining contingent protectionism and hub-and-spoke problems. Baldwin (1994) has made valuable proposals to address these issues. Because originally being made in the context of an estimated two decade accession time for all CEECs, Baldwin's proposals have received much critique. Their value rests, however, in pointing to the necessity of designing a non-discriminatory accession system, in particular when accession comes in tranches (probably with an ever increasing number of applicants). With respect to hub-and-spoke complications, Baldwin has suggested that the existing AAs should be embedded into an 'Association of Association Agreements' (AAA) through which CEECs would extend bilateral liberalisation with the EU to all other countries that have AAs. Although this would be a step in the right direction, it could be difficult to install the AAA in practice. Harmonising the content of AAs from the side of the hub could, however, be an important step not only towards installing an AAA, but also towards reducing the potential dangers of a hub-and-spoke system as such.[26] A second intermediate step proposed by Baldwin is to form an 'Organisation of European Integration' (OEI) that would establish some sort of an 'European Economic Area' with the CEECs that provides, loosely speaking, access to the EU's single market without the CAP, without EU voting rights, without access to funds, and (as opposed to the original EEA) without free migration. The OEI should, over time, rule out contingent protectionism and allow for mutual recognition of standards.

Whether or not one wishes to follow Baldwin's call for establishing new 'institutions' or 'organisations'—there are always good arguments against creating bureaucracies—a clear commitment to enlargement from the side of the Union with a clear timetable as well as clearer measurable accession criteria appear to be vital (Mayhew, 1998). Or as UNECE (1998, p. 14) put it:

> The EU itself can exert a major influence on the expectational environment in all the transition economies, not only those in the first wave of applications, by leaving no doubt as to either side's commitment to the ultimate objective of membership, but at the same time encouraging the adaptation of comprehensive and consistent strategies designed to enable the transition economies to meet the requirements of the acquis in the shortest feasible time (UNECE, 1998, p. 14).

Paving the roads into the European Union should ultimately contribute to a wider and deeper Union that could yield tremendous political and economic benefits from Eastern enlargement. This is not to say that this process is without risk. For the world trading system it is important that a deepened and widened EU will not become a 'Fortress Europe'. A strategy of 'inclusiveness' rather than 'exclusiveness' should make sure that the 'European house' stays open not only for less advanced CEECs, but also for all neighbours in the region (Emerson, 1998). Moreover, from the CEECs point of view, the EU must make sure that deeper integration will not become the enemy of a wider Europe. Inside the Union the issue of cohesion will have to be addressed, probably involving continuous policy reforms in all major policy fields. With the right policies Europe should be able to take advantage of Eastern Enlargement and re-invent itself politically and economically.

# Notes

[1] I will use term CEEC for the following ten countries: the CEEC4 (also known as the Visegrád groups comprising the Czech Republic, Hungary, Poland, and Slovakia), Bulgaria and Romania, plus the Baltic3 (Estonia, Latvia, Lithuania), and Slovenia. From time to time for reason of simplicity only I use the term 'Eastern Europe' for the before-mentioned group of countries. The following analysis will not deal with Albania and the former Yugoslav republics, with the obvious exemption of Slovenia.

[2] It is useful to recall the exact wording that the European Council in Copenhagen in June 1993 used:

'The associated countries in Central and Eastern Europe that so desire shall become members of the European Union. Accession will take place as soon as an associated country is able to assume the obligations of membership by satisfying the economic and political conditions required. Membership requires:

- that the candidate country has achieved stability of institutions guaranteeing democracy, the rule of law, human rights and respect for and protection of minorities;
- the existence of a functioning market economy as well as the capacity to cope with competitive pressure and market forces within the union;
- the ability to take on the obligations of membership, including adherence to the aims of political, economic and monetary union.

The Union's capacity to absorb new members, while maintaining the momentum of European integration, is also an important consideration in the general interest of both the Union and the Candidate countries'. (Quoted from *Agenda 2000, Commission Opinion on Application for Membership of the European Union*, European Commission DG 1A).

[3] According to the *Financial Times*, November 9 1998, 'for membership by January 1, 2002, a deal will have to be done by mid-2000, to give six months for member states to agree, and a year for all the countries to ratify it'.

[4] Next to the CEECs mentioned, Malta, Cyprus and Turkey are concerned.

[5] The signing of the Slovenia AA has been delayed because of unresolved restitution issues raised by the Italian government under Berlusconi.

[6] Quoted from the European Union's 'Europa Homepage' on the Internet: http://europa.eu.int.

[7] Calculations are made by comparing Denmark's 1994 GDP per capita measured in US $ with that of Bulgaria and Greece, respectively. Data are from the World Bank (1996).

[8] See eg. Hoekman and Djankov (1996), Weise, C. *et al.* (1997). The former argue that the increase of exports from CEECs to the EU was not so much a simple 'redirection' of traditional exports, but rather due to a growth of 'new' export goods and substantially upgraded and differentiated products, thus giving rise to more intra-industry trade.

9   The current EU criteria for receiving structural funds, which aim to increase regional economic and social cohesion, demand a per capita GNP of less than 75 per cent of the Union's average. The following figure may give an impression of the dimensions involved: adding the CEEC4 plus Slovenia to the EU15 would reduce the per capita GNP by 12.7 per cent from 19,759 US-$ to 17,243 US-$. Enlarging the Union by the CEEC10 would reduce average per capita income to 15,909 US-$, ie. by nearly 20 per cent (all figures are based on World Bank 1994 data, averages are population-weighted by the author).

10  Structural funds are focussed on six main objectives: 'Objective 1' regions, the major category, are those lagging behind in development—below the 75 per cent EU average of GNP, as per note 9.

11  All data are based on the author's calculations using 1994 data from World Bank (1996).

12  For references see footnote 8. UNECE (1995) also reports an increase in intra-industry trade as measured by an increase in the familiar Grubel-Lloyd index.

13  While the impact of distance on trade is evident not only from physical but also from cultural proximity, the impact of income is not. Specifically, the good results obtained from estimations of gravity equations seem to prove that richer economies are not only larger importer, but also larger exporters as the increase in per capita income goes together with an increase in product variety offered which in turn gives way to increased intra-industry trade.

14  Baldwin (1994) uses a somewhat different country sample: his CEEC12 includes Albania and Croatia. The actual figure for 1994 given by WTO (1995) is 36.9 billion dollar. The WTO country sample excludes, however, the Baltic states, Slovenia and Croatia.

15  One should however use such results with caution. Frankel *et al.* (1995) come up with similar results for their 1990 estimate, but over the time the absolute value of the parameter of an EU dummy as well as its significance varies considerably.

16  Earlier CGE models attempted to estimate the static impact of trade liberalisation only while later generations also allow for dynamic effects, like those coming from economies to scale. For a recent overview see Baldwin and Venables (1995). In Sander and Inotai (1996) various authors discuss the results of such models in relation to the Uruguay Round of the GATT.

17  I have elaborated on such ideas first in a seminar held at Centre for Public Policy at the Department of Political Science at the University of Melbourne, Australia, 25 September 1996 titled 'Flying Geese over Eastern Europe? Can Europe Learn from Asian Integration Experiences?'. For a more detailed coverage, see Sander (1999).

18  The European Commission's *Central and Eastern Eurobarometer* (No.6, March 1996) reports that in the Europe Agreement countries as a whole, 90 per cent of the citizens responded that in case of a referendum they would vote for joining the EU with Poles and Romanians most in favour of EU membership and anti-membership votes highest in Estonia and Slovenia.

19  The new theory of 'economic geography' is analysing such phenomena. One important result that is indirectly referred to here is the possibility of multiple equilibria (see Krugman, 1991a, 1995).

[20] Daviddi and Ilzkovitz (1997) argue that EMU should not be an immediate target for the majority of associated countries. According to them, the successful conclusion of the transformation calls for a certain degree of flexibility in the conduct of economic policy which the adoption of too strict criteria could actually prevent.

[21] As of 1994, the average per capita income in the CEECs amounts to some 20 per cent of the EU's poor countries' per capita income. In 1990 the corresponding figures for Czechoslovakia and Hungary were around 50 per cent.

[22] Calculations by Pinto/Ramakrishnan (1996) who are redoing a similar exercise provided by Baldwin (1994) point in the same direction. These authors caution—in a similar way as the author earlier—that dollar income data may be bad indicators for future developments since the dollar exchange rates of poorer EU incumbents and the EU applicants may not move in the same direction. My 'back-of-the-envelope' calculations are also mostly in line with the more recent economic growth regression scenarios.

[23] For example, housing was almost free in many countries in the early days of transition.

[24] According to the WTO *Trade Policy Review of the EU*, dated 18 July 1995, the EU remained one of the most frequent users of anti-dumping remedies in the GATT system. 156 cases were counted at the end of 1994, as opposed to two countervailing actions.

[25] Acquisition and joint venture investment accounted together for 67 per cent of 1990-93 investments in transition countries as opposed to the 23 per cent devoted to greenfield investment, according to the IMF (1995, p. 64). Moreover, often monopolies were overtaken to serve the local market at monopoly prices, and in some cases even evidence can be found that foreign investors pressed for protection in the local market (see UNCTAD, 1994).

[26] The July 1997 agreement on the pan-European cumulation of rules of origin provides one step in this direction (Mayhew, 1998).

# References

Baldwin, R.E. (1994), *Towards an Integrated Europe*, Centre for Economic Policy Research, London.

Baldwin, R.E. (1995), 'The Eastern Enlargement of the European Union', *European Economic Review*, Vol. 39, pp. 474–481.

Baldwin, R.E. and Venables, A.J. (1995), 'Regional Economic Integration', in G.M. Grossman, and K. Rogoff (eds), *Handbook of International Economics*, Volume 3, Elsevier, Amsterdam, pp. 1597–1644.

Brada, J. (1994), 'Regional Integration Versus Integration Into the World Economy: The Choices for Central and Eastern Europe', *The World Economy*, Vol. 17, pp. 603–618.

Brenton, P. and DiMauro, F. (1998), 'Is There Any Potential in Trade in Sensitive Industrial Products Between the CEECs and the EU?', *World Economy*, Vol. 21, No. 3, May, pp. 285–304.

Daviddi, R. and Ilzkovitz, F. (1997), 'The Eastern Enlargement of the European Union: Major Challenges for Macro-economic Policies and Institutions of Central and Eastern European Countries', *European Economic Review*, Vol. 41, Nos. 3–5, April, pp. 671–680.

Emerson, M. (1998), *Redrawing the Map of Europe*, Macmillan, London.

European Commission (1997), *Agenda 2000: For a Stronger Wider Union*, Directorate-General X, European Commission, Brussels.

Fischer, St. *et al.* (1998), 'How far is Eastern Europe from Brussels?', *IMF Working Paper*, 98/53, IMF, Washington D.C.

Francois, J.F. (1998), *Scale Economies, Imperfect Competition and the Eastern Expansion of the EU*, (mimeo), Tinbergen Institute, Tinbergen.

Frankel, J., Stein, E. and Shang-jin Wei (1995), 'Trading Blocs and the Americas: The Natural, the Unnatural, and the Super-natural', *Journal of Development Economics*, Vol. 47, pp. 61–95.

Herin, J. (1986), 'Rules of Origin and Differences Between Tariff Levels in EFTA and the EC', *EFTA Occasional Paper*, No. 13, EFTA, Geneva.

Hoekman, B. and Djankov, S. (1996), *Intra-Industry Trade, Foreign Direct Investment and the Reorientation of Eastern European Exports*, World Bank, Washington, D.C.

IMF (1995), *World Economic Outlook*, May, IMF, Washington D.C.

Inotai, A. (1995), 'The Economic Impacts of the Association Agreements: The Case of Hungary', *Russian and East European Trade and Finance*, January-February, pp. 48–73.

Inotai A. and Kiss, J. (1996), 'Central and Eastern Europe's Integration Into the World Trading System', in H. Sander and A. Inotai (eds), *World Trade after the Uruguay Round: Prospects and Policy Options for the Twenty-First Century*, Routledge, London, pp. 155–173.

Krugman, P.R. (1991a), 'Increasing Returns and Economic Geography', *Journal of Political Economy*, Vol. 99, pp. 183–199.

Krugman, P.R. (1991b), 'The Move Towards Free Trade Zones', in The Federal Reserve Bank of Kansas City (ed.), *Policy Implications of Trade and Currency Zones*, The Federal Reserve Bank of Kansas City, Jackson Hole, pp. 7–41.

Krugman, P.R. (1995), 'Increasing Returns, Imperfect Competition and the Positive Theory of International Trade', in G.M. Grossman, and K. Rogoff (eds), *Handbook of International Economics*, Volume 3, Elsevier, Amsterdam, pp. 1243–1277.

Lawrence, R.Z., Bressand, A. and Ito, T. (1996), *A Vision for the World Economy: Openness, Diversity and Cohesion*, Brookings Institution, Washington D.C.

Lorenz, D. (1996), *The Impact of Regional Integration on the International Division of Labour*, paper delivered at the Transatlantic Workshop: 'Towards Rival Regionalism', July 4–6, Stiftung Wissenschaft und Politik, Ebenhausen.

Martin, R. (1998), 'Financing EU Cohesion Policy in Central and Eastern Europe: A Budgetary Timebomb?', *Intereconomics*, Vol. 33, No. 3, pp. 103–112.

Mayhew, A. (1998), *Recreating Europe: The European Union's Policy Towards Central and Eastern Europe*, Cambridge University Press, Cambridge.

Murphy, R., Shleifer, A. and Vishny, R. (1989), 'Industrialization and the Big Push', *Journal of Political Economy*, Vol. 97, pp. 1003–1026.

Oman, Ch. (1994), *Globalisation and Regionalisation: The Challenge for Developing Countries*, OECD Development Centre, Paris.

Pinto, B. and Ramakrishnan, U. (1996), 'Wage Convergence to Western Levels: How Soon?', *Transition*, Vol. 7, Nos. 1–2.

Pisani-Ferry, J. (1997), 'Dealing with Diversity: The Challenges for Europe', *Briefing Paper No. 11*, for the conference 'Will there be a Unified European Economy, International Production Networks, Foreign Direct Investment, and Trade in Eastern Europe', organised by the Kreisky Forum for International Dialogue and The Berkeley Roundtable on the International Economy, Vienna.

Richter, S. (1996), 'The Visegrád Group Countries' Expectations *vis-à-vis* Western Europe', *Russian and East European Finance and Trade*, January-February, pp. 6–41.

Rollo, J. (1995), 'EU Enlargement and the World Trade System', *European Economic Review*, Vol. 39, pp. 467–473.

Sander, H. (1993), 'Wirtschaftliche Transformation in Osteuropa zwischen Stabilisierung und Restrukturierung', in I. Hauchle and L. Brock (eds), *Entwicklung in Mittel- und Osteuropa, Über Chancen und Risiken der Transformation*, Stiftung, Frieden und Entwicklung, Bonn, pp. 79–115.

Sander, H. (1995), 'Deep Integration, Shallow Regionalism, and Strategic Openness: Three Notes on Economic Integration in East Asia', in F.P. Lang and R. Ohr (eds), *International Economic Integration*, Physica Verlag, Heidelberg, pp. 211–244.

Sander, H. (1996), 'Multilateralism, Regionalism, and Globalisation: The Challenges to the World Trading System', in H. Sander and A.Inotai (eds), *World Trade after the Uruguay Round: Prospects and Policy Options for the Twenty-First Century*, Routledge, London, pp. 17–36.

Sander, H. (1999), 'Reunifying Europe Economically: Flying Geese over Rocky Roads?', in M.S.S. El-Namaki, *et al.* (eds), *Strategic Issues at the Dawn of a New Millennium*, Lansa, Leiderdorp.

Sander, H and Inotai, A. (eds) (1996), World Trade after the Uruguay Round: Prospects and Policy Options for the Twenty-First Century, Routledge, London.

Schott, J.J. (1991), 'Trading Blocs and the World Trading System', *The World Economy*, Vol. 14, pp. 1–17.

Schott, J.J. (1996), 'The Future Role of the WTO', in H. Sander and A. Inotai (eds), *World Trade after the Uruguay Round: Prospects and Policy Options for the Twenty–First Century*, Routledge, London, pp. 105–114.

UNCTAD (1994), *World Investment Report 1994*, United Nations, Geneva.

UNCTAD (1995), *World Investment Report 1995*, United Nations, Geneva.

UNCTAD (1997), *World Investment Report 1997*, United Nations, Geneva.

UNCTAD (1998), *World Investment Report 1998*, United Nations, Geneva.

UNECE (1995), *Economic Bulletin for Europe*, Vol. 47, United Nations, Geneva.

UNECE (1998), *Economic Survey of Europe*, No. 3, United Nations, Geneva.

Wagner, H. J. and Fritz, H. (1998), 'Transformation-Integration-Vertiefung, Zur politischen Ökonomie der EU-Osterweiterung', in H.-J. Wagner and H. Fritz (eds), *Im Osten was Neues: Aspekte der EU-Osterweiterung*, Dietz, Bonn, pp. 16–43.

Weise, C. *et al.* (1997), 'Ostmitteleuropa auf dem Wege in die EU', *Beiträge zur Strukturforschung 167*, Duncker and Humboldt, Berlin.

Wonnacott, R.J. (1996), 'Free-Trade Agreements: For Better or Worse?', *American Economic Review*, Vol. 86, No. 2, pp. 62–66.

Wonnacott, P. and Lutz, M. (1989), 'Is There a Case for Free Trade Areas?', in J.J. Schott (ed.), *Free Trade Areas and U.S. Trade Policy*, Institute for International Economics, Washington D.C., pp. 1–58.

World Bank (1996), *World Development Report 1996*, World Bank, Washington D.C.

World Bank (1998), *World Development Indicators 1998*, World Bank, Washington D.C.

World Trade Organisation (1995), *International Trade: Trends and Statistics*, World Trade Organisation, Geneva.

Zysman, J. and Schwartz, A. (1998), 'Reunifying Europe in an Emerging World Economy: Economic Heterogeneity, New Industrial Options, and Political Choices', *Journal of Common Market Studies*, Vol. 36, No. 3, September, pp. 405–429.

# 9 Legal Rights and State Responsibilities under the ECHR

DAVID KINLEY[1]

This chapter focuses on the essential legal dimension of the rights and responsibilities under European Convention on Human Rights (ECHR), while remaining mindful of the other important dimensions to human rights—namely, the moral, cultural, social, political, economic and gendered dimensions—with which the legal dimension necessarily interrelates (Kinley, 1998, pp. 1–26). It is in all these dimensions, albeit each differently weighted according the rights in question and the circumstances of their invocation, that the concept of human rights takes form and their practical effect is felt.

The principal concern of the chapter is to distinguish between court-enforced human rights and the scope for the implementation of rights outside the courts, as the significance of this distinction is not always appreciated by lawyers and non-lawyers alike.[2] In particular, the extra-curial responsibilities as well as opportunities for the protection of human rights are highlighted and discussed. None of this is to deny the crucial role that the courts play in the articulation and enforcement of all legal rights (including human rights) in the foundation and maintenance of social order. Rather, the intention is to warn of the dangers of adopting too blinkered a view of the nature of the responsibilities imposed on states by the Convention. The fundamental contention is, therefore, that to ignore or overlook the non-curial state responsibilities for the supervision of human rights expression, promotion and protection is seriously to undermine the operation and impact of such human rights instruments as the ECHR.

## The ECHR

The time and circumstances of the creation of the ECHR in 1950 has had much to do with the relative success of the venture as a binding international human rights instrument. Its stated objectives, like those of the Universal Declaration on Human Rights before it and its close cousin the International Covenant on

Civil and Political Rights after it, are impressively ambitious. What is more, the Convention situates its proclamations on human rights firmly within the context of the liberal, democratic ideals of the West.[3] The Preamble to the Convention declares:

> Fundamental Freedoms ... are the foundation of justice and peace in the world and are best maintained on the one hand by an effective political democracy and on the other by a common understanding and observance of the human rights on which they depend ...

In terms of the power and effect of the enforcement mechanisms of the ECHR, no other international human rights instrument bears comparison—not the *American Convention on Human Rights* (1969), nor the *African Charter on Human and Peoples' Rights* (1981) and not any of the United Nations' human rights covenants and conventions.[4] In fact, the ECHR's legal effect is aligned more closely with domestic human rights laws such as the *Canadian Charter of Rights and Freedoms* and the amendments to the United States Constitution that comprise its Bill of Rights, both in respect of its standing within the constituency it serves and its wider international influence.[5] Furthermore, the fact that the aspirational form of the Convention has been backed by the authority of its enforcement apparatus has been influential in the emergence of a new school of thinking in international relations and international law. The so-called cosmopolitan theorists see a defining characteristic of what is law as being based in the generic notion of human rights observance rather than by the simple, empirical recognition of the sovereignty of nation states (Gould, 1990, chapter 12; Téson, 1990, p. 15).

Too readily, however, the relative success of the ECHR is measured in terms first, of the instances in which the enforcement mechanisms and institutions are utilised, and second, the effects of the resultant decisions. In many respects, this is a strange way in which to measure success, as noting how heavily enforcement procedures are employed might be considered more a measure of failure than success. The 'policy objective horse' as it were—ie. the protection and promotion of human rights—if not already bolted, may be some way out of the stable door by the time the Court is called upon to close it. The ideal, of course, is to foster in society in general and in the institutions of government in particular, such regard for human rights that breaches, and certainly egregious breaches, do not occur in the first place.

It is a skewed and constricted way of viewing the Convention to concentrate on the dispute settlement and enforcement mechanisms at the end of the legal process that are the European Court of Human Rights and the domestic courts. Essential though the courts are to the implementation of human rights in any system governed by the rule of law, they are not alone sufficient. In States' efforts to meet the obligations placed on them by the Convention to guarantee human rights there are other means of compliance that are of equal importance and, potentially at least, capable of greater impact. If we are to take seriously the rhetoric of rights, we must ensure that a regard for human rights is actively promoted as well as their breach prevented. As such, a society cannot restrict its institutional response to curial enforcement that is largely reactive and less than comprehensive.

## A Fundamental Obligation

Article 1 of the ECHR provides: 'The High Contracting Parties shall secure to everyone within their jurisdiction the rights and freedoms defined in ... this Convention'. From these bare but apparently unimpeachable words flow a pair of fundamental questions that I wish to take up:

- how currently is this obligation honoured by signatory states and how better could it be met? And,
- what are the difficulties and challenges in meeting the obligation?

### Honouring the Article 1 obligation

Jurisprudential orthodoxy of international law holds that there are two dominant conceptual approaches to states honouring their treaty obligations: constitutional incorporation of the treaty, and transformation of the treaty provisions into domestic law.

*Constitutional incorporation* Constitutional incorporation is most easily facilitated by those jurisdictions that adhere to the so-called monist conception of legal systems. Under this notion international and domestic laws are considered to operate within the one legal hierarchy, with international law being constitutionally recognised as superior to domestic law. Typically this is the perspective adopted in the civil code jurisdictions of continental Europe. The consequence of the ratification of a legally binding international instrument by a monist jurisdiction is, seamlessly, to give domestic constitutional primacy to treaty comprising, as it does, part of international law. The Netherlands provides a clear example of this circumstance (van Hoof, 1996, pp. 186–203).

    The same formal recognition is also given to treaties under the French and German Constitutions. However, in respect to European Community (now European Union) law, the supreme curial bodies in both these countries were

for some time reluctant to give full force to these apparent constitutional intentions, before finally acknowledging the supremacy of European Union law
within their jurisdictions.[6] In fact, on account of its uniquely pervasive and
authoritative legal regime, the European Union has provided an arena in which
such jurisdictional tug o'wars have been played out most vividly, not only for
the above mentioned countries, but for all Member States of the EU (European
Parliament, 1995).

In terms, specifically, of the constitutional incorporation of the ECHR in
many European civil code countries, the Convention operates as a supplement
to, rather than a substitute for, pre-existing sets of rights entrenched in their
constitutions. It is true that there exists the potential for conflict between the
two sets of legally protected rights. In practice, however, this is rare, due to the
well-honed skills of juristic hair-splitting that allow the terms of domestic rights
to be distinguished from, or be read to be compatible with, ECHR rights (or
vice versa), and so avoid such conflict (Delmas-Marty, 1992; Gearty, 1997).

*Transformation into Domestic Law* The alternative, so-called transformation
method typically employed in the common law countries in Europe of the United
Kingdom and Ireland (and also in Australia), is based on the dualist approach
to the relationship between international law and domestic law. According to
this doctrine, domestic and international legal systems are not characterised as
belonging to a single hierarchical legal structure, but rather as belonging to
different legal structures. The matter of their relationship—in particular how
they recognise each other—is not (indeed, cannot be) hierarchical in form;
rather, it is based ultimately on the notion of their inherent separateness. When
the two intersect, as occurs when an international treaty is signed and ratified,
the consequences are not the same in the two systems.

From the perspective of international law, the fundamental demands of
subjugation to the conditions imposed by the treaty have been satisfied and
therefore the signatory state is bound. Thereby, domestic law must, where there
is a conflict, yield to the supremacy of the international law. From the perspective of the common law country on the other hand, domestic law is always
supreme and international law can never have precedence over domestic law.
For an international treaty to be given any binding status in the domestic legal
system it must be incorporated or 'transformed' into municipal law by statute;
and until such action is taken the treaty is considered to have direct legal effect
only in the international sphere. Ratification of the treaty does not constitute
such incorporation or transformation. Indeed, the very fact that ratification is
sufficient to bind the state in international law only goes to demonstrate the
perceived separateness of the two systems (Shearer, 1994, pp. 63–7).

## The Nature of the Obligation

In respect of both the dualist and monist strains of legal philosophy there is one important common thread. This is that the concept of the legality or bindingness of an international instrument such as the ECHR is defined in terms of its justiciability—that is, the extent to which its terms are arguable and enforceable in the *courts*, whether domestic or the European Court of Human Rights itself. For many that is the full extent of the fulfilment of the obligations imposed by the Convention; but that is to misread Article 1 of the Convention and to frustrate the intentions of its framers.

Under Article 1, as we have seen, it is the 'High Contracting Party'—that is, the State—that is obliged to secure the rights in the ECHR. But the High Contracting Party does not, when translated into a practical institutional form, equate to 'the courts'. At the minimum, the State comprises the executive and the legislature, as well as the judiciary; the bureaucracy might be considered a fourth arm of government if it is not included in the executive.

Such a tripartite characterisation of the organs of governmental authority forms the basis upon which the classic Montesquien 'separation of powers' doctrine has been established. It belies, however, the fact that the organs of state are often institutionally indistinct and operate in a continuum of policy formulation, legislative enactment, rule-making and implementation that comprises state governance. Thus, any reduction of the responsibility to fulfil the conditions of the ECHR to that which the courts can deliver is not just ineffective, it constitutes an abrogation of the responsibilities of the states' legislatures and executives. The fact that within democracies it is on the shoulders of the directly or indirectly elected legislatures and executives that the main responsibility of government rests adds still greater force to this argument.

Courts, in the main, operate *ex post facto*; their principal function being to provide redress for proven breaches of law. It is the legislators and the members of the executive who together or separately can protect and promote citizens rights proactively, through policy formulation, enactment and implementation of the law. The adage 'prevention is better than cure' applies as surely to the maintenance of a healthy corpus of human rights law as it does to living corporeal forms.

Mechanisms by which a culture of respect for human rights is established and sustained by legislatures and executives are crucial. Certainly, this goal cannot be left to their individual or collective consciences. Even with the best intentions, the pressures of political exigencies can at times override human rights principles. One option, at least, is the institution of cross-party parliamentary scrutiny committees that review all prospective legislation specifically for compliance with the ECHR. Under such a scheme human rights concerns would be highlighted in advance of the enactment of legislation, thereby better informing legislators, policy-makers and the bureaucracy (Kinley, 1993; Blackburn, 1998; Cooper and Bynoe, 1999). The nature and aim of this initiative was captured metaphorically in a statement made during a UK Parliamentary debate on the issue: 'whenever I travel on the underground I always intend to pay for the journey; but the fact that there is a ticket collector at the other end just clinches it'.[7]

An especially desirable effect of the implementation, or prospect of implementation, of such a preventive mechanism is the concern to instil in the policy-makers and legislators an awareness of the imperative of human rights observation. The UK *Civil Service Code*, for example, places ministers and civil servants under an express duty to take decisions that comply with the law 'including international law and treaty obligations'. There is a need alongside such a directive for the development of human rights education for politicians and bureaucrats, as well as, possibly, curial review of prospective policies or legislation for compliance. In fact this need is now acknowledged in the United Kingdom as a direct consequence of the incorporation of the ECHR by the *Human Rights Act* 1998 and in anticipation of it coming fully into force.

It must be said that there is little to suggest that the civil code countries are any more assiduous in their recognition of rights early in their legislative and policy-making processes. A number of civil code jurisdictions have records of breaches of the Convention similar, and in the case of Italy, exceeding that of the United Kingdom (ECHR, 1998). Still, it is fair to say that in civil code countries there is greater broad-based familiarity with rights discourse within and without legal circles and therefore, perhaps, a fuller understanding of their nature and demands within the ranks of the legislatures, executives and judiciaries.

## Challenges in Complying with the ECHR

There are two particular challenges facing all organs of government in the signatory states in regard to their compliance with Article 1 of the Convention. One is a relatively recent and growing phenomenon referred to as the 'privatisation of human rights'. The other is the existence of significant qualifications to many of the main rights under the Convention, including that they may be restricted in so far as the restriction is 'necessary in a democratic society'.

## Privatisation of the ECHR?

A concern that is common in all the 40 signatory states of the ECHR, albeit to varying degrees, is the question of the increasing exercise of public power by private entities. As a result of the corporatisation and privatisation of state agencies and enterprises, essentially private institutions with limited direct responsibility to the State are now able significantly to affect the rights of private individuals. Most dramatically, the 'shrinking state' is a prominent feature of the new democracies of Eastern Europe.

In the West, it is true that institutions and especially corporations in the private sector, both national and transnational, have always wielded considerable power. What is distinctive about the situation today is the unprecedented scale of the transfer of public functions and responsibilities away from state management and control. The push in Western Europe to privatise, corporatise, and contract-out core as well as peripheral state activities like public transport in France, electricity in Italy, or prisons in the United Kingdom is driven by domestic policy as well as EU competition policy. As such, the trend is seemingly irresistible.

The significance of this in respect of the ECHR lies in the manner in which, and the level at which, its provisions are made binding. The Convention's demands are, as Article 1 makes clear, directed at the signatory states alone. The obligations and responsibilities are imposed on a vertical axis— that is, they are owed by the state to the individuals within its jurisdiction. On the face of it, therefore, the Convention has no direct impact upon the human rights obligations that occur horizontally—that is, between private individuals or 'legal persons'.

This is significant because it provides a potential alternative to the otherwise reasonable assumption that the more the state sphere is reduced, the more restricted becomes the scope for pinning the obligation for human rights protection on the state. For where there exists the possibility of making the state also responsible for the horizontal protection of human rights (ie. by preventing breaches between private legal persons), the diminution of the state is of much less importance.

*Horizontal effect of human rights laws* There are two levels at which the horizontal application of human rights law can and does occur. The first is where domestic legislation protects individual and group rights against infringement both by state organs and agencies and by other individuals or groups. There already exist substantial provisions in the human rights laws of most European countries that apply both to vertical and horizontal societal, commercial and legal relations. Areas typically covered in this manner include:

- employment and industrial relations—employment laws that prohibit direct (and often indirect) discrimination on grounds of race, gender, political beliefs, religion, and disability, alongside trade union membership/non-membership laws;

- privacy and family life—data protection laws, and certain freedom of information and privacy laws extend to cover information held in the private as well as public sector; and

- freedom of expression—limitations to defamation laws, certain anti-discrimination laws (on the same grounds indicated above), and whistle-blower protection legislation.

The second stems from a more expansive reading of the Article 1 obligation under the Convention such that the state may be held indirectly responsible for the actions of non-state legal persons that infringe the rights of other private individuals. In recent years the European Court of Human Rights has taken very significant steps in this direction. In the 1993 *Costello-Roberts* case the Court first expressly entertained the possibility that Article 1 might be read to impose on the state *indirect* responsibility for the actions of private individuals that infringe Convention rights (*Costello-Roberts*, 1995, p. 112). The Court has since transformed that possibility into a reality in the case of *A v United Kingdom* (1998).

The question raised in the *Costello-Roberts* case concerned the administration of corporal punishment in a private school—specifically, whether the slippering of seven-year-old Jeremy Costello-Roberts violated his rights protected under the Convention. The complaint was made, by necessity, against the UK government, as it is the government, not the school, that is bound by the Convention. This point is crucial. For although, in the result, the complainant's contentions that the punishment meted out violated his right to be protected from inhuman and degrading treatment under Article 3 of the Convention, and/or his right to privacy under Article 8, failed before the Court, an important principle was nonetheless established. The Court followed the reasoning of the European Commission of Human Rights in the same case in holding that signatory states 'cannot absolve [themselves] from responsibility [under the ECHR] by delegating ... obligations to private bodies or individuals'. States, in other words, are to be held responsible *directly* for their own actions that infringe individual human rights, as well as *indirectly*, for the actions of private actors within the jurisdiction.

In holding this, the Court dismissed the counter-argument offered by the UK government which, it must be said, was somewhat disingenuous. The government's point was that because the private school concerned was not under the *direct* control of the state, then the state could not be held responsible for the school's actions. The deleterious consequences of such an argument would amount to permitting the state to remove itself from responsibility for anything done within its jurisdictional borders by non-state actors. The disingenuousness of such an argument lies in the fact that today there is hardly an aspect of the lives of citizens or the existence and operation of institutions in civil society that is not regulated or in some way affected by state action. Certainly this is the case with education and schools.[8] Even if it is recognised that there are certain limits to the extent of the state's vicarious liability, this does not change the fact of the ubiquity of, and potential for, state regulation.

In *A v United Kingdom*, the Court confirmed the line of reasoning it raised in the *Costello-Roberts* case by holding the UK responsible for the fact that a step-father was able successfully to plead 'reasonable chastisement' in defence of charges brought against him of assault after beating his step-son severely and often with a garden cane. The Court held that obligation under Article 1 of the Convention, taken together with the relevant articles of the rights in question, in this case Article 3 (again), 'requires States to take measures designed to ensure that individuals within their jurisdiction are not subjected to torture or degrading treatment or punishment, including such ill-treatment *administered by private individuals*', and that the fact that there existed under English law such a defence as 'reasonable chastisement' meant that 'the law did not provide adequate protection to the applicant against treatment or punishment contrary to Article 3' (*A v United Kingdom*, 1998, paras 22 and 24).

This privatisation of human rights has yet to develop fully, but it will likely be a growth area in the jurisprudence of the European Court of Human Rights and the domestic courts over the next decade or two (Clapham, 1995). Furthermore, such evolution will be affected by the continuing development of the relationship between European Union law and the ECHR, as the former applies both to horizontal and vertical legal relations. The impact that the ECHR will have on the Member States of the European Union (all 15 of which are signatories of the ECHR) is especially likely to increase as the ECHR is embraced ever more tightly by the more elaborate and directly effective legal regime of the European Union. In this regard, Article F of the 1993 Treaty on European Union (TEU) directs all organs of the EU to have regard for and to promote the ECHR. Indeed, there have been a number of decisions of the European Court of Justice, both before and after the coming into force of Article F of the TEU, that bear directly on the relationship between Community law and provisions of the ECHR (*Stauder v Ulm*, 1969; *Internationale Handelsgesellschaft v EVG*, 1970; *Nold v Commission*, 1972; *Rutili v French Minister of the Interior*, 1975).[9] The Court's use of the Convention is set to increase markedly following the direct inclusion of Article F within the express justiciable bounds of the Court by an amendment introduced by the Treaty of Amsterdam 1997.[10] As a result, the ECHR has been effectively incorporated in the EU legal regime in respect of those areas over which the EU has jurisdiction under its founding treaties.

The burden of the combined impact of the privatisation of human rights under the ECHR and the expansion of state responsibility that goes with it, will fall upon the legislatures, executives and bureaucracies of states more that the courts. For it is they, and not the courts, that can and must search out and repair the structural and substantive defects in laws and legal systems that might allow infringements of human rights to occur whether as a consequence of actions of public officials or the state itself, or private individuals.

## The limitation of rights 'where necessary in a democratic society'

The extent to which most of the rights guaranteed under the Convention must be protected is not unlimited. Limitations may be imposed where they are considered necessary to protect public health or morals, public order or national security or where 'necessary in a democratic society'. The last mentioned ground is found in a number of important articles: Article 6 (right to fair trial); Article 8 (rights to privacy and family life); Article 9 (rights to freedom of thought and religion); Article 10 (right to freedom of expression); and Article 11 (right to peaceful assembly).

The challenge that these qualifications pose for states—that is, specifically the law-makers, policy-makers and the courts—is how to determine when, and at what level, to employ such limitations to what are, after all, supposed to be fundamental and universal human rights. It must be noted that so commonplace are these limitations to rights within international treaties that some have argued that the label of a 'Bill of Rights' is a misnomer. Where the qualifications to the rights obtain as much significance as the rights themselves, it has been argued that it would be more appropriate to refer to a 'Bill of Limitations' (Hiebert, 1996).

That having been said, the 'necessary in a democratic society' qualification is an essential feature of any judicially enforceable rights instrument; if it were not expressly provided for in the European Convention it would almost surely be implied by courts and legislators. This device not only extends to policy-makers and legislators the necessary flexibility to implement human rights in a manner to suit societal demands. It also provides a way out of the very real dilemmas that are created when basic rights overlap and contradict one another in particular situations—for example, where free speech and free movement rights conflict with rights to privacy and family life, and where rights to freedom to hold and practice religious and political beliefs conflict with anti-discrimination rights.

The manner in which the European Court of Human Rights has approached the use of this particular limitation provides a valuable insight as to how states are to determine the nature and extent of their responsibility to protect the rights under the Convention. The basic line adopted by the Court has been to co-opt a notion familiar to many European legal systems—namely, that of the 'margin of appreciation' (Jones, 1995; Yourow, 1996). It is a common characteristic of administrative law jurisdictions that where Ministers and public servants are provided with a discretion whether and how to act, courts will only intrude upon the discretion where they believe the executive or administration has gone beyond the margins of discretion that the courts determine to be reasonable or proportionate to achieving the objects of the legislation in question.

One critical response to this proposition is to say that this appears to transfer to the courts the *ultimate*, rather than parallel, responsibility or power to determine what is reasonable in a democratic society. Indeed, this is precisely what can happen. In practice, however, whether the courts grant to themselves this authority in any particular instance depends on the circumstances of the case, at least as much as any philosophical or jurisprudential conviction the judiciary might hold.

Typically, the European Court on Human Rights has interpreted and applied the limitation in two ways. When faced with a state's justification for employing the limitation, the Court has adopted either:

- a wide margin of appreciation—that is, a formalistic, procedural view of the state's reasoning, which requires merely that the state's legislature or executive follow a fair and reasonable procedure in coming to the conclusion that the right in question has to be curtailed;[11] or

- a narrow margin of appreciation—that is, a substantive analysis of the state's reasoning, which requires not only that the implementing organ follow a fair decision-making procedure but also that its final decision be fair and reasonable.

Though there are examples of the Court declaring its adherence to both these approaches (*Sunday Times v King (No.1)*, 1979; *Handyside v UK*, 1979), the reasoning employed in judgments is barely distinguishable (Lavender, 1997).

For example, in the watershed *Sunday Times* case, the majority (of ten) supporting the imposition of a narrow margin of appreciation on national authorities, argued that the term as used in the Convention:

> does not mean that the Court's supervision is limited to ascertaining whether a respondent state exercised its discretion reasonably, carefully and in good faith. Even a Contracting State so acting remains subject to the Court's control as regards the compatibility of its conduct with the engagements it has undertaken under the Convention (*Sunday Times v UK*, 1979, p. 36).

The reasoning employed by the minority (of nine) judgment in the same case, though favouring a wider margin of appreciation, is not manifestly different. After establishing that the margin of appreciation 'involves a certain discretion' on the part of the domestic authorities, the minority qualifies this base principle by holding that the notion:

> does not give the Contracting State an unlimited power of appreciation ... The domestic margin of appreciation ... goes hand in hand with European supervision. This supervision is concerned, in the first place, with determining whether the national authorities have acted in good faith, with due care and in a reasonable manner ... (*Sunday Times v UK*, 1979, p. 50).

In this case and others like it, the Court talks of the 'reasonableness' of the state's decision to limit the right at issue. In the context of a judgment of the Court, whether the decision was taken in a reasonable manner or not can be read to mean the same thing as whether in the view of the judges or judges the decision finally reached was reasonable.[12] That is so, despite the Court's effort in the *Sunday Times* case to objectify the criteria of what is reasonable, by enunciating two of the essential features of the companion notion of 'in accordance with the law'—namely, that the law be 'adequately accessible' and that it be 'formulated with sufficient precision to enable a citizen to regulate his conduct' (*Sunday Times v UK*, 1979, p. 31).

The closely related interpretive principle of 'proportionality'—which holds not only that the taking of action be necessary, but that it be proportionate to the end sought—is also relevant (Louciades, 1995, pp. 197–200). This principle has been embraced in a number of cases before the Strasbourg Court (*Belgian Linguistic Case* 1968; *Rasmussen v Denmark*, 1984; *Abdulaziz, Cabales and Balkandali v UK*, 1984; *Inze v Austria*, 1987) where its use tends to lead one to conclude that it is 'reasonableness' by another name.

The potential for the European Court of Human Rights as well as the domestic courts to exercise such a powerful tool as that of determining what is reasonable in democratic society can create difficulties for the functioning of democracy itself. The limiting factor on its use would appear to be the extent to which, in reaching decisions to curtail rights guaranteed under the Convention, legislators and policy-makers weigh up the advantages and disadvantages to democratic society of invoking the limitations. It might be supposed that the more earnest they are in this respect, the less likely will the courts feel inclined to second-guess their resultant decision.

If this is the manner in which the principle is applied by the courts (and there is no guarantee that it is or will be) then curiously, it would have the desirable effect of pressurising legislatures, executives and bureaucracies to honour more fully their obligations under the Convention.

## Conclusion

The theme of the chapter has been to caution against an over-reliance on that aspect of the legal expression of human rights that comprises court enforcement—whether by domestic courts or the European Court of Human Rights. Though there is, as I have intimated, an important qualification to this cautionary tone that must be revisited in conclusion.

It is true that the courts are oriented towards the resolution of disputes that come before them according to the specific facts of the case and the particular legal rights and duties involved. In this respect, judgments have a singular and limited effect. However, it is not the case that all court decisions or all aspects of them are devoid of normative effect. Important legal principles associated with the way in which human rights are interpreted and applied by individuals as well as by organs of state have been developed by the courts. For example, the notions of proportionality and reasonableness of a decision; natural justice (that is, fairness in decision-making); and the fledgling notion that states are responsible, even if indirectly, for the actions of those whom they control or have the potential to control (that is, the 'privatisation' of rights) are all judge-made. Each, clearly, has preventive effect on individuals and governmental actors. The normative role of judicial pronouncements may be fractured and less comprehensive than that played by the legislative and policy statements that emanate from the other arms of government, but they are significant nonetheless.

The importance of these innovations cannot be denied. Yet it remains the case that the main responsibility for the protection and promotion of human rights in all states, but certainly those within the embrace of the ECHR, lies with the elected legislators and officials of state. The courts' responsibility must, in other words, be placed in perspective. To engender in all an understanding of, and a respect for, the freedom and integrity of individuals in society is the only sure way in which to achieve a just and humane social order. Few would disagree with that. But to pin one's hopes on achieving such an end on the retroactive sanctions of the courts alone, whether normative or not, is to jeopardise the whole enterprise. The governing institutions of the nation-states in Europe, as well as the supra-national organs of European government, are not themselves perfect, but they are more accessible, more responsive, more representative and potentially more comprehensive than courts. It is through them that the human rights cause must, in the main, be actively pursued.

## Notes

1   This chapter is an edited version of a paper delivered at the 'Rewriting Rights in Europe' Conference, CESAA Annual Symposium, Melbourne University, 30 September 1996. My thanks go to Julia Grix for assisting with the editing of the chapter.

2   I yield to the temptation here to comment on the merits of being a non-lawyer by repeating the insightful remark made by an eminent British constitutional lawyer in the Preface of a seminal text: that this 'book is intended primarily for those who take examinations in law ... But the attempt has been made to make the book readable by the 'intelligent layman' whose intelligence is manifested by avoiding examinations in law altogether', (Hood-Phillips, 1939).

3   That is even if the liberalist focus on the individual (and especially on individual rights) has been somewhat qualified. 'It is arguable,' as one commentator has put it, 'that in so far as liberal societies have been successful over the last two centuries, it has been because they have been constructed as approximations to the communitarian model rather than because of their dependence on rights based individualism' (Brown, 1997, pp. 41, 51).

4   It is claimed that the ECHR has instituted 'the most effective enforcement regime yet known, regional or universal', (Lillich, 1991, p. 646).

5   Such influence, both actual and potential, extends to the development of rights jurisprudence in Australia and New Zealand. See Jones, 1994, p. 56.

6   In respect of France, see the decision of the *Conseil D'Etat* in *Nicolo* in 1989 that established the primacy of EU law over inconsistent domestic administrative law (the decision is reported in English in *Common Market Law Reports*, 1990, p. 173). In respect of Germany, see the decision of the Constitutional Court in *Entscheidungen des Bundesverfassungsrecht* (judgment of 12 October 1993), regarding the compatibility of the Treaty on European Union (the 'Maastricht Treaty') with the Basic Law of the German Constitution (an English version of the judgment is reported in *Common Market Law Reports*, 1994, p. 57).

7   Attributed to Archbishop Temple; quoted by Lord Lester during his Maiden Speech to the House of Lords regarding the UK's record of compliance with the ECHR, *House of Lords Debates*, Vol.550, col.169, 23 November 1993.

8   Indeed, the UK's *Education Act 1944* which was at the centre of the *Costello-Roberts* case dealt with independent or private schools as well as state schools, though a 1987 amendment to the Act abolishing corporal punishment in state schools was expressly not extended to independent and private schools.

9   For a post-TEU reiteration of this principle see *Kremzow v Austria* (Case-299/95), judgment of 29 May 1997.

10  By way of Article 1(13) of the Treaty of Amsterdam, Article L of the TEU (which stipulates the jurisdictional boundaries of the Court of Justice) has been amended so as to include Article F of the TEU.

11  Otherwise known—to adopt an American tag—as the 'deference' model; that is, judicial deference, where appropriate, to the reasoning of the legislature or administration.

12  It has been noted in this respect that the preference for widening the national authorities' discretion has led, effectively, to the reasonableness test becoming a 'not-unreasonable' test; for discussion of this trend, including analysis of relevant cases, see van Dijk and van Hoof, 1990, p. 591.

# References

Blackburn, R. (1998), 'A Human Rights Committee for the UK Parliament–The Options', *European Human Rights Law Review*, 534.

Brown, C. (1997), 'Universal Human Rights: A Critique', *International Journal of Human Rights*, Vol. 1.

Clapham, A. (1995), 'The Privatization of Human Rights', *European Human Rights Law Review*, 20.

Cooper, J. and Bynoe, I. (1999), *Scrutiny and Accountability: Democratic Compliance with International Human Rights Standards,* The Institute of Public Policy Research, London.

Delmas-Marty, M. (ed.) (1992), *The European Convention for the Protection of Human Rights*, Martinus Nijhoff, Dordrecht.

van Dijk, P. and van Hoof, G.J.H. (1990), *Theory and Practice of the European Convention on Human Rights*, 2nd edition, Kluwer, Deventer.

European Court of Human Rights (1998), *Table Showing Referrals to and Judgments and Decisions of the Court 1960-1998* (dated 25.8.98), at ECHR website at <www.dhcour.coe.fr>.

European Parliament, Directorate of General Research (1995), 'Relationship between International Public Law, Community Law and the Constitutional Law of the Member States', *Working Paper, Legal Affairs Series M-6*, European Parliament, Luxembourg.

Gearty, C.A. (ed.) (1997), *European Civil Liberties and the European Convention on Human Rights*, Martinus Nijhoff, The Hague.

Gould, C.C. (1990), *Rethinking Democracy*, Cambridge University Press, Cambridge.

Hiebert, J. (1996), *Limiting Rights: The Dilemma of Judicial Review*, McGill-Queen's University Press, Montreal.

Hood-Phillips, O. (1939), *The Principles of English Law and the Constitution*, Sweet and Maxwell, London.

van Hoof, F. (1996), 'The Impact of International Law in the Legal order of the Netherlands: The Role of the Judiciary', in C. Saunders (ed.), *Courts of Final Jurisdiction: The Mason Court in Australia*, Federation Press, Sydney, pp. 186–203.

Jones, T. (1994), 'Legal Protection for Fundamental Rights and Freedoms: European Lessons for Australia', *Federal Law Review*, Vol. 22, pp. 57–97.

Jones, T. (1995), 'The Devaluation of Human Rights under the European Convention', *Public Law*, pp. 430–449.

Kinley, D. (1993), *European Convention on Human Rights: Compliance without Incorporation*, Dartmouth, Aldershot.

Kinley, D. (1998), 'The Legal Dimension of Human Rights', in D. Kinley (ed.), *Human Rights in Australian Law*, Federation Press, Sydney, pp. 2–25.

Kinley, D. (1999), 'The Parliamentary Scrutiny of Human Rights: Duty Neglected?', in P. Alston (ed.), *Promoting Human Rights Through Bills of Rights: Comparative Perspectives*, Oxford University Press, Oxford, 1999.

Lavender, N. (1997), 'The Problem of the Margin of Appreciation', *European Human Rights Law Review*, 380.

Lillich, R.B. (1991), *International Human Rights: Problems of Law, Policy and Practice*, 2nd edition, Little, Brown, Boston.

Loucaides, L.G. (1995), *Essays on the Developing Law of Human Rights*, Martinus Nijhoff, Dordrecht.

Shearer, I.A. (1994), *Starkes' International Law*, 11th edition, Butterworths, London.

Téson, F.R. (1990), 'International Obligation and the Theory of Hypothetical Consent', *Yale Journal of International Law*, Vol. 15, pp. 16–22.

Yourow, H.C. (1996), *The Margin of Appreciation Doctrine in the Dynamics of Human Rights Jurisprudence*, Martinus Nijhoff, The Hague.

## Cases

*A v United Kingdom* [1998] 5 British Human Rights Cases 137 (Judgment of 23 September 1998).

*Abdulaziz, Cabales and Balkandali v UK* [1984] Series A, No. 94, *European Human Rights Reports*.

*Belgian Linguistic Case* [1968] Series A, No. 6, *European Human Rights Reports*

*Costello-Roberts* [1995] Series A, No. 247-C, 19 *European Human Rights Reports*.

*Handyside v UK* [1979] Series A, No. 25, (1979-80) 1 *European Human Rights Reports*.

*Internationale Handelsgesellschaft v EVG* [1970] ECR 1125.

*Inze v Austria* [1987] Series A, No. 127, *European Human Rights Reports*.

*Nold v Commission* [1972] ECR 491.

*Rasmussen v Denmark* [1984] Series A, No. 87, *European Human Rights Reports*.

*Rutili v French Minister of the Interior* [1975] ECR 1219.

*Stauder v Ulm* [1969] ECR 419.

*Sunday Times v King, (No.1)* [1979] Series A, No. 30, (1979-80) 1 *European Human Rights Reports*.

*Sunday Times v UK, (No.1)* [1979] Series A, No. 30, 1 *European Human Rights Reports*.

# 10 The International Criminal Court and State Sovereignty

HELEN DURHAM

This chapter reviews the development of the Statute for an International Criminal Court. It briefly examines the reasons behind the creation of the Court and the previous historical attempts to advance such an international legal institution. The *ad hoc* International Criminal Tribunals for the former Yugoslavia and Rwanda are dealt with as precedents, encouraging the international community to acknowledge that international prosecutions *are* possible. It examines the issues raised at the 1998 Rome Diplomatic Conference, including the significant but at times fragmented role played by the European Union (EU). Finally, the chapter surveys the Statute of the International Criminal Court, highlighting the most important judicial elements of the treaty and some implications for the EU.

International criminal law has undergone spectacular advances in the last 50 years. At midnight on July 17 1998 in Rome, a Statute for an International Criminal Court (ICC) was agreed upon. This was the result of over 50 years of discussion, five years of debate at the United Nations (UN) and an intense five-week Diplomatic Conference. The new Court has the capacity to try individuals accused of the most serious international offences, both human rights breaches and international humanitarian law (often referred to as 'the law of war') breaches. It is a major step forward for international criminal law, and brings the world closer to ending impunity for those who commit atrocities.

Traditionally States are the subjects of international regulations. International criminal law can be seen to be unique as it imposes criminal responsibility upon individuals rather than states. It takes the political and makes it personal. It puts names and faces to horrible and complex historical events. It dissects activities often sanctioned by States and lays blame upon individual citizens. The relationship between international criminal law and State sovereignty is thus a complex one. International criminal prosecutions enforce fundamental notions of human rights in the broadest sense. Within the international criminal legal system, leaders and powerful figures in States are not immune from being held accountable for their actions. They cannot avoid responsibility for the commission of atrocities by hiding behind State sovereignty.

International criminal law highlights the fact that 'crimes against international law are committed by men, not by abstract entities, and only by punishing individuals who commit such crimes can the provisions of international law be enforced' (International Military Tribunal, 1947, p. 221).

Over 160 States participated at the Rome Conference as well as a number of Non-Governmental Organisations (NGOs) and international organisations such as the International Committee of the Red Cross (ICRC) and the United Nations High Commission for Refugees. Negotiations at the Conference often lasted late into the night, due to the complexity of developing a Court that satisfied as many countries as possible, without creating a weak and ineffective institution. The Statute itself is necessarily a compromise reflecting the diverse interests, opinions and standards throughout the world for dealing with the prosecution of those who plan or commit actions that cause profound and horrific human suffering. It is not a perfect institution; however, as stated by Kofi Annan, the UN Secretary-General, at the ceremony adopting the Statute:

> The establishment of the Court is still a gift of hope to future generations, and a giant step forwards in the march towards universal human rights and the rule of law. It is an achievement which, only a few years ago, nobody would have thought possible (Annan, 1998, p. 4).

Located in The Hague with links to the United Nations, the ICC will enter into force after 60 States have ratified the Statute. The ICC does not replace national war crimes prosecution, but rather will complement such activities. Article 17 states that the ICC will only have jurisdiction when a State is 'unwilling or unable genuinely to carry out the investigation or prosecution'. The permission of either the State on whose territory the crime occurred or the State of which the person accused is a national is required before the ICC can exercise jurisdiction (Article 12).[1]

The Court will have jurisdiction over the crimes of genocide, crimes against humanity and war crimes. The crime of aggression will also be included in the ICC Statute, after further work has been done to create a clear legal definition of this crime. There are three methods for a case to be referred to the ICC. Article 13 allows a case to be referred to the ICC by the Security Council acting under Chapter VII of the Charter of the United Nations, and referrals can also be made by a State Party and by the Prosecutor.

There have been claims that international criminal trials erode the rights of the State. This sentiment was strongly expressed by Dr Jahreiss, a German defence counsel for one of the accused in his opening address at the first international war crimes trials in Nuremberg:

What the prosecution is doing, when in the name of the world community as an entity it desires to have individuals legally sentenced for their decisions regarding war and peace, is destroying the spirit of the State (King, 1994, p. 175).

Although State sovereignty is alive and well today, there is little doubt that the developments in international criminal law, in particular enforcement mechanisms, highlight the fact that individuals have international duties which transcend their national obligations of obedience imposed by States. With this in mind, questions must be asked as to when and how the international community is able to 'trump' State sovereignty. When is a crime deemed so serious that it concerns the international community as a whole? (see Thiam, 1989). Historically, the prosecution of those accused of crimes under international criminal law, both domestically and internationally, raises grave issues of partiality, legal credibility, cultural and historical relativity and conceptual difficulties associated with international criminality.[2] During the many years of debates leading to the development of the ICC Statute these matters were visited on numerous occasions. However, at the final hour of the Diplomatic Conference, over 120 States—despite the inherent flaws in the treaty and the concept—voted to support the Statute for the first permanent legal institution dedicated to enforcing international criminal law. 'The question in the end becomes not whether we are privileged to judge but whether we have the tools, the capacity and the will to do so consistently and fairly' (Simpson, 1997, p. 8).

## Why Create an International Criminal Court?

There is a plethora of legal, political, intellectual and even emotional arguments on the need for an international criminal court. The creation of the *ad hoc* Tribunals for the former Yugoslavia (ICTY) and Rwanda (ICTR) by the United Nations Security Council in 1993 and 1994 respectively injected massive momentum to the development of a permanent institution. The proceedings of the ICTY and ICTR demonstrate to the international community that international trials are possible. They also indicate the capacity for such bodies to develop rigorous and fair international criminal jurisprudence. At the same time, the end of Cold War paralysis of the Security Council resulted in States realising that a treaty-based court may protect national interests more than a Security Council Resolution. Added to this political dimension were the rowdy cries from civil society and NGOs demanding an end to impunity of those who had been party to the carrying out of atrocities.[3] (Pol Pot died a frail old man after a questionable domestic trial.) The media and information technology allowed citizens increased access to global events. Time was ripe for a dramatic international legal development.

Arguments advanced on the benefits of an ICC include the capacity to provide 'justice' and thus help the healing of survivors of atrocities and victims' families (Bronkhorst, 1995), the development of international law (Meron, 1994), and the assistance such a mechanism provides attempts to move towards international peace and security.[4] There is also a belief by many that recording what has happened during horrific periods of history creates understanding of what has occurred and is essential in national reconciliation. The Nuremberg Trials, for example, thoroughly documented the activities of the Nazis making it more difficult to refute the horrors of that regime. As Zuroff and Ferencz write:

> The public trials of (Nazi) criminals have played an important role in educating the public regarding the Holocaust and undermining the propaganda of Holocaust deniers (Zuroff, 1994, p. 224).

> Just as domestic penal law was invented to maintain peace and security in national societies so too international penal law must be created to help maintain peace and security on an international level (Ferencz, 1980, p. 22).

The correlation between the *raison d'être* of domestic criminal systems and international criminal law is obvious. In undertaking this comparison the need for an international enforcement mechanism is highlighted. Providing a deterrent to potential aggressors based on fear of personal liability, establishing a system to curb 'retributive' justice and symbolically stating what the international community deems wrong and right are roles the ICC will hopefully fulfil. As Madeleine Albright stated in relation to the ICTY:

> (It will not) revolutionize human behavior ... but it will at least place the force and prestige of international law squarely on the side of the victim ... it will enhance the prospects for a durable peace. It will add a measure of caution to the scales in the minds of would-be aggressors (Albright, 1994, p. 4).

## The Historical Development of the International Criminal Court

International criminal law encompasses a range of legal norms dealing with international criminal responsibility. It is neither a coherent nor an autonomous system and has wider jurisdiction than previous international tribunals such as Nuremberg and Tokyo and the current *ad hoc* institutions for the former Yugoslavia and Rwanda (Sunga, 1997). International criminal law is based on customary international rules which prohibit a range of activities deemed to harm the fundamental interests of the international community as a whole. International crimes include activities such as piracy;[5] war crimes;[6] crimes against peace;[7] crimes against humanity[8] (including genocide);[9] enslavement and slave trade;[10] traffic in persons for prostitution;[11] and production and sale of narcotic drugs and aircraft hijacking.[12] Only international offences can be subject to universal jurisdiction, which allows offenders to be tried in any country, irrespective of the locus of the offence and the nationality of the offender and the victims.[13] Furthermore, contracting States are bound to prosecute international offenders. In most jurisdictions this requires incorporation of the international crime within the domestic law. However, even those countries with such legislation rarely prosecute their own citizens or others for these crimes. The recognition by the international community that national courts have failed to prosecute or deter the commission of international crimes was one reason leading to the call for a permanent international criminal court.

## First War Crimes Trials

The idea for an international criminal court has been mooted for over 100 years (Hall, 1998). Discussions were held during and after World War I in relation to trying individuals responsible for international crimes committed during the armed conflict. Particular focus was given to the atrocities committed by the Turkish in attempts to exterminate the Armenian people. No such prosecutions were held and despite serious discussions at the 1919 Preliminary Peace Conference for such an international legal institution, it did not eventuate. The Allied Governments proposed that the German Government would try their own people in German courts. This resulted in the Leipzig Trials which were subsequently deemed unsuccessful due, among other factors, to the Allied Governments' belief that extremely lenient sentences were handed down.[14]

Debate ensued on the need to set up an international penal enforcement mechanism over the next few decades (Ferencz, 1980). The International Law Association (ILA) completed a Draft Statute for an International Criminal Court in the mid-1920s (ILA, 1926). However it was not until after World War II that the idea of international criminal trials became reality.

In August of 1945 the four major victorious Allies of World War II agreed in London upon the Charter for an International Military Tribunal. This Tribunal was empowered to try major German officials accused of war crimes, crimes against the peace, and crimes against humanity. Not long after this, a Charter for the Far East was created through a proclamation to establish a similar Tribunal in Tokyo to try Japanese officials (1945). Despite the criticism that these were victors' courts involving selective and retrospective justice, these were the first international criminal proceedings. For many years they remained the last.

It is relatively easy to criticise these Tribunals for their lack of due process and extremely limited rules of procedure. However, the impact of these cases on the development of international law cannot be overstated (Wolfe, 1998). As well as developing the subject matter jurisdiction still utilised today, the post World War II trials quashed any dispute on whether individuals could be subjects under international law.

Momentum was gained from the experiences of the Nuremberg and Tokyo Trials. In the early 1950s the UN General Assembly requested the International Law Commission (ILC) to draft a statute establishing an International Criminal Court (Draft Statute for an International Criminal Court Report, 1952), as well as a Draft Code of Crimes Against the Peace and Security of Mankind; in an attempt to codify this area of international law. Drafts were undertaken and reviewed, but difficulties arose with attempts to define the crime of 'aggression' and the General Assembly concluded that further consideration should be deferred until this matter was resolved (Sunga, 1997). The advent of the Cold War stifled any prospects for the practical development of an international criminal court due to the fact that many States perceived it as an institution requiring them to surrender elements of their sovereignty. In summary, the Cold War reduced the capacity of the UN Security Council to pass resolutions relevant to the enforcement of international criminal law.

## *The Ad Hoc International Criminal Tribunals*

All was quiet on the international front relating to the development of enforcement mechanisms for international criminal law for a couple of decades, despite numerous trials being held in domestic courts all over the world.[15] However, in the 1990s the reported activities occurring in the conflicts in Rwanda and the Balkans resulted in a re-assessment of the need for national security matters to be tempered by the international legal system. As Professor Bassiouni noted:

> The events in Yugoslavia and Rwanda shocked the world out of its complacency and the idea of prosecuting those who committed international crimes acquired a broad base of support in world public opinion and in many countries (quoted in Butler, 1998, p. 6).

The Tribunal for the former Yugoslavia was established by the Security Council pursuant to unanimous UN Resolutions 808 of February 1993 and 827 of May 1993. This was implemented under Chapter VII of the United Nations Charter and, accordingly, creates a binding obligation on all Member States to assist and cooperate fully with the Tribunal, if so requested (Article 29 of the Statute). The Tribunal has attempted to balance States' concerns over issues of sovereignty, against responding appropriately to the international outcry over violations of international humanitarian law committed in the former Yugoslavia. Thus it can have concurrent jurisdiction with national courts in relation to war crimes and crimes against humanity committed in the territory of the former Yugoslavia since 1991 (Article 91).

However, while attempts have been made to deal with such concerns within the structure of the Tribunal, there are criticisms from many States of the process used to create the ICTY. One controversial issue is that while the Security Council has direct representation from only a few States, all States are technically bound to assist. Furthermore, in appropriate circumstances the Tribunal can exercise primacy over national courts (Article 92). It is also important to note that the Federal Republic of Yugoslavia and other key parties to the Balkan conflict strongly opposed the establishment of the Yugoslav Tribunal.

In November of 1994, pursuant to Security Council Resolution 955, a similar international criminal Tribunal was created to try breaches of international criminal law in Rwanda. Although the Security Council established separate Tribunals for these two regions, it recognised the need to make institutional and organisational links. Thus, the Appeals Chamber of both Tribunals is the same and the Prosecutor for the Yugoslavia Tribunal also serves as a Prosecutor for the Rwanda Tribunal, although extra staff is available and Rwanda has a separate Deputy Prosecutor.

The two International Criminal Tribunals also share the same Rules of Procedure and Evidence. Unlike the Yugoslav government, the Rwandan government supported, at least initially, the establishment of an *ad hoc* international criminal jurisdiction within its own boundaries. However Rwanda eventually voted against the creation of the Tribunal in the Security Council due, among other things, to the international institution's lack of the death penalty.[16] Here rises another irony in the interface between domestic and international war crimes prosecutions. For countries like Rwanda those prosecuted domestically can receive capital punishment while those who stand trial internationally do not face such a penalty.

Due to the fact that the *ad hoc* Tribunals were created through the speedy process of Security Council resolutions rather than the drafting of a treaty, there was limited opportunity for lengthy debate on much of the legal technicalities. The vast bulk of drafting for both Tribunals was done by the United Nations Department of Legal Affairs, thus accounting for the greater influence of common law rather than civil law (Tavernier, 1997).

Perhaps an area where the Tribunals differ most is in subject matter jurisdiction. Both Tribunals have the capacity to try individuals for genocide and the definition is reproduced from the Genocide Convention. Both can try individuals who perpetrate crimes against humanity, although the Rwandan Statute does not require a nexus with armed conflict. While the Tribunal for the former Yugoslavia also has jurisdiction over grave breaches of the Geneva Conventions and war crimes, the fact that the Rwandan conflict is not characterised as 'international' results in the exclusion of these two crimes from its Statutes. Instead, Article 4 of the Rwandan Statute deals with violations of Article 3 common to the Geneva Conventions and Additional Protocol II.

By late 1999, the former Yugoslavian Tribunal had indicted in excess of 91 individuals and had 31 in custody. Recent significant indictments include Slobodan Milosevic, President of the Federal Republic of Yugoslavia, Milan Milutinovic, President of the Republic of Serbia, Nikola Sainovic, Deputy Prime Minister of the Federal Republic of Yugoslavia, Dragoljub Ojdanic, Chief of the General Staff of the Armed Forces of the Federal Republic of Yugoslavia, and Vlajko Stojiljkovic, Minister of Internal Affairs of the Republic of Serbia. The Rwandan Tribunal had indicted 48 persons and had 38 in custody, including individuals such as Jean Kambanda, the former Prime Minister of Rwanda. The judgments from these Tribunals to date have made significant advances in international criminal jurisprudence on topics such as the Security Council's authority to create such bodies; their relationship with national courts; jurisdiction; trials in absentia; evidentiary matters; challenges to Judges and elements of the crimes to name a few.[17] Decisions from these Tribunals have also had a crucial impact on the way the international community views and prosecutes sexual violence (see Askin, 1999).

## The International Criminal Court Statute

### *ILC 1994 Draft Statute*

On 25 November 1992 the General Assembly (GA) requested the International Law Commission to draft a statute for an international criminal court (GA Resolution, 1992). This request was prompted by a specific call from a coalition of Caribbean States, who perceived an international criminal court could assist them with the transnational problem of drug traders (Ferencz, 1992). In 1994 the ILC provided the GA with a Draft Statute (International Law Commission, 1994).

This Draft Statute has been at the core of all recent deliberations on the ICC. The ILC had numerous precedents to consider including the Nuremberg and Tokyo Tribunal Statutes, the 1951 and 1952 draft statutes as well as the ICTY and ICTR Statutes. It also considered the other broad range of crimes under international criminal law such as crimes defined in Conventions dealing with Apartheid;[18] Torture;[19] Hijacking[20] and Drug Trafficking.[21] The five major principles in the ILC draft were:

1) that the ICC should be established by treaty, rather than by resolution of a UN organ (such as the *ad hoc* Tribunals) or as a Charter amendment;

2) that the ICC's subject matter be limited to crimes already articulated in international treaties in force;

3) that the ICC have jurisdiction over private persons as distinct from States;

4) that the ICC should not have compulsory jurisdiction. Rather, jurisdiction would be consensual, thus supplementing rather than substituting national criminal systems;

5) that the ICC not be a full-time standing body, but rather, only be called into operation when it was required.[22]

In submitting the Draft Statute the ILC recommended that the Assembly call a conference to finalise the process. However due to a lack of agreement among the States on a number of issues, an *Ad Hoc* Committee was created to continue discussions. When this Committee failed to arrive at a consensus on the ICC, the GA established a Preparatory Committee (PrepCom) to work with the Draft Statute and to develop 'a widely accepted consolidated text of a convention for an international criminal court as a next step towards consideration by a conference of plenipotentiaries' (GA Resolution, 1995).

Six PrepComs were held at the United Nations in New York from March 1996 until April 1998, discussing at length the proposal and additional elements (for details see Bassiouni, 1997). Not long after the 5th PrepCom of December 1997, the General Assembly proclaimed that a United Nations Conference of Plenipotentiaries on the establishment of an international criminal court would be held in Rome from 15 June to 17 July 1998. The task of this Conference was to finalise the Statute and work towards the establishment of an international criminal court (GA Resolution, 1998).

In order to assist in the consolidation of a text for the purposes of deliberations at the Conference, an inter-sessional meeting was held in January 1998 and a revised 'Zutphen' text was created, gaining its name from the location of the meeting (Report of the Inter-Sessional Meeting, 1998). This text, covered in a mass of square brackets reflecting the huge number of unresolved issues, formed the basis for the 5 weeks of negotiations in Rome.

## The Rome Conference: June-July 1998

The Rome Conference commenced with broad State agreement on the structure of the Draft Statute, the basic framework of the international criminal justice system (including the merging of civil and common law systems) and some of the substantive issues, such as 'complementarity' (the relationship between the ICC and national courts) (Kirsch and Holmes, 1999).

However, much remained to be agreed upon. In order to deal with the mass of work needed to complete its task the Conference created three major organs: the Committee of the Whole, the Drafting Committee and the Plenary. The Committee of the Whole undertook the development of the Statute; the Draft Committee's task was to ensure consistent drafting was used through-out the process; the Plenary was responsible for the organisation of the work, the delivery of States' policies and the formal adoption of the Statute. Numerous informal working groups were held concurrently with the coordinators of these groups reporting the results of their work to the Committee of the Whole. Negotiations and drafting lasted late into the evenings and in the last week, often all night.

Very few of the issues relating to the ICC were uncontroversial. The nature of the institution to be created through the conference touched on a mass of issues layered together—from the obvious State sovereignty concerns and various criminal legal systems, to culturally relative views of matters such as the concept of punishment.[23] As Philippe Kirsch, Chairman of the Committee of the Whole has expressed: '(T)he conference was characterised by a mosaic of positions that transcended political and regional groupings' (Kirsch and Holmes, 1999, p. 4).

However, we can identify a number of 'groupings', including the 'like-minded group' (LMG), which favored a robust and independent ICC. This group was created during the *Ad Hoc* Committee stage and grew significantly at the Rome Conference to over 60 States from all corners of the globe, including a large number of countries from the European Union.[24] The other clear group consisted of the permanent members of the Security Council, which on the whole pushed for a strong role for the Security Council in International Criminal Court matters, particularly relating to jurisdictional matters of the court. States traditionally suspicious of the Security Council and members of the Non-Aligned Movement, in particular countries from the Asian region, wished for the role of the Security Council to be extremely limited and generally pressed the need for an ICC with restrictive powers.

At the Conference the United Kingdom joined the 'like-minded group' despite having previously been a strong player in the Permanent Five, which was often at odds with the like-minded group. It was interesting to note the role the European Union played in negotiations. Fragmented due to France and the UK being members of the Permanent Five, the EU would at times speak as a whole despite differences expressed by the other groups containing its members. Whether it was this internal complexity or the inexperience of the 'new union' at multilateral negotiations, there is no doubt that the EU could potentially be a powerful force during treaty negotiations in the future. However, at the Rome Conference the EU did not come close to rivaling the power of the United States. The split caused by (two) members of the EU also being members of the Permanent Five will require careful analysis in future attempts to develop a single strong policy on international legal and political matters.

The 'mosaic of positions' was most obvious during debates on Part 2 of the Draft Statute which deals with issues of jurisdiction, admissibility and applicable law. This section contains the heart of the ICC, including the list of crimes, State consent requirements and the powers of the Prosecutor. Accordingly, States felt strongly about Part 2 and it was the most sensitive and complex area to negotiate. On the issue of the list of crimes, while the ILC draft had suggested a list including a range of international criminal treaty crimes, there was early discussion that the ICC's jurisdiction should be limited to the 'core' crimes of genocide, crimes against humanity and war crimes. However a large number of States, including Germany, advocated that the crime of aggression should be included despite lack of agreement on definition. Others, including the Caribbean States and Turkey, wished to see treaty crimes such as terrorism and regional drug trafficking remain in the Statute.

The definition of the 'core' crimes was a matter of heated dispute. In the PrepComs suggestions had been made that the definition of genocide, found in the 1948 Genocide Convention, was limited as it excluded intent to destroy political or social groups. Early in the Conference it was agreed that the Genocide Convention definition should stay and that crimes against humanity should 'catch' crimes which would not fall under the strict definition of genocide. Dispute over whether crimes against humanity could be committed in times of peace as well as times of armed conflict reflected the range of varied jurisprudence on this topic. While the Nuremberg and Tokyo proceedings required a strict nexus between such crimes and crimes against peace, the Yugoslav Tribunal does not demand concurrent prosecution of these two crimes and the Rwandan Tribunal cuts the connection altogether. The crimes to be listed under crimes against humanity as well as whether the intent would be 'widespread or systematic attacks' or 'widespread and systematic attacks' were also matters of lengthy deliberations.

The crimes to be listed under the war crimes provision also demonstrated the diversity of States' views. There was little contention on the inclusion of the 'grave breach' provision of the Geneva Conventions[25] nor many concerns expressed relating to the serious violations of the laws and customs applicable in international armed conflict. However the position of crimes committed during non-international armed conflict, other than those listed in common Article 3 of the Geneva Conventions, created great discord. The 'like-minded group' as well as a range of other States argued passionately that the ICC must reflect the reality of massive violations occurring in a great number of non-international armed conflicts currently being waged. However, many countries were not comfortable with the thought of the court having jurisdiction over internal disputes. The proposal that the Prosecutor should be able to initiate investigations on her/his own behalf was also hotly contested as the ILC draft only contemplated States Parties or the Security Council being able to 'trigger' the Court.

Most highly controversial were matters relating to the jurisdiction of the ICC. Issues included whether a ratified State automatically accepted ICC jurisdiction over the listed crimes and which States' consent was required before a case could go before the court. In relation to the former, the ILC draft outlined an intricate 'opt in' system where countries could ratify the Statute choosing on which crimes to accept jurisdiction. With reference to the latter issue, heated debate ensued on whether the consent of the State of the nationality of the accused, the territory where the crimes took place, the nationality of the victims or the State with custody of the accused was required. Some States argued for none of the above, thus giving the ICC 'universal' jurisdiction. Other powerful countries insisted that the consent of the State of the accused was essential.

As the Conference drew to an end, there was still little agreement on much of the substantial area, particularly that found in Part 2. With only two days remaining, and under apprehension that without consensus the negotiation process over the previous five years would unravel, the Bureau of the Conference advised that they would provide a 'package' text. The 'package' was developed by the Chairman and other members of the Bureau in consultation with various delegations, taking into account the various options canvassed over the last five weeks of debate. The 'package' was eagerly awaited by all State delegates and NGOs and became available on the morning of the last day of the Conference. That evening a meeting of the Committee of the Whole was called and India and the United Nations proposed amendments to the 'package' that were not widely supported. The Conference then moved to the Plenary where, due to concerns primarily relating to the State consent requirements of the 'package', the United States called for a vote, whereupon 120 countries voted in favor, 21 abstained and 7 voted against. The world had a Statute for an ICC which had gained overwhelming support.

## The Rome Statute, 1998

The Rome Statute is divided into 13 parts consisting of 128 Articles fronted by a preamble.[26] Two major principles underlying the creation of the ICC are mentioned in the preamble as well as being articulated in specific Articles. The first is that it is not a legal institution which aims to replace domestic courts. Several references are made to the fact that the ICC is complementary to national criminal jurisdictions and the preamble recalls: 'that it is the duty of every State to exercise its criminal jurisdiction over those responsible for international crimes' (Rome Statute of the International Criminal Court, 1998, Preamble). The second is that the Rome Statute has jurisdiction over only the most serious crimes of concern to the international community as a whole. The preamble recognises that 'such grave crimes threaten the peace, security and well-being of the world'. The preamble reaffirms the purpose and principles of the Charter of the United Nations and mentions 'States' and 'peoples'. No reference is given to individuals, nor is the connection between peace and justice, deterrence, or protection of victims mentioned.

Part 1 of the Statute determines that the ICC will be a permanent institution and will be established in The Hague with the ability to sit elsewhere when desirable. International legal personality is given to the Court and the 'legal capacity as may be necessary for the exercise of its functions and the fulfillment of its purposes' (Article 4). The relationship between the ICC and the United Nations is not stipulated and rather will be agreed upon by the Assembly of States Parties to the Rome Statute.

As noted, Part 2 is the heart of the ICC, dealing with jurisdiction, admissibility and applicable law, and was by far the most controversial and highly negotiated section. Thus this part will be dealt with in more detail than other provisions. Article 5 of the Statute lists the crimes within the jurisdiction of the ICC including: the crime of genocide, crimes against humanity, war crimes, and the crime of aggression. As States could not reach consensus on the definition of aggression, Article 5(2) states: 'The Court shall exercise jurisdiction over (this crime) once a provision is adopted ... defining the crime and setting out the conditions under which the Court shall exercise jurisdiction with respect to this crime'.

The definition of genocide reflects that of the Genocide Convention (Article 6). The definition of crimes against humanity does not demand a nexus to armed conflict and requires 'widespread or systematic attack directed at any civilian population'. The list of such crimes includes murder; extermination; forcible transfer of population; torture; persecution; enforced disappearance; Apartheid and 'other inhumane acts of a similar nature' (Article 7). Article 7 also includes a specific and detailed list of crimes concerning sexual violence, including rape, sexual slavery, and enforced pregnancy.

The war crimes provision states that the ICC shall have jurisdiction in respect of 'war crimes in particular when committed as part of a plan or policy or as part of a large-scale commission of such crimes', thus not creating a strict threshold (Article 8(1)). Grave breaches of the Geneva Conventions are included as well as other serious violations of the laws and customs applicable in international armed conflict (Article 8(2)). Article 8 also lists the provisions of Article 3 common to the four Geneva Conventions, as well as a range of crimes committed in non-international armed conflict such as attacking civilians not taking part in hostilities (Article 8(2)(i)); attacking humanitarian workers (Article 8(2)(ii)); sexual violence (Article 8(2)(vi)) and actively using children under the age of 15 in hostilities (Article 8(2)(vii)).

In order for the ICC to exercise jurisdiction, either the State on the territory in which the act occurs or the State of which the person being investigated is a national must be a State Party (Article 12). A State Party, the Security Council or the Prosecutor can initiate an investigation (Article 13) but only when a State with primary jurisdiction over the matter is 'unwilling or unable genuinely to carry out the investigation or prosecution' (Article 17). The applicable law is listed as not only the Statute but also: 'Applicable treaties and principles and rules of international law, including the established principles of international law of armed conflict' (Article 20).

Part 3 covers general principles of criminal law laying down the required mental element as well as the grounds for excluding criminal responsibility. Purporting the principle of *nullum crimen sine lege*[27] the Rome Statute makes it very clear that the ICC will not have retroactive jurisdiction nor be subject to any statute of limitations. The Court will not be able to prosecute individuals who, at the time of committing the crime, are under the age of 18 years. Military commanders and other superiors are liable for their acts and omissions in relation to subordinates (Article 25). Furthermore the claim of superior orders will not ordinarily relieve an individual of criminal responsibility (Article 32).

Part 4 deals with the composition and administration of the ICC, setting out the organs of the Court which include the Presidency; an Appeals, Trial and Pre-Trial Division; Office of the Prosecutor and the Registry (Article 35). Details relating to the qualification and election of the 18 judges are articulated. The need for judges to be independent is noted (Article 41) as well as the need to select judges with equitable representation based on principal legal systems, geography and gender (Article 37(8)). Candidates for election to the Court need to have competence in criminal law and procedure or international law and will be elected by the highest number of votes at a secret ballot of the Assembly of States Parties. The Prosecutor will be elected by an absolute majority of a secret ballot of the Assembly of States Parties and shall head the Office of the Prosecutor which is deemed to act independently as a separate organ of the ICC (Article 43). Part 4 also states that Rules of Procedure and Evidence will enter into force upon the adoption by a two-thirds majority of the members of the Assembly of States Parties (Article 52).

Part 5 focuses upon the area of investigation and prosecution including the initiation of an investigation (Article 53) as well as the rights to persons during investigations (Article 55). In relation to the duties and powers of the Prosecutor with respect to investigations, reference is made to the need for the Prosecutor to potentially enter into arrangements with States, intergovernmental organisations and persons (Article 54(3)). Following this, Part 6 requires that the accused be present at a fair and expeditious trial and that full respect is accorded to the rights of the accused (Article 64) as well as the protection of victims and witnesses (Article 68). There will be a presumption of innocence in all cases (Article 66) and the ICC shall establish principles of reparation to victims (Article 75).

Part 7 outlines the applicable penalties which include imprisonment not exceeding a maximum of 30 years or a term of life 'when justified by the extreme gravity of the crime' (Article 75(1)). The ICC can also impose a fine and forfeiture of proceeds, property and assets derived directly or indirectly from the crime (Article 75(2)). A Trust fund shall be established for the victims, and their families (Article 79). Part 8 lists the grounds on which the Prosecutor and convicted person can appeal (Article 80). Judgments by the Trial Chamber may be revised by the Appeals Chamber (Article 83) and compensation for an unlawfully convicted individual may also be granted (Article 84).

Part 9 addresses international cooperation and judicial assistance stating that States Parties shall cooperate fully with the ICC in investigations and the prosecution of relevant crimes (Article 86). States Parties shall ensure that there are domestic procedures available under their national laws to facilitate cooperation (Article 88). Matters such as the surrender of persons to the Court (Article 89) as well as competing requests (Article 90) are dealt with. When a State Party fails to comply with a request from the ICC the court will refer the matter on to the Assembly of States Parties or the Security Council if this is where the matter was referred from (Article 87(7)). Part 10 provides that the sentence of imprisonment shall be served in a State chosen by the ICC from a list of States indicating their willingness to accept the prisoner (Article 103). Part 11 sets out the role of the Assembly of States Parties allowing each State Party one representative with one vote and those who have signed the Statute observer capacity (Article 112).

Finances are covered in Part 12 with funds provided by assessed contributions made by States Parties and the United Nations (Article 115) and voluntary contributions from Governments, international organisations, individuals, corporations and other entities (Article 116). Part 13 deals with final clauses. No reservations may be entered into (Article 120), however there is the capacity for States to declare that they do not accept the ICC's jurisdiction over war crimes (Article 8) for a period of 7 years (Article 124). State Parties can propose amendments seven years after the Rome Statute enters into force and these would be adopted by a vote of two-thirds of the majority of States Parties (Article 121). The ICC will enter into force on the first day of the month after the 60th ratification.[28]

## Conclusion

It is naive to assume that the development of the International Criminal Court will result in the complete eradication of breaches of international criminal law or revolutionise human behaviour. However, such a court reflects the reality that crimes are committed by individuals rather than by abstract entities and that it is thus essential to develop an international system that punishes individuals. Due to the fact that the ICC will be created through a treaty and includes carefully drafted requirements of State consent, it may be argued that it does not dramatically erode State sovereignty. It does however reflect the growing realisation of the need to protect fundamental human rights, both during times of armed conflict and 'peace'. It also reflects a shift from 'national security' to 'human security'—leaders can no longer do what they want with their own people. The rule of law, which protects individuals, can be enforced.

As the year 2000 marks the end of the most violent century in history, the development of the Statute for the ICC indicates that a vast number of States acknowledge the need for a permanent international legal institution to end impunity for those who commit atrocities.

# Notes

1    Articles refer to the relevant section of the *Rome Statute of the International Criminal Court*, 1998.

2    Raising the historical and political complexities of the Eichmann trial, Hannah Arendt (1994), wrote: 'it was history that, as far as the prosecution was concerned, stood in the center of the trial'. See also Simpson (1997).

3    In 1993 Amnesty International wrote: 'the real danger is that *ad hoc* tribunals will be no more than a token political gesture, set up to satisfy short-term political interests of States' (Amnesty International, 1993, p.ii.).

4    Meron (1994, p.87) writes: 'the reaction of the international community to the appalling abuses in the former Yugoslavia has brought about certain advances in international criminal and humanitarian law'.

5    *Geneva Convention on the High Seas*, opened for signature 29 April 1958, entered into force 30 September 1962. As at 11 May 1999, there were 62 States Parties.

6    *Geneva Convention for the Amelioration of the Condition of the Wounded and the Sick in Armed Forces in the Field*, (First Geneva Convention); *Geneva Convention for the Amelioration of the Condition of Wounded, Sick and Shipwrecked Members of Armed Forces at Sea*, (Second Geneva Convention); *Geneva Convention Relative to the Treatment of Prisoners of War*, (Third Geneva Convention); *Geneva Convention Relative to the Protection of Civilian Persons in Time of War*, (Fourth Geneva Convention). All opened for signature 12 August 1949; entered into force on 21 October 1950; as at 28 October 1998, there were 188 States Parties.

7    *Agreement for the Prosecution and Punishment of Major War Criminals of the European Axis*, 8 August 1945, art 6(c) (*'Nuremberg Charter'*).

8    *Agreement for the Prosecution and Punishment of major War Criminals of the European Axis*, 8 August 1945, art 6(c) (*'Nuremberg Charter'*).

9    *Convention on the Prevention and Punishment of the Crime of Genocide*, opened for signature 9 December 1948; entered into force 12 January 1951. As at 11 May 1999, there were 129 States Parties.

10   *Supplementary Convention on the Abolition of Slavery, the Slave Trade and Institutions and Practices Similar to Slavery*, opened for signature 7 September 1956.

11   Convention for the Suppression of the Traffic in Persons and of the Exploitations of the Prostitution of Others and Final Protocol, opened for signature 21 March 1950, entered into force 25 July 1951. As at 11 May 1999, there were 72 States Parties.

12   *Single Convention on Narcotic Drugs, 1961, as amended by the Protocol of 25 March 1972 amending the Single Convention on Narcotic Drugs, 1961*, 8 August 1975; as at 11 May 1999, there were 154 States Parties. *Convention on Psychotropic Substances*, opened for signature 21 February 1971, entered into force 16 August 1976; as at 11 May 1999, there were 159 States Parties. *Convention Against Illicit Traffic in Narcotic Drugs and Psychotropic Substances*, opened for signature 20 December 1988, entered into force 11 November 1990; as at 11 May 1999, there were 153 States Parties.

[13] For a detailed analysis of these crimes see Alston and Steiner (1996).

[14] For a full examination of post World War I and World War II Developments see McCormack (1997).

[15] For details on trials held in Europe see Marschik (1997).

[16] The vote of Resolution 955 was adopted with 13 votes for, China abstained and Rwanda voted against (Sunga, 1997, p.5).

[17] For a detailed examination of recent legal developments in the ICTY see Murphy (1999).

[18] *International Convention on the Suppression and Punishment of the Crime of Apartheid* (1973).

[19] *Convention Against Torture and Other Cruel, Inhuman or Degrading Treatment or Punishment.*

[20] *Convention for the Suppression of Unlawful Acts against the Safety of Civil Aviation* (1971).

[21] *Convention against Illicit Traffic in Narcotic Drugs and Psychotropic Substances* (1988).

[22] For a full discussion on the ILC draft see Crawford (1995).

[23] For example a number of countries advocating, unsuccessfully, for the death penalty were adamant that sentences involving life imprisonment were too cruel to contemplate.

[24] The number of countries who are members of the 'like-minded' group is always in a state of flux, however it encompasses all corners of the globe. In June 1998 it numbered approximately 60 and included a large number of members of the European Union (excluding France) as well as nations such as Australia, Canada, Chile, Egypt, Finland, Malawi, New Zealand, Republic of Korea, Uruguay and Venezuela.

[25] *Geneva Conventions*, see note 6 above.

[26] The thirteen parts consist of 1) Establishment of the Court; 2) Jurisdiction, Admissibility and Applicable Laws; 3) General Principles of Criminal Law; 4) Composition and Administration of the Court; 5) Investigation and Prosecution; 6) The Trial; 7) Penalties; Appeal and Revision; 9) International Cooperation and Judicial Assistance; 10) Enforcement; 11) Assembly of States Parties; 12) Financing; and 13) Final Clauses.

[27] A person shall not be criminally responsible under this Statute unless the conduct in question constitutes, at the time it takes place, a crime within the jurisdiction of the Court' (Article 21(1)).

[28] As of May 1999 over 87 States have signed the Rome Statute; four States—San Marino, Senegal, Trinidad and Tobago, and Italy—have ratified.

# References

Albright, M. (1994), 'Address at the US Holocaust Museum', *USIA Wireless File* EUR 303, 13 April 1994, p. 4.

Alston, P. and Steiner, H. (1996), 'Universal Jurisdiction and International Crimes', in *International Human Rights in Context: Law, Politics, Morals*, Clarendon Press, Oxford, pp. 1021–1040.

Amnesty International (1993), *The question of Justice and Fairness in the International War Crimes Tribunal for the Former Yugoslavia*, AI International Secretariat, London.

Annan, K. (1998), 'The Gift of Hope to Future Generations', *International Criminal Court Up-date 4*, Australian Red Cross, Melbourne.

Arendt, H. (1994), E*ichmann in Jerusalem—A Report on the Banality of Evil*, Penguin Books, New York.

Askin, K. (1999), 'Sexual Violence in Decisions and Indictments of the Yugoslav and Rwandan Tribunals: Current Status', *American Journal of International Law*, Vol. 93, No. 1, pp. 97–123.

Bassiouni, C. (1997), 'Observations Concerning the 1997-98 Preparatory Committee's Work' (Report of the International Law Association), *Denver Journal of International Law and Policy*, Vol. 25, No. 2, pp. 397–421.

Bronkhorst, D. (1995), *Truth and Reconciliation: Obstacles and Opportunities for Human Rights*, Amnesty International (Dutch Section), Amsterdam.

Butler, A. (1998), *The Establishment of a Permanent International Criminal Court: A Selective and Annotated Bibliography*, Rutgers, State University of New Jersey, New Jersey.

Crawford, J. (1995), 'The ILC Adopts a Statute for an International Criminal Court', *American Journal of International Law*, Vol. 89, No. 2, pp. 405–416.

Ferencz, B. (1980), *An International Criminal Court: A Step Towards World Peace—A Documentary History and Analysis,* Oceana Publications, New York.

Ferencz, B. (1992), 'An International Criminal Code and Court: Where They Stand and Where They're Going', *Columbia Journal of Transnational Law,* Vol. 30, No. 3, pp. 375–399.

Hall, C. (1998), 'The First Proposal for a Permanent International Criminal Court', *International Review of the Red Cross,* pp. 57–74.

ILA (1926), 'Proposal for an International Criminal Court', *Report of the Thirty-Fourth Conference of the International Law Association*, ILA, Vienna, August 11.

International Law Commission (1994), *Report of the International Law Commission on the Work of its 49th Session*, GAOR 49th Session, Supp.10/90, UN Doc. A/49/10.

International Military Tribunal (1945), 'Rules of Procedure of the International Military Tribunal', *Trial of Major War Criminals,* Vol. 1, pp. 19–23.

International Military Tribunal (1947), 'Trial of the Major War Criminals Before the International Military Tribunal, Nuremberg (1945-46), Judgement', reprinted in 'Judicial Decisions', *American Journal of International Law*, Vol. 41, Winter, p. 17.

King, H. (1994), 'The Limitations of Sovereignty from Nuremberg to Sarajevo', *Canada-United States Law Journal*, Vol. 20, pp. 167–175.

Kirsch, P. and Holmes, J. (1999), 'The Rome Conference on an International Criminal Court: The Negotiating Process', *American Journal of International Law,* Vol. 93, No. 1, pp. 2–12.

Marschik, A. (1997), 'The Politics of Prosecution: European National Approaches to War Crimes', in T. McCormack and G. Simpson (eds), *The Law of War Crimes: National and International Approaches*, Kluwer Law International, The Hague, pp. 65–101.

McCormack, T. (1997), 'From Sun Tzu to the Sixth Committee', in T. McCormack and G. Simpson (eds), *The Law of War Crimes: National and International Approaches*, Kluwer Law International, The Hague, pp. 31–63.

McCormack, T. and Simpson, G. (eds) (1997), *The Law of War Crimes: National and International Approaches*, Kluwer Law International, The Hague.

Meron, T. (1994), 'War Crimes in Yugoslavia and the Development of International Law', *American Journal of International Law*, Vol. 88, No. 1, January, pp. 78–87.

Murphy, S. (1999), 'Progress and Jurisprudence of the International Criminal Tribunal for the Former Yugoslavia', *American Journal of International Law*, Vol. 93, No. 1, pp. 57–97.

Simpson, G. (1997), 'War Crimes: A Critical Introduction', in T. McCormack and G. Simpson (eds), *The Law of War Crimes: National and International Approaches*, Kluwer Law International, The Hague.

Sunga, L.S. (1997), *The Emerging System of International Criminal Law—Developments in Codification and Implementation*, Kluwer Law International, The Hague.

Tavernier, P. (1997), 'The experience of the International Criminal Tribunals for the former Yugoslavia and for Rwanda', *International Review of the Red Cross*, Vol. 321, pp. 605–621.

Thiam, D. (1989), 'The need to better clarify the concept of Crimes of States', in J. Weiler, A. Cassese and M. Spinedi (eds), *International Crimes of State: A Critical Analysis of the ILC's Draft Article 19 on State Responsibility*, De Gruyter, Berlin, pp. 279–82.

Wolfe, R. (1998), 'Flaws in the Nuremberg Legacy: An Impediment to International War Crimes Tribunals' Prosecution of Crimes Against Humanity', *Holocaust and Genocide Studies*, Vol. 12, No. 2, pp. 434–53.

Zuroff, E. (1994), *Occupation: Nazi-hunter—the Continuing Search for the Perpetrators of the Holocaust*, KTAV in association with the Simon Wiesenthal Center, New Jersey.

## Charters, Conventions and Statutes

*Agreement for the Prosecution and Punishment of Major War Criminals of the European Axis* (1945), 8 August, 8 UNTS, 279 ('*Nuremberg Charter*').

*Charter of the United Nations* (1945), United Nations, New York, Chapter VII.

*Charter of the International Military Tribunal* (1945), 8 August, 56 Stat. 1544, 82 UNTS 279.

*Charter of the International Military Tribunal for the Far East* (1945), August, TIAS No. 1589.

*Convention Against Illicit Traffic in Narcotic Drugs and Psychotropic Substances* (1988), 20 December, UN Doc. E/CONF.82/15.

*Convention Against Torture and Other Cruel, Inhuman or Degrading Treatment or Punishment* 39 UN GAOR, UN Doc. A/RES/39/46.

*Convention for the Suppression of the Traffic in Persons and of the Exploitations of the Prostitution of Others* and *Final Protocol* (1950), 21 March, 96 UNTS 271.

*Convention for the Suppression of Unlawful Acts against the Safety of Civil Aviation*, Montreal (1971), 23 September, 974 UNTS 177.

*Convention on Psychotropic Substances* (1971), 21 February, 1019 UNTS 175.

*Convention on the Prevention and Punishment of the Crime of Genocide* (1948), 9 December, 78 UNTS 277.

*Draft Code of Crimes Against the Peace and Security of Mankind* (1954), 9 UN GAOR (Supp. No. 9), UN Doc. A/2693.

*Draft Statute for an International Criminal Court Report* (Annex to the Report of the Committee on International Criminal Jurisdiction (1952), 31 August 1951, GAOR Supp. 11, UN Doc. A/2136.

*GA Resolution 47/33*, UN GAOR, 47th Sess., (1992), Agenda Item 3, UN Doc. A/RES/47/33.

*GA Resolution 49/53*, UN GAOR, 49th Sess., (1994), Supp. No. 49, UN Doc. A/49/49.

*GA Resolution 50/46*, UN GAOR, 50th Sess., (1995), Agenda Item 142, 2, UN Doc. A/RES/50/46.

GA Resolution 52/207, UN GAOR 52nd Sess., (1998), Agenda Item 150, 3, UN Doc. A/RES/52/160.

*Geneva Convention for the Amelioration of the Condition of the Wounded and the Sick in Armed Forces in the Field* (1949), 12 August, 75 UNTS 31.

*Geneva Convention for the Amelioration of the Condition of Wounded, Sick and Ship-wrecked Members of Armed Forces at Sea* (1949), 12 August, 75 UNTS 85.

*Geneva Convention on the High Seas* (1958), 29 April, 450 UNTS 82.

*Geneva Convention Relative to the Protection of Civilian Persons in Time of War* (1949), 12 August, 75 UNTS 287.

*Geneva Convention Relative to the Treatment of Prisoners of War* (1949) 12 August, 75 UNTS 135.

*International Convention on the Suppression and Punishment of the Crime of Apartheid* (1973), 30 November, GA Resolution 3068, 28 UN GAOR (Supp.30), UN Doc. A/RES/3068.

*Report of the Inter-Sessional Meeting from 19-30 January 1998* (1998), UN Doc. A/AC.249/1998/L.13, Zutphen, The Netherlands.

*Revised Draft Statute for an International Criminal Court* (1954), (Annex to the Report of the Committee on International Criminal Jurisdiction, 20 August 1953), 9 GAOR Supp.12, UN Doc. A/2645

*Rome Statute of the International Criminal Court* (1998), adopted by the United Nations Diplomatic Conference of Plenipotentiaries on the Establishment of an International Criminal Court on 17 July; 37 ILM 1002, Rome.

*Single Convention on Narcotic Drugs, 1961, as amended by the Protocol of 25 March 1972*, (1975), 8 August, 976 UNTS, 105.

*Statute of the International Tribunal for the Prosecution of Persons Responsible for Genocide and Other Serious Violations of International Humanitarian Law Committed in the Territory of Rwanda and Rwandan Citizens Responsible for Genocide and Other Violations Committed in the Territory of Neighbouring States, Between 1 January 1994 and 31 December 1994*, SC Resolution 955, 49 UN SCOR (3453rd meeting), UN Doc. S/RES/955 (1994); ('*Statute of the ICTR*').

*Statute of the International Tribunal for the Prosecution of Persons Responsible for Serious Violations of International Humanitarian Law Committed in the Territory of the Former Yugoslavia since 1991* (1993), SC Resolution 827, 48 UN SCOR (3217th meeting), UN Doc. S/Res/827; ('*Statute of the ICTY*').

*Supplementary Convention on the Abolition of Slavery, the Slave Trade and Institutions and Practices Similar to Slavery* (1956), 7 September, 266 UNTS 3.

# 11 Fundamental Rights, National Sovereignty and Europe's New Citizens

STEPHEN HALL

The fieriest ingredients spicing public debates about European integration are undoubtedly those which most clearly engage aspects of national sovereignty. The stubborn attachment by most Europeans to their own states as a primary focus of allegiance is a momentous obstacle to the achievement of that federal European *patria* which was the principal motivating impulse of the European Union's founders half a century ago.[1] This attachment persists as an article of faith for a large section of the European political class. It seems clear, however, that the EU's Member States 'remain, for their peoples, the principal focus of collective loyalty and the principal forum of democratic political activity' (Dashwood, 1996, p. 113).

Indeed the European continent has, especially since the end of the Cold War and the decline of liberal Europe's principal external threat, witnessed a resurgence of national aspirations. This manifests itself increasingly in the very nineteenth century desire to make the 'nation' co-extensive with the state. In this connection one may consider German reunification, national separations in Yugoslavia, Czechoslovakia and the Soviet Union and an intensification of fissiparous nationalist or quasi-nationalist developments in Belgium, Italy, Spain and the United Kingdom. Like their nineteenth century progenitors, these developments are mostly embedded in a broadly liberal and democratic context, rather than in the setting of the twentieth century's totalitarian perversions.

Parallel and complementary to these strands is an increased awareness of Europe's possibilities, and especially the many-faceted success of the European Union. The fact that the EU has helped deliver an unprecedented level of economic prosperity, and hence of political stability, to its Member States is a rightly prized achievement. It is also a powerful attraction to aspiring members most of whom are struggling to repair the vast damage wrought on their societies by decades of brutality and neglect. Equally prized and attractive is the fact that the EU 'is an economic community, of course, but is also a security community—a group of states that do find it unthinkable to resolve their own differences by war' (Garton Ash, 1998, p. 61).

This confluence of European and resurgent national aspirations throws into sharper relief the question of the extent to which the nation state can exist inside the EU while simultaneously retaining that vital attribute of statehood—national sovereignty. This is not at all a new issue, and it is of course widely understood that joining the EU is a step of the most profound importance for a state's national sovereignty in fields such as foreign and security policy, immigration, and most aspects of economic policy including monetary policy.

My present purpose is to show that important diminutions of national sovereignty result not only from these 'usual suspect' areas of EU competence, but also from the gradual emergence of the individual as the beneficiary of the Community's unwritten and steadily-unwinding code of fundamental rights, and the establishment of a *de jure* citizenship of the Union. We will see, furthermore, that the diminution of national sovereignty involved in EU membership is, as a matter of Community law, a permanent transfer or loss of sovereignty and not a temporary arrangement which can be reversed by an exercise of national sovereign will.

## Fundamental Rights in Community Law

The peoples of the European Union, some 370 million in number, are the subject of human rights law over a wide range of topics and at an impressive number of levels. Indeed they are, in purely legal terms, probably the most human rights-protected people in world history. Each of the fifteen EU Member States has its own national system of human rights protection, almost all of them extending beyond the ordinary law to national constitutional entrenchment.[2] Sub-national sovereign units such as the Austrian *Bundesländer* and the German *Länder* provide complementary constitutional guarantees of fundamental rights, while regional and municipal authorities in all the Member States typically adopt and apply ordinary laws protecting the civil and political rights of the individual.

Additionally, the EU's peoples are the subject of international legal regimes protecting human rights. All the Member States of the EU are parties to the United Nation's International Covenant on Civil and Political Rights and the International Covenant on Economic Social and Cultural Rights. More significantly still, the Fifteen are also parties to the Council of Europe's Convention for the Protection of Human Rights and Fundamental Freedoms (ECHR) and the European Social Charter.

However the legal protection of human rights for the peoples of the EU is not limited to the national, sub-national and classically international levels. The mostly dry and economically technical law of the European Communities has, over the last thirty years, been increasingly informed by a jurisprudence of human rights protection. This process has now advanced to the point where it is possible to characterise the Community legal order, which is neither a national nor a classically international system, as an important additional source of human rights law. European Community law's ever-increasing reach, combined with the emergence of a European Community human rights jurisprudence, has transformed this once seemingly arcane and remote legal system into one which is much more clearly perceived to be of direct and increasing concern to hundreds of millions of Europeans.

There is no legally binding written charter of human rights in European Community law. Although there has over the years been some official consideration given to the Community becoming a party to the ECHR, the European Court of Justice[3] has recently ruled that the Community may not take this step (Opinion 2/94, 1996).

This does not mean that there is not a system of fundamental rights protection in the Community's constitutional law. There has emerged a fairly extensive array of constitutional human rights principles with which laws made under or pursuant to the Community treaties must conform. Once again, the Court of Justice is responsible for this development.

After some reluctance to admit fundamental principles of human rights protection at the very early stage of the Community's history, (*Friedrich Stork & Co v High Authority*, 1959 and *Geitling Ruhrkohlen-Verkaufsgesellschaft mbH v High Authority*, 1960), the Court in 1969 forever changed the complexion of Community law. In a case about whether certain details of Community legislation providing subsidised butter to social welfare recipients violated the German *Grundgesetz*'s (Basic Law) protection of human dignity, the Court declared that the Community legislation properly interpreted 'contains nothing capable of prejudicing the fundamental human rights enshrined in the general principles of Community law and protected by the Court' (*Stauder v City of Ulm Sozialamt*, 1969, p. 425).

In writing these words the Court left tantalisingly uncertain the sources and content of Community law's enshrined fundamental human rights. Lawyers were left to ponder, worry and argue about this issue for another thirteen months until the Court partly lifted the veil by saying that the Community's principles of fundamental rights are 'inspired by the constitutional traditions common to the Member States' (*Internationale Handelsgesellschaft mbH v Einfuhr- und Vorratsstelle für Getreide und Futtermittel*, 1970, p. 1134). We were more fully initiated into the Court's mysteries after a further delay of over three years when we were told that, in addition to fundamental rights being inspired by the Member States' constitutional traditions, 'international treaties for the protection of human rights on which the Member States have collaborated or of which they are signatories, can supply guidelines which should be followed within the framework of Community law' (*J Nold, Kohlen- und Baustoffgrosshandlung v Commission*, 1974, p. 507).

Since these initial three cases spanning the period 1969-1974, the Court of Justice has considered arguments based on Community law's protection of fundamental rights on a large number of occasions. In so doing the Court has said that it will in principle protect a wide range of interests as falling within the scope of fundamental rights, including *inter alia* religious freedom, (*Prais v Council*, 1976); right to respect for private and family life, (*Demirel v Stadt Schwäbisch Gmünd*, 1987); property rights (*Hauer v Land Rheinland-Pfalz*, 1979; *SpA Ferriera Valsabbia v Commission*, 1980; *Hermann Schräder HS Kraftfutter GmbH & Co v Hauptzollamt Gronau*, 1989); right to a fair hearing, (*Pecastaing v Belgian State*, 1980; *SA Musique Diffusion Française v Commission*, 1983); right to privacy (*National Panasonic (UK) Ltd v Commission*, 1980); and freedom of expression. (*Vereniging ter Bevordering van het Vlaamse Boekwezen v Commission*, 1984; *Oyowe v Commission*, 1989; *Elliniki Radiophonia Tileorassi AE v Dimotiki Etairia Pliroforissis*, 1991).

The vast majority of these cases have not resulted in any Community law or administrative action being successfully challenged for inconsistency with the Community's system of fundamental rights protection. Indeed, the infrequency with which a plea based on infringement of fundamental rights has been accepted by the Court has led some observers to conclude that the Court does not take fundamental rights seriously and that it adopts a purely instrumentalist approach to fundamental rights protection (Coppel and O'Neill, 1992, p. 227). According to this view the Court will allow a fundamental right to trump a legislative or executive act only where such a course would assist, or at least not in any way impede, the big-picture project of European integration.

It is not presently my task to evaluate this unflattering view of the Court's approach to fundamental rights protection; suffice it for present purposes to say that it has been vigorously and comprehensively contested (Weiler and Lockhart, 1995). There are, however, not many examples which can be given of Community law fundamental rights being successfully pleaded. Two examples will serve to illustrate this exceptional phenomenon.

Community fundamental rights principles were successfully pleaded in *R v Kirk* (1984) in which a Council regulation authorising the United Kingdom to impose penal sanctions in respect of certain fishing activities was annulled to the extent that it purported to authorise such sanctions retrospectively. The Court held that protection from retrospective penal sanctions is among the general principles of Community law protecting fundamental freedoms. Another rare example is to be found in *Razzouk v Commission* (1984) in which a Commission decision was annulled. The decision granted the husband of a deceased Commission employee a widower's pension at a rate lower than a widow's pension payable to an employee's surviving wife in materially identical circumstances. The Court held that the decision violated the fundamental Community principle of equal treatment of both sexes.

The Court has referred to a number of international treaties and national constitutional provisions in the course of expounding the Community's fundamental rights principles. The most important of these sources is undoubtedly the ECHR, and there are now numerous examples of the Court referring to the text of the ECHR in order to assist in the formulation of a corresponding Community law principle. The Court of Justice has however significantly declined ever to refer to the case law of the European Court of Human Rights, although it has noted the lack of such case law on a particular point (*Hoechst AG v Commission*, 1989).

It is important to remember that the ECHR, other human rights treaties and national constitutional provisions are not as such binding in Community law or on the Court of Justice. They merely furnish guidelines which the Court of Justice may employ in developing the Community's own autonomous principles of fundamental rights protection.[4]

## Loss of National Sovereignty and Community Fundamental Rights

The emergence of a Community system of human rights protection does not, of itself, necessarily imply any restriction on the national sovereignty of the individual Member States additional to those required by other branches of Community law. To the extent that the principles of Community human rights law act simply as a restriction on the legislative and executive power of the Community's own institutions, the existence of such a body of law will not affect the Member States' sovereign freedom of action.

On the contrary a system such as this would, if anything, tend to enhance the Member States' sovereignty by placing potentially important restrictions on the extent to which Community institutions could affect the lives and affairs of the Member States' citizens. This was essentially how the United States Bill of Rights worked until the US Supreme Court's landmark 1925 decision in *Gitlow v New York*[5] 'nationalised' the Bill of Rights by extending its applicability from the federal government to the acts of the country's constituent States.

Has the Community's unwritten Bill of Rights, inspired mainly by the ECHR and national constitutional traditions, been 'nationalised' in the sense that it operates as a legal restraint on the Member States' freedom of action, or does it simply impose restrictions on the Community's powers?

Up until the mid-1980s no decision of the Court of Justice even suggested that national laws could be invalid or inapplicable by virtue of conflict with a Community fundamental rights principle. In 1984 the Court of Justice in *R v Kirk* held, as we have seen, that the fundamental freedoms protected by Community law prevented a Community regulation from retrospectively authorising the adoption of a national law imposing criminal liability. Without the authorising Community regulation, the national law was inconsistent with Community law and could not be applied by the national courts. Thus national measures can be *indirectly* struck down when an authorising Community measure fails to meet the Community's human rights standards.

The following year the Court of Justice, in *Cinéthèque SA v Fédération nationale des cinémas français* (1985) signalled that this might be as far as it was prepared to go. The Court refused to declare as inconsistent with the Treaty, French measures forbidding the commercial release on video of cinematographic works within one year of issue of their cinema performance certificates. The complaint was that the restriction was inconsistent with Community law's guarantee of freedom of expression.

In this connection, the Court said that although it had a duty to ensure the observance of the Community's fundamental rights 'in the field of Community law', it had no power to do so in 'an area which falls within the jurisdiction of the national legislator' (p. 2627). The impugned French measures did 'enter the field of Community law'; the Court expressly acknowledged that measures of the sort under challenge 'may create barriers to intra-Community trade in video-cassettes' (p. 2626). But they were still measures which the Member State was entitled to adopt. The *Cinéthèque* Court was therefore saying that any attack on grounds of human rights violations must be directed at measures adopted by the Community institutions themselves, and that national measures are unimpeachable on these grounds even if they 'enter the field of Community law'.

There has since been a subtle, but highly significant, reorientation in the Court's approach to the application of the Community's fundamental rights principles to national measures. A hint of a change in the Court's direction appeared in 1987 in *Demirel v Stadt Schwäbisch Gmünd* (1987), two years after *Cinéthèque*. The Court of Justice was asked whether Article 8 ECHR (right to respect for private and family life) affected a decision by German authorities to order a Turkish national, the wife of a Turkish worker resident in Germany, to leave the country. The Court held that no relevant provision of the EEC-Turkey Association Agreement was directly effective and there was no legislation adopted under that agreement which could confer on the Turkish woman a right to remain in the Community on family reunion or other grounds. After repeating the formula in *Cinéthèque* the Court said:

> In this case ... there is at present no provision of Community law defining the conditions in which Member States must permit the family reunification of Turkish workers lawfully settled in the Community. It follows that the national rules at issue in the main proceedings did not have to implement a provision of Community law. In those circumstances, the Court does not have jurisdiction to determine whether national rules such as those at issue are compatible with the principles enshrined in Article 8 of the European Convention on Human Rights (*Ibid.*, p. 3754).

Although apparently following *Cinéthèque*, the Court was actually signalling an imminent departure. Now it was suggested, for the first time, that certain national measures could be tested against the Community's human rights standards. National measures implementing Community rules might have to pass the test.

The Court's reorientation manifested itself openly in 1989 in *Wachauf v Federal Republic of Germany* (1989). The Court of Justice was invited to invalidate a Council regulation which allegedly authorised the adoption of a German order depriving compensation to tenant farmers who, without their landlords' consent, surrendered their milk production quotas. The regulation was asserted to be invalid for violation of a fundamental right against unconstitutional expropriation without compensation:

> [I]t must be observed that Community rules which, upon the expiry of the lease, had the effect of depriving the lessee, without compensation, of the fruits of his labour and of his investments in the tenanted holding would be incompatible with the requirements of the protection of fundamental rights in the Community legal order. Since those requirements are also binding on the Member States when they implement Community rules, the Member States must, as far as possible, apply those rules in accordance with those requirements (*Ibid.*, pp 2639-2640).

The Court ruled that the regulation, properly construed, did not have the effect imputed to it and that it did not permit landlords to deprive tenants of the fruits of their labours. The Council regulation was therefore valid. However the German order was, by necessary implication, incompatible with Community law for violation of fundamental rights and could not be applied by the national court.

The next encroachment made by the Court of Justice into state jurisdiction came two years after *Wachauf*, on a reference from the Thessaloniki Regional Court in *Elliniki Radiophonia Tileorassi AE ('ERT') v Dimotiki Etairia Pliroforissis* (1991). The Court of Justice was asked whether a Greek law conferring a broadcasting monopoly on a state broadcasting company (ERT) contravened Article 10 of the ECHR and, if so, what were the implications in Community law.

The *ERT* Court started by putting a gloss on its decision in *Wachauf*, which case was interpreted as meaning that 'the Community cannot accept measures which are incompatible with observance of the human rights ... recognized and guaranteed' in the constitutional traditions common to the Member States, international treaties which they have signed or on which they have collaborated, and especially the ECHR (*Ibid.*, pp. I–2963-I–2964). The passage in *Wachauf* to which the *ERT* Court refers in making this comment indicates that its use of the word 'measures' is a reference to both national and Community measures.

The Court then said that while it has no power to examine the compatibility with the ECHR of national rules which do not fall within the scope of Community law;

> ... where such rules do fall within the scope of Community law, and reference is made to the Court for a preliminary ruling, it must provide all the criteria of interpretation needed by the national court to determine whether those rules are compatible with the fundamental rights the observance of which the Court ensures and which derive in particular from the European Convention on Human Rights (*Ibid.*, p. I–2964).

In particular, the Court said, when a Member State relies on the public policy provisos to derogate from a fundamental Community freedom, any derogations must not infringe the general principles of law and particularly fundamental rights. Whether an infringement was actually involved in the present case was a matter left to the Greek court.

Thus any national measure which 'falls within the scope of Community law', in the sense of derogating from a Community right on grounds permitted by Community law, must be consistent with the Community's general principles on fundamental rights.[6] A national measure will 'fall within the scope of Community law' if it implements a Community rule (*Demirel, Wachauf*) or if it derogates from a Community rule on grounds permitted by Community law (*ERT*). Thus the potential for national measures to fall foul of the fundamental rights protected by Community law is now wider than it appeared in the early days of the Court of Justice's construction of fundamental rights principles.

We can therefore perceive a progressive expansion in the types of measures which will be subject to Community control on fundamental rights grounds. Jason Coppel and Aidan O'Neill have commented that:

> The only Member State actions which the Court might decline to vet on human rights grounds are ... those which occur in an area of exclusive Member State jurisdiction. This concept of Member State jurisdiction may itself be open to future redefinition by the Court (Coppel and O'Neill, 1992, p. 236).

To the extent that the laws and administrative acts of Member States 'fall within the scope of Community law' they will be applicable only to the extent that they conform to the fundamental rights protected as general principles of Community law protected by the Court of Justice. These national measures will need to satisfy a test imposed from without by Community law, enforceable by courts within the states themselves, and in respect of which the Member States lack a legal power to disapply. The development of a fundamental human rights jurisprudence by the Court of Justice has, consequently, further diminished the national sovereignty of the Member States; albeit within a fairly narrow range of activities for the time being.

## EU Membership and National Sovereignty

By 'national sovereignty' in this context I mean the exclusive right of a state to exercise official powers, unfettered by external legal obligations. The scope *ratione materiae* of those powers are 'matters which are essentially within the domestic jurisdiction' of states;[7] that is, matters which are not the subject of legally binding international obligations.[8] A state's national sovereignty, in this sense, is therefore compromised whenever it enters into an arrangement under which it assumes obligations to other entities in international law, or when a customary rule of international law emerges which imposes obligations upon the state.

National sovereignty is not an absolute quantity. Its scope can diminish as the state's international obligations expand without the state's national sovereignty being thereby abandoned. The significance of particular attributes of national sovereignty can also change with time.[9] A state's national sovereignty may be seriously circumscribed by membership of some sorts of international organisations. In exceptional circumstances, membership of such organisations may strike at core attributes of national sovereignty in such a way as to place in question the state's independent international personality. According to

Brownlie:

> If an organization encroaches on the domestic jurisdiction of members to a substantial degree the structure may approximate a federation, and not only the area of competence of members but their very personality will be in issue. The line is not easy to draw, but the following criteria of extinction of personality have been suggested: the obligatory nature of membership; majority decision-making; the determination of jurisdiction by the organization itself; and the binding quality of decisions of the organization apart from the consent of member states (Brownlie, 1990, pp. 290–91).

These tentatively suggested 'criteria of extinction of personality' are useful but insufficient, for they need to be considered together with the competences exercised by the international organisation in question. It is entirely conceivable that an international organisation might satisfy all the above mentioned suggested criteria, but possess competence in such a narrow or technical field as to pose no threat to the core attributes of national sovereignty in such a way as to place in question the state's independent international personality. Euratom, considered as a separate legal entity, is clearly such an organisation.

Some attributes of national sovereignty are clearly more important than others and, beyond a certain point, the divestment of sovereignty may threaten a state's independence and thus its continued existence as an entity possessing personality in international law. Among the significant attributes of national sovereignty is possession by the state of, 'particularly important, a nationality law of its own' (Brownlie, p. 74).

Becoming a party to the treaties constituting the EU involves a number of definite, extensive and well-known restrictions on a state's domestic jurisdiction and national sovereignty, not all of which need to be rehearsed here.

In connection specifically with the criteria referred to by Brownlie, we may simply note that a qualified majority decision-making procedure has long been part of the EU's legislative processes and has been extended to an increasing number of policy areas as a result of the Single European Act (SEA) and the Treaty on European Union (TEU). The Treaty of Amsterdam continues this trend. The EC determines its own jurisdiction subject to the juridical control only of its own judicial organs.[10] It is now an unremarkable and long-established Community law principle that national law, even national constitutional law protecting fundamental rights, must give way to an inconsistent Community law regardless of its form or subject matter (*Costa v ENEL*, 1964; *Internationale Handelsgesellschaft mbH v Einfuhr- und Vorratsstelle für Getreide und Futtermittel*, 1970), and even if the state affected opposed the duly adopted measure in the Council. Indeed Community law goes further than classical international law by insisting that certain types of Community legislation are directly effective and are thus enforceable in national courts by individual litigants.

## National Sovereignty and the Direct Effect of Community Law

This last point, though by now an entirely familiar and well-worn piece of furniture in the EU's legal order, merits a little further consideration in connection with national sovereignty. According to the Court of Justice:

> [T]he EEC Treaty, albeit concluded in the form of an international agreement, none the less constitutes the constitutional charter of a Community based on the rule of law. As the Court of Justice has consistently held, the Community treaties established a new legal order for the benefit of which the States have limited their sovereign rights, in ever wider fields, and the subjects of which comprise not only Member States but also their nationals... (Opinion 1/91 Re *Draft EEA Treaty*, 1991, p. I–6102).

This represents a dramatic break with previous international legal practice and sprang from the portals of the Court of Justice in 1963 when, in one of its most important judgments, it held that a private person could rely on certain Community law rights before a Netherlands tribunal to defeat an inconsistent provision of national law. In so ruling the Court of Justice said:

> The objective of the EEC Treaty, which is to establish a Common Market, the functioning of which is of direct concern to interested parties in the Community, implies that this Treaty is more than an agreement which merely creates mutual obligations between the contracting states.

> The conclusion to be drawn from this is that the Community constitutes a new legal order of international law ... Independently of the legislation of Member States, Community law therefore not only imposes obligations on individuals but is also intended to confer upon them rights which become part of their legal heritage (*NV Algemene Transport- en Expeditie Onderneming van Gend en Loos v Nederlandse administratie der belastingen*, 1963, p. 12).

National courts work in cooperation with the Court of Justice. They are given an important role in the application and enforcement of Community law, and individuals are entitled to a vindication of their Community law rights at the national court level. The Member States cannot in all circumstances regard themselves as the channels through which Community law rights are mediated, and through which such rights can be effectively interpreted, granted, modified or denied *in accordance with their own sovereign policy choices*. A Member State's own courts and tribunals may, in a sense, be used against it to ensure the observance of legal rights formulated by institutions and processes outside the state's territory and control.

It is the fact that Community law itself treats not only states but also their citizens as subjects that most clearly and practically distinguishes it from classical international law, and from other more orthodox international organisations. Subject status for the Member States' citizens means that Community law rights and obligations may apply directly to them in much the same way that federal Australian, United States and Canadian law applies directly to the citizens of the constituent states or provinces.

## National Sovereignty and the Right to Secede from the Union

But what of the first criterion mentioned by Brownlie, that is, the obligatory nature of membership? Here there is perhaps more uncertainty.

Whether the Member States, in joining the EU, have *permanently* abdicated any part of their national sovereignty is a matter of political dispute. Convinced federalists and convinced nationalists frequently argue, albeit for opposed purposes, that membership of the EU involves a progressive and eventually irreversible transfer of national sovereignty to Community institutions.

The middle ground tends to describe the process less starkly: the Member States have not 'lost' or 'transferred' their sovereign rights but have merely 'pooled' them. This comforting characterisation portrays each Member State as having gained more than it has lost; the United Kingdom may have foregone exclusive power to determine its own environmental standards, but has acquired a say in the formulation of standards applying throughout the Union. This approach also avoids the knotty question as to whether a Member State remains 'ultimately sovereign' to resume its fully independent status by unilaterally withdrawing from Community membership.

International law envisages that there may be treaties from which unilateral withdrawal is simply not expressly or impliedly permitted.[11] Where a treaty does provide for denunciation or withdrawal, a party may withdraw 'in conformity with the provisions of the treaty' or 'at any time by consent of all the parties after consultation with the other contracting States'.[12] The fact that a treaty is also the constitution of an international organisation does not take it outside these principles (Schermers and Blokker, 1995, pp. 134-135).

Although the TEU expressly provides for the admission of new members (Article 49 TEU),[13] and does not expressly provide for withdrawals,[14] and although the EC Treaty, the Euratom Treaty and the TEU were concluded for an 'unlimited period',[15] it is nevertheless legally possible for a Member State to withdraw from the Union. An applicant state becomes a member of the EU by completing a treaty of accession with the existing Member States after the prescribed admission procedure has been followed, according to Article 49 TEU.[16] A treaty of accession will provide for various adjustments to the founding treaties in order to accommodate the new member's entry. There is no legal reason why a Member State's withdrawal could not be effected also by making accommodating adjustments to the founding treaties.

This could be done, however, only by adherence to the treaty amendment procedure contained in Article 48 TEU:[17] essentially, consultation by the Council with the European Parliament (and possibly the Commission and the European Central Bank) followed by unanimous consent of the Member States at a specially convened conference resulting in an amendment to the treaties which must then be ratified in accordance with each Member State's constitutional requirements.

The mere consent of all the other Member States would not be sufficient because, as we have seen, the constituent treaties are the constitutional charter of a Community based on the rule of law concluded in the form of international agreements. Purported amendments to the treaty otherwise than in accordance with the prescribed amendment procedure are simply unlawful. (*Defrenne v Société Anonyme Belge de Navigation Aérienne Sabena*, 1976, p. 478). There is a precedent for withdrawal from the Community. Greenland, part of the Kingdom of Denmark's territory, effectively withdrew in 1985 but only after Denmark had observed the prescribed treaty amendment procedure (Harhoff, 1983; Weiss, 1985). At no stage did Denmark openly claim that it could effect Greenland's withdrawal by unilateral sovereign action.

The legal conditions for withdrawal are therefore strict. No Member State, as a matter of Community law, has a unilateral right of withdrawal. As a matter of Community law, then, the Member States have really transferred large parts of their sovereignty to the Community. They can get it back only with the other Member States' unanimous consent and in accordance with their respective constitutional requirements.

It is, of course, politically very unlikely at the current stage of European integration that a Member State manifesting a clear desire to withdraw, particularly if it were armed with evidence of majority popular support for withdrawal, would be blocked by any of the other Member States. The future, however, may be a different matter as the Union expands and becomes in some ways less homogeneous and more unpredictable, especially by taking in new members some of whose democratic experiences are so recent as not to have hardened into traditions.

Thus, although there is a *mechanism* for withdrawal from membership of the Union, there is as a matter of Community law, no *right* to withdraw. Membership of the EU is obligatory for all its Member States. From a constitutional perspective the Member States have really transferred, and not simply pooled, their sovereignty

## Europe's New Citizens

All the general fundamental rights principles developed by the Court of Justice apply regardless of the nationality of any person relevantly affected. Thus in *Demirel* the individual's Turkish nationality was not the reason for the failure of her argument based on a right to respect for private and family life. The Court of Justice's general fundamental rights principles will apply to any person affected by the operation of Community law. These principles are not, therefore, strictly to be classified simply as rights of citizenship—they are truly human rights.[18]

At Maastricht, however, the Member States established a new legal citizenship status, to be conferred on citizens of the Member States, and agreed upon a set of non-economic rights which are linked to that status. As a result of changes agreed at Maastricht, Article 17 EC[19] formally establishes citizenship of the Union.

None of the Union treaties defines what is meant by 'nationality of a Member State', although a Declaration on Nationality of a Member State adopted by the Intergovernmental Conferences on Political Union and on Economic and Monetary Union states that wherever in the EC Treaty;

> ... reference is made to nationals of the Member States, the question whether an individual possesses the nationality of a Member State shall be settled solely by reference to the national law of the Member State concerned. Member States may declare, for information, who are to be considered their nationals for Community purposes by way of a declaration ... and may amend any such declaration when necessary (Article 1 of the Final Act of the conference).

The principal citizenship provisions in Part Two of the Treaty grant three types of rights: Articles 19 and 21 grant some political rights; freedom of movement and residence is granted by Article 18; certain rights to diplomatic and consular protection are dealt with by Article 20.[20]

- Under Article 19(1), every Union citizen living in a Member State of which he is not a national shall have the right to vote in and stand for elections at the municipal level under the same conditions applying to nationals of that Member State. The same Union citizens, pursuant to Article 19(2), are to enjoy a similar right in respect of elections to the European Parliament. Both rights are to be exercised subject to detailed arrangements to be adopted unanimously by the Council on a proposal from the Commission after consulting the European Parliament. In each case, the detailed arrangements may provide for derogations where warranted by problems specific to Member States.[21]

- Article 18 provides that '[e]very citizen of the Union shall have the right to move and reside freely within the territory of the Member States, subject to the limitations and conditions laid down in this Treaty and by the measures adopted to give it effect'.

- Article 20 entitles Union citizens, while in the territory of a third country where his own Member State lacks consular or diplomatic representation, to receive consular and diplomatic protection by the authorities of other Member States on the same conditions as nationals of those other Member States.

- Article 21 (first paragraph) guarantees every citizen of the Union the right to petition the European Parliament in accordance with Article 194 which in turn confers a right of parliamentary petition on every Union citizen and on every natural or legal person residing or having its registered office in a Member State. The second paragraph of Article 21 provides that every citizen of the Union may apply to the Ombudsman established in accordance with Article 195. The Ombudsman is, by Article 195, appointed by the European Parliament and is empowered to receive complaints from the same categories of persons entitled to petition the Parliament.

- Article 22[22] obliges the Commission to make regular reports on the application of these provisions and authorises the adoption of 'provisions to strengthen or to add to the rights laid down' in Part Two.

What implications does all of this have for the remaining national sovereignty of the Member States?

It is clear that the new rights of Union citizenship relieve Member States of their previously sovereign power to restrict a range of important political and civil rights to their own nationals. Of most importance in this regard are the rights of democratic participation, movement and residence.

The ability to decide who is eligible to participate in the political life of the state is intimately related to the power to make dispositions of nationality and goes very close to the heart of national sovereignty (Brownlie, 1990). Article 19 and its implementing legislation *require* Member States to extend important political rights to foreign nationals from elsewhere in the Union. These rights will be enforceable directly before courts in the Member States themselves, and the Member States cannot legally opt out of these obligations.

Similarly, an essential sign of national sovereignty is the ability to refuse entry to the national territory of persons who are not citizens of the state. Australia, the United States and Canada have this ability but New South Wales, California and Ontario do not.

The European Court of Justice has recently expressly left open the question as to whether Article 18 EC confers a right on Union citizens to take up residence in a Member State whose nationality they do not possess (*Martínez Sala v Freistaat Bayern*, 1998). At the very least, according to the Court of Justice, Article 8 renders all Union citizens already lawfully resident in a host Member State within the scope *ratione personae* of the EC Treaty, even if the lawfulness of their residence stems from national law alone on grounds outside the scope of Community law. Such Union citizens are thereby protected by, *inter alia*, the non-discrimination entitlements enshrined in Article 12 EC.

In other words, Article 17 EC extends Community law rights to Union citizens resident in a host Member State even where those Union citizens cannot trace their claim through an economic status covered by the treaties, *and* where their residence in the host Member State's territory is authorised by national law alone. The better view is that this Article confers a new and directly effective constitutional right on Union citizens to take up residence in host Member States subject to limitations and conditions objectively justified on grounds of public policy, public security and public health and (because the Article 18 right is not an economic one) for the protection of the host Member States' systems of social assistance (Hall, 1995, pp. 182–207).

However there are implications for national sovereignty which are perhaps more fundamental than the Treaty rights attaching to the new citizenship of the Union. They arise from the establishment of Union citizenship itself. This new category of citizenship, established in the Community's constitutional charter, has been conferred in such a way as to affect the hitherto sovereign capacity of Member States to deprive persons of their nationality.

Article 17 EC not only establishes a citizenship of the Union, it also declares that '[e]very person holding the nationality of a Member State shall be a citizen of the Union'. We have already seen that national laws which fall 'within the scope of' Community law will be subject to supervision by the Court of Justice for compliance with the fundamental rights which the Court protects as general principles of law. National measures will fall within the scope of Community law if they implement a Community rule or derogate from a Community rule on grounds permitted by Community law. The only national measures exempt from Community supervision on fundamental rights grounds are those which fall within the Member States' exclusive jurisdiction.

Citizenship of the Union is a status created by and held under Community law. It is Article 17 EC which both creates the status and determines who possesses it. The Treaty chooses to make this determination by referring to national law, which in turn determines the conditions for acquisition and loss of nationality. Any national of a Member State is, by force only of Article 17, a citizen of the Union. National law does not of its own force create, confer or withdraw citizenship of the Union. A national measure which withdraws a person's nationality is one *which produces effects in* an area covered by Community law. But at the current stage of development of the law this is not enough to place it 'within the scope of Community law'.

Such a measure does more, however, than simply produce effects in an area covered by Community law. Rather, it affects the very operation of Community law itself by excluding certain persons from access to the benefits conferred by Community law. It is therefore comparable in its effects to a national measure purporting to define a class of persons as falling outside the Community status of 'worker', or one of the other functional criteria determining Community economic rights.[23] Accordingly, it falls 'within the scope of Community law'. Falling within the scope of Community law, it is subject to the Court of Justice's supervision for consistency with the fundamental rights which Community law protects, including those set out in the European Convention on Nationality (Hall, 1999).

Community law does not, however, limit a Member State's power to withdraw its nationality from a person consistently with the general principles of law protected by the Court of Justice. Thus if a Member State withdraws its nationality from a person without infringing fundamental human rights, proportionality, the right to be heard, legal certainty or the other general principles of Community law, then the Court of Justice will have no basis upon which to impugn the Member State's action.

But where a national measure deprives an individual of his Member State nationality, in violation of the fundamental rights or other general principles protected by the Court of Justice, the national authorities (including national courts) will be under an obligation not to enforce that measure. The result would be that the individual affected would retain *both* Member State nationality and Union citizenship. This outcome would be consistent with Article 17's declaration that every person holding the nationality of a Member State shall be a citizen of the Union.

What if such a national measure remained fully valid at the level of national law? A citizen of the Union would retain that status throughout the Union, including in his/her (former) own Member State. Such a Community law status could not be withdrawn in violation of the fundamental rights and other general principles of law protected by the Court of Justice. The affected individual would remain entitled to all the Community law rights attaching to Union citizenship, including residence rights (Hall, 1996).

## Conclusion

Europe is in a time when there is renewed evidence of the 'logic that leads peoples who speak the same language and share the same culture and tradition to want to govern themselves in their own state' (Garton Ash, 1998, p. 64). It is also a time of clamour from Europe's East to join the EU and share in its economic, political and social benefits. Of the many issues challenging Europeans in the next decade, how to reconcile the popular goals of national self-government and some degree of European integration will be an increasingly complicated and important one.

There is a vision which seeks to resolve this tension by erecting a 'Europe of the Regions', in which the power of the European centre and regional units would be strengthened at the expense of the Member States. This vision is genetically identical to the older idea of a federal European *patria*. In some parts of Europe, this project would tend to complement aspirations for enhanced national self-government although, in other more homogeneous Member States, it would tend in the opposite direction. The only clear winner from such a process would be the Union's own power centres.

The increased centralisation of power which would result from the realisation of such a vision runs counter to the liberalising currents now dominant in most of Europe, and would not any time soon stand to be mitigated by the emergence a genuine European democracy.

Citizenship of the Union is a juridical reality, but not a social, civic or patriotic reality. Probably the most striking evidence for this is the absence of any EU-wide political parties, notwithstanding that there have now been five directly elected European Parliaments during the last 21 years. Indeed elections to the European Parliament are conducted in separate national campaigns by national (or regional) political parties and are generally treated, by politicians and voters alike, as opportunities for expressing popular opinion of national governments.

The tension between an expanding field of EU competence and popular attachment to sovereign government through Member States is addressed by two treaty provisions agreed at Maastricht. Article F(1) TEU provided that '[t]he Union shall respect the national identities of its Member States, whose systems of government are founded on the principles of democracy'.[24] Article 5 EC[25] commits the Community to act 'within the limits of the powers conferred upon it' in the Treaty, to refrain from going 'beyond what is necessary to achieve the objectives' of the Treaty, and establishes a truncated principle of subsidiarity in the following terms:

> In areas which do not fall within its exclusive competence, the Community shall take action, in accordance with the principle of subsidiarity, only if and in so far as the objectives of the proposed action cannot be sufficiently achieved by the Member States and can therefore by reason of the scale and effects of the proposed action, be better achieved by the Community.[26]

The principle of subsidiarity as expressed in Article 5 is truncated, and truncated in a revealing way, because it applies to distribute powers only as between the Community and the Member States. The principle, however, finds its origins in Catholic social doctrine (Cass, 1992, p. 1107) as 'an injustice and at the same time a grave evil and disturbance of right order to assign to a greater and higher association what lesser and subordinate organisations can do'.[27] An unqualified application of subsidiarity would therefore have extended to all levels of official authority within the Community, including regional and local administrations (Kapteyn and Verloren van Themaat, 1998).[28]

The fact that the Article 5 principle is restricted to relations between the Community and the Member States is indicative of the sensitivities powerfully felt in at least some of those states that the on-going process of transferring attributes of national sovereignty to the Union has neared domestic political limits.

The diminution in national sovereignty was not in any way intensified when the Court of Justice began constructing its general principles of fundamental rights protection between 1969 and the mid-1980s. On the contrary, while the Court of Justice's fundamental rights jurisprudence operated only on Community legislation, national sovereignty was, if anything, enhanced. However, now that the Court of Justice has extended the application of these principles to certain legislative and executive acts of the Member States, there has been a further encroachment on national sovereignty.

If the Court of Justice were ever to fully 'nationalise' the Community's unwritten Bill of Rights there would be a significant further diminution of Member State sovereignty. It is very unlikely, on the Court of Justice's current form, that such a development will occur in the foreseeable future. Such a development would not be strictly necessary to achieve either the single market or the euro-federalist project, and would severely test the legitimacy of the Court of Justice and its vital partnership with the national courts.

Although the foreseeable limits on national sovereignty imposed by the general fundamental rights principles have already probably been reached, the institution of a citizenship of the Union has made further important incursions into Member State sovereignty.

Not only does Community law now entitle certain non-nationals to participate in the electoral life of a host Member State and oblige Member States to accept into their territory such people; it also affects a Member State's ability to say who will be considered a full member of the national community. In a Union of democracies in which the people are politically sovereign, Community law now places constitutional restrictions on the hitherto sovereign right of States to exclude an individual from membership of 'the people'.

Furthermore, the Court of Justice has extended Community law *ratione materiae* to cover Union citizens already lawfully present in a host Member State on grounds entirely unconnected to any economic activity regulated by Community law. It has also left open the question as to whether Union citizens have a Community constitutional right to take up residence in a host Member State independently of any such economic activity.

Because of their essentially rights-enhancing character, these are not encroachments on national sovereignty which are likely to meet much, if any, resistance from Europe's people (although neither have they been warmly embraced). Nevertheless, they illustrate a larger point about Community law; there is in many areas a quiet and, to the citizen, invisible seepage of power from the Member States to the Union. Bit by bit, national sovereignty continues to seep away from the Member State capitals to the EU. The trickle is one way and irreversible, at least in the sense that no Member State may unilaterally and lawfully withdraw from the 'ever closer union' (Preambles to the EC Treaty and the TEU) which the EU was established to advance.

I would argue, however, that a centralised Europe will not be democratic, while a democratic Europe will not be centralised. We should also bear in mind that the 'ever closer union' envisaged by the treaties is to be 'among the *peoples* of Europe' (*Ibid.*, emphasis added).[29] In this connection Germany's federal constitutional court has remarked:

> The Union Treaty ... establishes a federation of States for the purpose of realising an ever closer union of the peoples of Europe (organised as States) and not a state based on the people of one European nation (*Brunner v The European Union Treaty*, 1994).

Subsidiarity may well emerge as the most felicitous addition ever made to the EU's structure. Used wisely as an aspect of justice for which it was originally identified, subsidiarity can help ensure that the EU builds a home, and not a bureaucratic empire, for her families of people to inhabit. This would be a fitting quest as Europe emerges from her worst century in history, her long dark night of the soul.

## Notes

1   According to French Foreign Minister Robert Schuman, in publicly proposing the establishment of a European Coal and Steel Community, the 'pooling of coal and steel production will immediately assure the establishment of common bases for economic development, which is the first state for the European federation'. See 'The Schuman Declaration', 9 May 1950, in Patijn, 1970, pp. 46 et seq.

2   The United Kingdom, whose constitution is sometimes unfairly said to be 'not worth the paper it isn't written on', is the sole exception.

3   The European Court of Justice is a major Community institution whose principal function is to ensure that Community law is correctly interpreted and applied.

4   Article F(2) TEU, however, provides as follows: 'The Union shall respect fundamental rights, as guaranteed by the European Convention for the Protection of Human Rights and Fundamental Freedoms signed in Rome on 4 November 1950 and as they result from the constitutional traditions common to the Member States, as general principles of Community law'. This provision is not, however, justiciable by the Court of Justice; Article L TEU. See also Articles J.1(2) and K.2(1) TEU and the preamble to the SEA. The following renumbering is effected by the Treaty of Amsterdam: Article F(2) becomes Article 6(2); Article L becomes Article 46; Article J.1 becomes Article 11; Article K.2 becomes Article 30.

5   268 US 652 (1925).

6   See also the opinion of Advocate General Van Gerven in Case C-159/90, *Society for the Protection of Unborn Children Ireland Ltd v Grogan*, 1991, p. I–4723.

7   The phrase is taken from Article 2(7) of the Charter of the United Nations. Article 15(8) of the Covenant of the League of Nations was to similar effect.

8   A matter falling within a state's domestic jurisdiction, and hence lying within the realm of its national sovereignty, may exceptionally be removed from that realm by United Nations Security Council measures adopted under Chapter VII of the United Nations Charter: 'Action with Respect to Threats to the Peace, Breaches of the Peace, and Acts of Aggression', Articles 39–51. Article 25 of the Charter provides: 'The Members of the United Nations agree to accept and carry out the decisions of the Security Council in accordance with the present Charter'. Article 103 of the Charter provides: 'In the event of a conflict between the obligations of the Members of the United Nations under the present Charter and their obligations under any other international agreement, their obligations under the present Charter shall prevail'.

9    For example, it was once regarded as an essential attribute of national sovereignty that states had a right to wage war on their enemies. During the course of this century, however, this attribute has not only lost all its importance as an element and a signifier of national sovereignty, but is now unlawful: Article 2(4) of the United Nations Charter prohibits 'the threat or use of force against the territorial integrity or political independence of any state, or in any other manner inconsistent with the Purposes of the United Nations'; Article 51 of the Charter tempers this prohibition by preserving 'the inherent right of individual or collective self-defence if an armed attack occurs'.

10    Article 16 EC; formerly Article 219, before the Treaty of Amsterdam.

11    Article 56(1) of the Vienna Convention on the Law of Treaties provides: 'A treaty which contains no provision regarding its termination and which does not provide for denunciation or withdrawal is not subject to denunciation or withdrawal unless: (a) it is established that the parties intended to admit the possibility of denunciation or withdrawal; or (b) a right of denunciation or withdrawal may be implied by the nature of the treaty'. Withdrawal under Article 56(1) can be effected only upon the giving of twelve months' notice (Article 56(2)).

12    Article 54 of the Vienna Convention on the Law of Treaties.

13    Formerly Article O, before the Treaty of Amsterdam.

14    Like the United Nations Charter, but unlike the vast majority of treaties constituting international organisations. Most international organisations permit termination of membership by unilateral withdrawal, though a period of prior notice—often twelve months—is usually required. See Schermers and Blokker, 1995, §120.

15    Article 36 EC (formerly Article 240 before the Treaty of Amsterdam), Article 208 Euratom, Article 51 TEU (formerly Article Q before the Treaty of Amsterdam).

16    Formerly Article O before the Treaty of Amsterdam.

17    Formerly Article N before the Treaty of Amsterdam.

18    This is to be contrasted with the EC Treaty-based economic freedoms guaranteeing movements of workers (Article 39), services (Article 49) and the right of establishment (Article 43).

19    Formerly Article 8 before the Treaty of Amsterdam.

20    Articles 18, 19, 20 and 21, formerly numbered respectively Articles 8a, 8b, 8c and 8d before the Treaty of Amsterdam.

21    Both directives permit special limited derogations in respect of any Member State (in fact only Luxembourg) 'where the proportion of citizens of voting age who reside in it but are not nationals of it exceeds 20 per cent of the total number of citizens of the Union residing there who are of voting age': Article 12(1) of Directive 94/80 and Article 14(1) of Directive 93/109.

22    Formerly Article 8e before the Treaty of Amsterdam.

23    As to the impermissibility of allowing national measures or practices exclusively to define the concept of 'worker' for the purposes of Article 48 EC see eg. *Hoekstra v Bestuur der Bedrijfsvereniging voor Detailhandel en Ambachten*, 1964; *Levin v Staatssecretaris van Justitie*, 1982; *Kempf v Staatssecretaris van Justitie*, 1986; *Lawrie-Blum v Land Baden-Württemberg*, 1986.

24  The Treaty of Amsterdam changes the text of Article F(1) TEU as follows: 'The Union is founded on the principles of liberty, democracy, respect for human rights and fundamental freedoms, and the rule of law, principles which are common to the Member States'. A new Article F(3) provides: 'The Union shall respect the national identities of its Member States'. Article F is renumbered Article 6 by the Treaty of Amsterdam.

25  Formerly Article 3b before the Treaty of Amsterdam.

26  The extent of the Community's 'exclusive competence' is a matter of some debate. According to John Temple Lang (1995, p. 98), the Community has exclusive power over only four areas: commercial policy, conservation of marine biological resources, treaties on supply of nuclear materials and certain mergers. Implementation of the TEU's provisions on monetary union extend the Community's exclusive competence to the common currency. See also Alan Dashwood, 1996, p. 113 for an even more restrictive view.

27  Pope Pius XI, *Quadragesimo Anno* (papal encyclical, 1931) para 79. See also; Pope John XXIII, *Pacem in Terris* (papal encyclical, 1963) para 140; the Catechism of the Catholic Church (1994) at paras 1883-1885.

28  They argue (p. 27) that the Catholic doctrine of subsidiarity is 'exclusively concerned with the relationship between the public authorities, citizens, families and intermediate organisations' and that in its origin 'it thus has no relevance to relationships between the different territorial administrative layers of a State, even within a federal State'. This view is not supported by either the language or context of the authorities referred to in the previous footnote, which are clearly wide enough to embrace all levels of official authority and the relationships between them.

29  The preamble to the TEU also records the Member States' desire 'to deepen the solidarity between their peoples while respecting their history, their culture and their traditions'.

# References

Brownlie, I. (1990), *Principles of Public International Law*, 4th edition, Clarendon Press, Oxford.

Cass, D.Z. (1992), 'The Word that Saves Maastricht? The Principle of Subsidiarity and the Division of Powers within the European Community', *Common Market Law Review*, Vol. 29, pp. 1107–1136.

Coppel, J. and O'Neill, A. (1992), 'The European Court of Justice: Taking Rights Seriously?', *Legal Studies*, Vol. 12, pp. 227–245.

Dashwood, A. (1996), 'The Limits of European Community Powers', *European Law Review*, Vol. 21, pp. 113–128.

Garton Ash, T. (1998), 'Europe's Endangered Liberal Order', *Foreign Affairs*, Vol. 77, No. 2, pp. 51–65.

Hall, S. (1995), *Nationality, Migration Rights and Citizenship of the Union*, Nijhoff, Dordrecht.

Hall, S. (1996), 'Loss of Union Citizenship in Breach of Fundamental Rights', *European Law Review*, Vol. 21, pp. 129–143.

Hall, S. (1999), 'The European Convention on Nationality and the right to have rights', *European Law Review*, Vol. 24, pp. 584–602.

Harhoff, F. (1983), 'Greenland's Withdrawal from the European Communities', *Common Market Law Review*, Vol. 20, pp. 13–33.

Kapteyn, P.J.G. and Verloren van Themaat, P. (1998), *Introduction to the Law of the European Communities*, 3rd edition, Kluwer, Boston.

Lang, John Temple (1995), 'What powers should the European Community have?' *European Public Law*, Vol. 1, No. 1, pp. 90–110.

Patijn, S. (ed.) (1970), *Landmarks in European Unity*, A.W. Sijthoff, Leyden.

Schermers, H.G. and Blokker, N.M. (1995), *International Institutional Law*, 3rd edition, Nijhoff, The Hague.

Weiler, J.H.H. and Lockhart, N.J.S. (1995), '"Taking rights seriously" seriously: The European Court and its fundamental rights jurisprudence', *Common Market Law Review*, Vol. 32, pp. 51–94, and 579–627.

Weiss, F. (1985), 'Greenland's Withdrawal from the European Communities', *European Law Review*, Vol. 10, pp. 173–185.

## Cases

*Brunner v The European Union Treaty* [1994], Cases 2134/92 and 2159/92, 1 CMLR 57.

*Cinéthèque SA v Fédération nationale des cinémas français* [1985], Joined Cases 60 and 61/84, ECR 2605.

*Costa v ENEL* [1964], Case 6/64, ECR 585.

*Defrenne v Société Anonyme Belge de Navigation Aérienne Sabena* [1976], Case 43/75, ECR 455.

*Demirel v Stadt Schwäbisch Gmünd* [1987], Case 12/86, ECR 3719.

*Elliniki Radiophonia Tileorassi AE v Dimotiki Etairia Pliroforissis* [1991], Case C-260/89, ECR I–2925.

*Friedrich Stork & Co v High Authority* [1959], Case 1/58, ECR 17.

*Geitling Ruhrkohlen-Verkaufsgesellschaft mbH v High Authority* [1960], Cases 36–8, 40/59, ECR 423.

*Hauer v Land Rheinland-Pfalz* [1979], Case 44/79, ECR 3727.

*Hermann Schräder HS Kraftfutter GmbH & Co v Hauptzollamt Gronau* [1989], Case 265/87, ECR 2237.

*Hoechst AG v Commission* [1989], Cases 46/87 and 227/88, ECR 2859.

*Hoekstra v Bestuur der Bedrijfsvereniging voor Detailhandel en Ambachten* [1964], Case 75/63, ECR 177.

*Internationale Handelsgesellschaft mbH v Einfuhr- und Vorratsstelle für Getreide und Futtermittel* [1970], Case 11/70, ECR 1125.

*J Nold, Kohlen- und Baustoffgrosshandlung v Commission* [1974], Case 4/73, ECR 491.

*Kempf v Staatssecretaris van Justitie* [1986], Case 139/85, ECR 1746

*Lawrie-Blum v Land Baden-Württemberg* [1986], Case 66/85, ECR 2121.

*Levin v Staatssecretaris van Justitie* [1982], Case 53/81, ECR 1035.

*Martínez Sala v Freistaat Bayern*, Case C-85/96, judgement of 12 May 1998.

*National Panasonic (UK) Ltd v Commission* [1980], Case 136/79, ECR 2033.

*NV Algemene Transport- en Expeditie Onderneming van Gend en Loos v Nederlandse administratie der belastingen* [1963], Case 26/62, ECR 1.

*Oyowe v Commission* [1989], Case C-100/88, ECR 4285.

*Pecastaing v Belgian State* [1980], Case 98/79, ECR 691.

*Prais v Council* [1976], Case 130/75, ECR 1589.

*R v Kirk* [1984], Case 63/83, ECR 2689.

*Razzouk v Commission* [1984], Cases 75, 117/82, ECR 1509.

*SA Musique Diffusion Française v Commission* [1983], Cases 100-103/80, ECR 1835.

*Society for the Protection of Unborn Children Ireland Ltd v Grogan* [1991], Case C-159/90, ECR I-4685.

*SpA Ferriera Valsabbia v Commission* [1980], Cases 154, 205-6, 226-8, 263-4/78, ECR 907.

*Stauder v City of Ulm Sozialamt* [1969], Case 29/69, ECR 419.

*Vereniging ter Bevordering van het Vlaamse Boekwezen v Commission* [1984], Cases 43 and 63/82, ECR 19.

*Wachauf v Federal Republic of Germany* [1989], Case 5/88, ECR 2609.

Opinion 1/91 *Re Draft EEA Treaty* [1991] ECR I-6079.

Opinion 2/94 [1996], ECR I-1759.

# Index

absolute rights *see* rights as absolute
affirmative action, 82
*African Charter on Human and
    Peoples' Rights*, 9, 152
aggression (crime), 170, 174, 179, 181
Akobé, Véronique, 37
*Alerte Orange*, 64
aliens *see* resident aliens
*American Convention on Human
    Rights*, 152
Amsterdam Treaty *see* Treaty of
    Amsterdam
anti-dumping, 136
apartheid, 177, 182
'Asian values', 96
Association Agreements,121, 123-4,
    135-6, 138-40, 143-4, 146*n*
autonomy versus heteronomy, 17-19

Bangkok Declaration, 40
bilateralism *see* hub-and-spoke
    bilateralism

*Cairo Declaration of Human Rights in
    Islam*, 40
*Canadian Charter of Rights and
    Freedoms*, 152
capital punishment *see* death penalty
Carribean and Latin American Com-
    mittee for the Defence of Women'
    Rights, 46*n*
Catholic natural law theory, 16
censorship, 80-1
    *see also* library censorship
Central Europe
    *see* Eastern Europe
citizenship, 1, 2, 6, 7, 204-8
    *see also* nationality rights
    supranational, 2, 7, 8*n*, 204-8
civil rights, 2
    United States, 3
coercion, 10, 15
    needed to protect freedom, 11-12
    versus rational consent, 10-11

communitarianism *see* individual
    rights versus group rights
Community law, 4, 192-5
    versus national sovereignty, 195,
        200-2, 206-8, 211
constitutionalism, 92, 94-8
Convention of the Elimination of All
    Forms of Discrimination Against
    Women, 40, 47*n*
Convention on Transfrontier Broad-
    casting, 30
Court of Justice *see* European Court of
    Justice
crimes against peace *see* war crimes
crimes against humanity, 173, 179,
    181-2
cultural determinism, 102-4
cultural diversity see multiculturalism
cultural relativism, 41, 44
customs unions, 138
Czech Republic, 75, 79-80

death penalty, 175
decision-making, 28
Declaration on the Elimination of All
    Forms of Intolerance and   Discrimi-
    nation Based on Religion or Belief, 40
democracy, 3, 6, 11, 16, 69-86, 210
    Bohemia, 99, 101
Diop, Aminata, 43
direct investment *see* foreign direct
    investment
domestic law versus international law
    *see* international law versus
    domestic law
drug trafficking, 173, 177, 179

Eastern Europe 3, 4, 5-6
    *see also* Central Europe
    benefits of, 131-2
    exports, 137
    integration into the European Union,
        123-32, 143-4
    minority rights, 69-88

economic rights, 2, 3, 4, 109-19
  United States, 3
equality, 2, 3, 15
  gender aspects, 25, 27-30, 38-9
  France, 30-3
  in the workplace *see* labour equality
  of resources, 20
ethnic minorities, 6, 25-6, 86
  Czech Republic, 79-80
  Slovak Republic, 78-9
Europe Agreements *see* Association
  Agreements
European Central Bank, 4
European Commission, 122, 130
European Community law
  *see* Community law
European Convention on Human
  Rights, 1, 4, 9, 40, 82, 151-60,
  163, 192, 211*n*
European Court of Human Rights, 8,
  152, 158-9, 161-3, 195-6, 198
European Court of Justice, 1, 4, 21,
  159, 195-9, 201, 204, 206, 209-10
  versus national courts, 201-2
European Free Trade Association, 123,
  138
European Monetary Union, 4, 7, 125,
  132
European Monitoring Centre on
  Racism, 5
European Network of Women, 29
European Parliament, 5, 28, 205
  Ombudsman, 205
  Women's Rights Committee, 25
European Social Charter, 192
European Union, 1, 21-2, 191
  Action Programs, 28, 29
  anti-discrimination laws, 27, 158
  expansion, 1-2, 121-2, 126
    *see also* Association Agreements
  absorptive capacity of, 127-30
  benefits of, 133
  gender policy, 25
  law, 131, 154
    transformation into domestic
    law, 154

membership criteria, 124
  economic, 127, 146*n*
  human rights, 5, 6
  income convergence, 133-5
  membership versus national
    sovereignty, 199-200, 210
  secession from, 202-4
European Women's Union, 25

family law, 158
female genital mutilation, 33, 41, 43
force *see* coercion
foreign direct investment, 140-3
free market economics, 3, 110-2, 130
free trade areas, 138-9
  *see also* European Free Trade
    Association
free will *see* self-sovereignty
freedom *see* liberty
'freedom from' *see* negative freedom
freedom of expression, 158
'freedom to' *see* positive freedom
French National Front, 6, 47, 53-66
  in local government, 63-65

Geneva Conventions, 43, 44, 180,
  182, 185*n*
genocide, 173, 179, 181
globalisation, 3, 6, 109-10
group rights versus individual rights
  *see* individual rights versus
    group rights
Gypsies *see* Romanies

heteronomy versus autonomy *see*
  autonomy versus heteronomy
hijacking, 173, 177
hub-and-spoke bilateralism, 138-40,
  142, 144

immigrant rights, 1, 2, 6
  France, 54-60
income catch-up *see* European Union,
  criteria for membership, income
  convergence
indifference, 75-7

individual liberty *see* liberty
individual rights, 12-20
  *see also* self-sovereignty
  versus group rights, 26, 70, 87*n*, 192
  versus national sovereignty, 26, 192
inflation, 115-6
institutionalism, 93, 95, 99
International Covenant on Civil and
  Political Rights, 151-2, 192
International Covenant on Economic
  Social and Cultural Rights, 192
International Criminal Court, 2, 169-87
  *see also* Rome Statute of the
  International Criminal Court
  jurisdiction over individuals, 170, 184
  relations with United Nations
  Security Council, 178
International Criminal Tribunals, 169,
  174-6, 179
international law, 153, 156, 193
  compensation under, 183
  versus domestic law, 153-4, 181,195
International Law Association, 173
International Law Commission, 174, 176
International Military Tribunal, 173
international trials versus national
  trials, 170-1, 173, 178

Joan of Arc as French nationalist
  symbol, 60-2

Keynesian economics, 110-11

labour equality, 27, 29-30
legal rights, 2, 3-4, 151-64
  *see also* privatisation of human
  rights; rule of law
  court-enforced, 151
  Eastern Europe, 92-3
Leipzig Trials, 173
liberal democracy *see* democracy
liberal nationalism *see*
  multiculturalism versus nationalism
liberalisation of trade *see* trade
  liberalisation

liberty, 2, 9-10
  *see also* negative freedom;
  positive freedom as natural right, 11
  based on equal respect, 11
  versus compassion, 16
library censorship, 64-5

Maastricht Treaty, 5, 41-2, 132, 204, 209
masculinist definition of rights *see*
  rights as 'men's rights'
*Mères d'Alger*, 44-5
Migrants Forum, 44, 48
minority rights, 1, 2, 5, 6
  France, 6
monist conception of law, 153, 155
moral individualism *see* individual rights
moral rights, 11
multiculturalism, 70, 76-80
  Australia, 77, 87*n,* 88*n*
  Central Europe, 78-86
  versus nationalism, 71-5, 84-5

national preference *see* immigrant rights
national sovereignty, 1-2, 6-7, 191
  *see also* subsidiarity
  over criminal trials, 170-1
  versus Community law
  *see* Community law versus national
    sovereignty
  versus individual rights *see*
    individual rights versus national
    sovereignty
  versus transnational institutions, 1-2,
    6-7, 22
  versus universal rights, 61, 152
  versus women's rights
  *see* women's rights versus national
    sovereignty
nationalism, 191
  versus multiculturalism *see*
    multiculturalism versus nationalism
nationality rights, 206
negative freedom, 2-3, 11
Northern Ireland, 76
Nuremberg Trials, 172, 174

*Parité*, 30-2
personal rights *see* individual rights
piracy, 173
political asylum *see* refugees
political morality, 9-10, 21, 22*n*
political rights, 2, 12, 17, 27, 104
    Eastern Europe, 91
    France, 30
    exercised by consent, 13, 15, 21, 70
    United States, 3
positive freedom, 3, 10, 13
post-communist states, 91-105
    *see also* Central Europe; Eastern
    Europe
power, arbitrary *see* coercion
power, individual *see* positive freedom
privacy law, 158
private conscience, 12-13
private property, 20, 22*n*
privatisation of human rights, 157-60
prostitution, 37-8, 173
protectionism, 135-6
Protestant philosophy, 12

Quebec, 72-4, 75

racist violence
    France, 62-3
rape, 37
rational assent versus coercion *see*
    coercion versus rational assent
recognition *see* multiculturalism
    versus nationalism
Reformation, 12-14
refugees, 3
regional economic integration, 125-6, 131
religious liberty, 12-13
resident aliens, 3
Resolution on Violence Against
    Women, 30
rights as absolute, 17
rights as 'men's rights', 26-7, 36, 46
rights as 'Third World' problem, 25, 38
'rights as trumps', 16, 17, 19, 20
Romanies, 79-80, 82-3, 88*n*
Rome Conference (1998), 170, 178-81
Rome Statute of the International

Criminal Court (1998), 181-4
rule of law, 93-4, 96-8, 101, 153
Rwanda Tribunal *see* International
    Criminal Tribunals

self-sovereignty, 6, 14, 19, 26
sexual violence, 47, 182
single European currency
    *see* European Monetary Union
slavery, 173
Slovak Republic, 74-5, 78-80
social rights, 2, 27
    United States, 3
social structure, 15
social welfare, 110, 111, 117-9
sovereignty *see* national sovereignty
state sovereignty *see* national
    sovereignty
subsidiarity, 209-11, 213*n*
Summit of Women in Power, 27-8

terrorism, 179
'think for yourself' *see* autonomy
    versus heteronomy
Tokyo Trials, 174
torture, 177
trade liberalisation, 137-8, 140
    *see also* free trade areas
traditions, 101-2
transnational institutions versus
    national sovereignty *see* national
    sovereignty versus transnational
    institutions
Treaty of Amsterdam, 5, 200
Treaty on European Union, 159, 200,
    202-3, 209
Treaty of Rome, 27, 47
unemployment, 112-8

United Nations, 9
    Covenants on Civil and Political
    Rights, 1
    Department of Legal Affairs, 175
    Division for the Advancement of
    Women, 25, 40
    Security Council, 178
United States Constitution, 152

Universal Declaration of Human
  Rights, 1, 9, 25, 40, 151
universal rights versus national
  sovereignty *see* national sovereignty versus universal rights
utilitarianism, 16

Vienna Convention on the Law of
  Treaties, 212*n*

war crimes, 170, 173, 179-81
War Crimes Trials, 179
  *see also* Leipzig Trials; Nuremberg

Trials; Tokyo Trials
Women in Decision-making, 28
women's rights, 2, 3, 8*n*, 25-8, 39-46
  France, 26-7, 42-3
  versus national sovereignty, 41-2
  violations of, 26
    *see also* prostitution; rape,
    sexual violence
  Bosnia, 34
  France, 33-9, 44-5

Yugoslavia Tribunal *see* International
  Criminal Tribunals